Sing Them Over Again to Me

Religion and American Culture
Series Editors

David Edwin Harrell Jr.
Wayne Flynt
Edith L. Blumhofer

Sing Them Over Again to Me

Hymns and Hymnbooks in America

Edited by Mark A. Noll and Edith L. Blumhofer

THE UNIVERSITY OF ALABAMA PRESS
Tuscaloosa

Copyright © 2006
The University of Alabama Press
Tuscaloosa, Alabama 35487-0380
All rights reserved
Manufactured in the United States of America

Typeface: Minion

∞
The paper on which this book is printed meets the minimum requirements of American
National Standard for Information Sciences-Permanence of Paper for Printed Library
Materials, ANSI Z39.48–1984.

Library of Congress Cataloging-in-Publication Data

Sing them over again to me : hymns and hymnbooks in America / edited by Mark A.
    Noll and Edith L. Blumhofer.
        p. cm. — (Religion and American culture)
    Includes index.
    ISBN-13: 978-0-8173-1505-4 (cloth : alk. paper)
    ISBN-10: 0-8173-1505-5 (cloth : alk. paper)
    ISBN-13: 978-0-8173-5292-9 (pbk. : alk. paper)
    ISBN-10: 0-8173-5292-9 (pbk. : alk. paper)
    1. Hymns, English—United States—History and criticism. 2. Protestant churches—
United States—History. I. Noll, Mark A., 1946- . II. Blumhofer, Edith Waldvogel.
III. Series: Religion and American culture (Tuscaloosa, Ala.)
    BV313.S56 2006
    264′.230973—dc22
                                                                    2005027013

Contents

III. Understanding the Classical Era of American Protestantism
through Hymns

Introduction

T HIS BOOK DEMONSTRATES how much can be learned about the broad sweep of American religious life from studying the writing, publishing, and singing of Christian hymns. Its academic premise is that scholarship has fallen far short of capturing the immensely important role of hymns and hymn singing for American experience. This scholarly deficiency is particularly regrettable in light of the worthy efforts historians have made in recent decades to recover the ordinary lives of ordinary people in their ordinary experiences. It is thus a special irony that one of the most protean of ordinary religious activities—the singing of hymns—remains so seriously understudied. Throughout American history—for men, women, and children, for members of almost every ethnic group, for practitioners of high, low, and middle-brow culture, especially for the great numbers of Americans associated with Protestant churches, and at all the critical moments of the life cycle—hymns have created and sustained community, expressed fundamental human aspirations, invigorated religious convictions with moving emotional force, promoted religious fellowship among disparate peoples, allowed otherwise inarticulate people to voice their most ardent longings, summarized with power the often recondite opacity of doctrinal formulas, comforted the grieving, nerved vast numbers for religious and social service, and—it must also be conceded—offered more than ample resources to parodists, satirists, and naysayers eager to subvert the pieties of mainstream religious cultures.

The three sections of this book represent efforts to remedy the scholarly lack of attention. The first traces complex transformations in the use of three well-known individual hymns. The second examines the shape of hymnbooks and hymn texts as critical cultural icons. And the third section documents the way that hymnody gave shape to American Protestantism during the great age of its cultural preeminence during the nineteenth century.

This book reveals the many, often unitive, functions that hymns have exercised among many types of Protestants throughout American history. Unlike any other source, the hymns that have been sung, reprinted, and sung again throughout the generations reveal the center of lived Protestant spirituality. They also open a window into the deepest emotions of the laity. They provide a singular guide to the spirituality of women, who wrote many of the most reprinted hymns and were also a majority of those who sang them. They reveal more about the actual convictions of Protestants than most formal theological writings. And they offer one of the clearest ways of understanding Protestant perceptions of "others" outside their churches.

Because hymns open such a broad window onto religious experience, they provide unusually rich sources for many different academic enterprises. The essays presented in this book show the many possibilities of such projects. For cultural, social, and intellectual historians, hymns can be barometers of ideological and emotional climate—as illustrated by Bruce Hindmarsh's account of the very different uses to which the hymn "Amazing Grace" has been put. For historians of the book, hymnbooks themselves offer one of the most persistent but also revealing types of printed text—as illustrated by the surprisingly substantial insights that Mary Louise VanDyke draws from studying the evolution of topical indexes over the years. For literary scholars, hymns open up the way in which popular metaphors define selves, create social expectations, reinforce hierarchy, or spark liberation—as illustrated, again for the nineteenth century, by Susan Gallagher's examination of domestic themes, Heather Curtis's study of hymns for children, and Candy Brown's exploration of motifs of pilgrimage. With this book we hope that all such lines of academy inquiry will be advanced, and more besides.

Our claim is not that hymns have been entirely neglected as ripe historical sources, for as we indicate below there is a lively and growing body of scholarship devoted to hymnody. Rather, we are suggesting that historians have usually not appreciated the breadth of insight to be gained from systematic attention to hymn texts, their transmission, and their use. This book does not by any means exhaust what can be done with the study of hymns. It does, however, indicate better than earlier attempts how broadly and deeply the study of hymns illuminates the religious past.

Historiography

Writing about hymns and their authors has long been a well-established enterprise in the English-speaking world. Monuments to biographical, textual, and musical study are provided in a number of both older and newer works of reference.[1] The availability of these well-organized bodies of mass information has also found a welcome complement in the informed writings of a distinguished corps of hymnologists whose ranks in the twentieth century included Louis F. Benson, Henry Wilder Foote, Eric Routley, and Paul Westermeyer.[2] Knowledgeable editors have also prepared several helpful collections.[3] In addition, those who value the genre sustain a number of worthy periodicals, including for Britain the *Bulletin of the Hymn Society* and in America *The Hymn*, both of which skillfully bridge the concerns of interested amateurs and learned professionals.

Until fairly recently, however, most of the serious writing on hymnody has been "internal," devoted to the texts, tunes, and authors themselves rather than to the capacity of hymnic sources to shed light on the contexts of church, society, belief, community, and religious aspiration for which hymns have always been so important. This volume, by contrast, is oriented toward these "external" relationships. With this intent it takes advantage of a gratifying range of recent historical scholarship and also extends the contributions of that work.

Three focal points of historical interest have already yielded especially insightful writing. First is a steady tradition of literary-cultural studies on English hymns in their religious and social settings during the eighteenth and nineteenth centuries. The best of this work has interpreted the hymns of Isaac Watts, Charles Wesley, John Newton, William Cowper, and other eighteenth-century evangelicals, and of many hymn writers from the Victorian era as consequential poetry, heartfelt social statement, complex religious expression, or a mixture of all three.[4] Alongside this outstanding work on English hymn texts and hymn writers has appeared also creative essays on the social significance of hymn singing, especially for working-class communities and in connection with major changes in English society.[5] Although use of hymns as historical sources is not as well developed for Ireland and Scotland as for England, the English scholarship points a way for all serious students to follow.

The two exceptions to underutilization of hymns for writing American religious history concern African American communities and the gospel hymns of the late nineteenth century. Since at least 1925 and the publication of James Weldon Johnson's "Preface" to his innovative collections of black spirituals, there has been widespread recognition of how important the creation, adaptation, and singing of religious songs has been for black religious experience.[6] To be sure, a few scholars interpret African American hymnic history as another arena of white oppression.[7] But most suggest that African American hymnody has provided not only a space for the deepest possible religious meditation but also for significant musical creativity, self-expression, and community strengthening. Solid studies by James Cone, Wyatt Walker, Dena Epstein, Michael Harris, and others have used hymns, religious songs, and spirituals to show how singing provided some control over religious expression under slavery and in the postbellum South, how hymns and the blues combined for unusual effect in African American communities, and how apparently otherworldly singing has regularly carried distinctly this-worldly implications in black churches.[8] Guided by such published work, students of African American religious experience also have access to a surprisingly extensive reservoir of unpublished doctoral research as well.[9] An intriguing expansion of this study of African American hymnody is now being carried out by students of Native American religious experience. Significant studies from, for example, Thomas McElwain and Michael McNally have shown that when Indians appropriate mainstream Protestant hymns, significant adaptation results in Native American ownership of the hymns' presentation of foundational religious realities.[10]

The other segment of American religious history with a tradition of serious study through hymns is the urban revivalism of the late nineteenth century. For this effort, Sandra Sizer's book from 1978, *Gospel Hymns and Social Religion,* was a pacesetter.[11] It showed how popular gospel hymns created a community of common sentiment in which the stereotypically feminine virtues of the nineteenth century could be appropriated by men as well. Sizer's appendix, which explained her "Methods of Analyzing Hymns" by identifying and assessing dominant patterns of metaphor, remains a particularly helpful guide to how patient attention to hymns can yield a large historical dividend.[12] Since Sizer's pioneering study, others have also explored ways in which the gospel hymns of urban revivalists mediated between rural traditions and industrial imperatives, redefined gender expectations, and pushed evangelical theology toward a stress on personal religious experience.[13]

Once the rewarding study of hymns for African American religion and for the sensibilities of late-nineteenth-century revivalism has been noted, however, it is difficult to find other themes for which the rich resources of the hymnbook have been as well deployed. To be sure, promising preliminary work does exist for a number of other subjects—for example, connections between hymn use and revival patterns in colonial New England, and nineteenth-century attitudes toward death and dying.[14] And there also exists a wealth of more broadly significant information hidden away in the many publications on individual hymn writers, hymns, and hymnals within the various denominational traditions.[15] Such a smattering of interest does not, however, come close to exploiting the full potential awaiting careful research into the full range of American hymnody.

The Shape of the Book

Sing Them Over Again to Me (these words are from a popular hymn by Philip P. Bliss first published ca. 1870) seeks to show how that potential might be realized from the serious study of the most frequently sung and often-reprinted hymns from the most representative Protestant traditions in American history. While no single volume can open up a field of study on its own, we do hope that the following chapters demonstrate how inadequate any broad study of American religion must be that does not consider what has been sung and how that singing has reflected the most basic religious realities for the broadest range of participants.

As indicated above, the book is divided into three parts. Its first major section offers an advertisement as well as historical research. The advertisement promotes the value of patient attention to the multiple uses—and inevitably multiple textual variants—of the most popular hymns. By charting the incredibly diverse ways in which individuals, churches, and larger communities employ a popular hymn, historians can discover compelling records of both continuity and discontinuity. That congregations—and in some instances whole communities—are still singing hymns at the start of the twenty-first century that were written more than two centuries ago testifies to remarkable stability in religious conviction and religious sensibility. That these enduring hymns now appear with many variant texts, set to new tunes, and appropriated for religious and civic purposes their authors could never have imagined sheds light on some of the most important differences that now separate ordinary religious practices from their counterpart in the eighteenth century.

Bruce Hindmarsh's study of the hymn "Amazing Grace" shows that its meaning changed over its first century from the original design of its author, John Newton, to inculcate biblical theology in his evangelical parish in the English Midlands into an American testimony of wholly individual conversion. But then Hindmarsh proceeds to detail the hymn's remarkable twentieth-century retransformation into a polyvalent symbol of redemption, appropriated by pop musicians and the creators of *Star Trek,* for a religiously diverse American society.[16] John Tyson's treatment of Charles Wesley's "O, For a Thousand Tongues to Sing" fully justifies his calling this hymn "The Methodist National Anthem." By showing how Methodist reprintings (and abridgments) of this hymn marked distinct stages in the course of this denomination's theological and liturgical development, and by noting when and under what circumstances Wesley's hymn was adopted for use by other denominations, Tyson demonstrates how the history of one hymn can become a road map clarifying a very broad set of more general religious developments.[17] Mark Noll's study of the variant printings of "All Hail the Power of Jesus' Name" found in over 1,200 American hymnbooks demonstrates the way that the use of different versions, modifications, and tunes for a single hymn can define distinct and even competing movements within American religious life.

The book's next section features four inter-disciplinary studies that demonstrate the cultural insights to be found in studying the organization of hymnals and the specific wording of individual hymns. It begins with a clash of opinion between Mary De Jong, who applauds editorial changes made in successive hymnbooks as revealing much helpful information about the interests, commitments, and convictions of succeeding eras of American believers and Samuel Rogal, who argues that the poetic worth of hymns deteriorated steadily over the nineteenth century as meddling compilers edited away the vigor from hymns' original compositions. In both cases, the authors carry forward long-standing commitments to serious hymnological study. De Jong's essay advances upon her earlier work by showing that hymnologists' debates over the portrayal of Jesus as Lover and Bridegroom and over appropriate language for representing the body (e.g., breast, bosom, bowels) powerfully reflected contemporary ideologies of class and gender.[18] For his part, Rogal's concern for the integrity of hymn texts grows out of painstaking earlier efforts to catalogue the sources put to use in some of America's most popular hymnbooks.[19]

Mary Louise VanDyke, the energetic director of the "Dictionary of American Hymnology" headquartered at Oberlin College, once explained in an interview how much could be learned by paying attention to changes in the topical indexes of hymnbooks over time.[20] Her contribution to this book shows what treasures she herself has found in such research. By analyzing seventeen hymnals of various denominations over 130 years, she shows how much can be gleaned from the very structure of hymnbooks about a denomination's shift in worship practices, a particular leader's distinctive style, or the gradual evolution of doctrine. Her study is a pioneering effort at taking seriously the way in which hymns are organized in printed collections as well as what appears on the hymnal page.

The final chapter in this section is Edith Blumhofer's on the hymn-writing career of Fanny Crosby and her collaboration with William Doane. It offers the necessary reminder that hymn publishing was a very big business in nineteenth-century America. Because Fanny Crosby was probably the best-known American hymn writer of her era, Blumhofer's study is especially important for revealing the way in which hymns contributed to the expanding empire of American business and also for how the business of hymns shaped (and reflected) perceptions of gender, uses of sentiment, and construction of economic networks.

The third section of the book is made up of chapters that use hymns to tell the story of America's main Protestant constituencies during the nineteenth century—for, that is, the period when Protestants came close to exercising a near cultural hegemony over American public life. Historians have long since rung the changes on Protestant involvements with politics, education, economic development, mercantile expansion, diplomacy, urbanization, and many other spheres of public life.[21] The chapters in the book's third section supplement these well-known accounts but also amend, modify, and expand them by paying attention to the hymnody of the era. Through that attention, the essays provide fresh readings of important subjects, especially as experienced by ordinary people, that have hitherto remained on the margins of historical interest.

The first chapter in this section is Dennis Dickerson's account of Richard Allen establishing and developing the African Methodist Episcopal Church. By examining Allen's wider concerns as well as his specific publishing projects, Dickerson can show that hymns played a shaping role from the founding of the AME Church in 1816, especially because of Allen's "quintessentially Wesleyan" fascination with the positive role of Christian hymnody. Candy Brown ranges still more widely as she identifies a broad array of narratives, enacted in hymns, that open up the inner meaning of evangelical cultures. Brown argues that the pilgrim narratives presented in countless hymns were important not only for their doctrines of initial salvation but also for the progression of the story itself. Through their hymns, Brown can show that nineteenth-century Protestant evangelicals were driven by their concern for individual salvation and also by interest in communal relationships and a lifelong process of sanctification.

The section's next two chapters study the way that specific populations of American Protestants appropriated the broader themes charted by the previous chapters. Heather Curtis finds a similarly central role for hymns in shaping the religious and social identities of children in the early American republic. By drawing on Sunday school reports, tracts, devotional books, hymnbooks targeted at children, and novels, Curtis suggests that the practice of hymn singing incorporated children into multiple communities—familial, civil, religious—even as they offered children both cultural integration and spiritual transformation. Susan Gallagher's study of hymns and Victorian domestic ideals draws still further conclusions about the cultural power of hymns. Her argument is that many aspects of nineteenth-century hymnody quietly subverted the ideology of separate spheres that confined women to private realms of domestic spiritual development. Rather, she finds that nineteenth-century hymns did not always idealize home life, that they were sometimes vehicles for female liberation, and that hymns could deconstruct as well as reinforce the mentality of separate gender spheres. The common thread that joins the studies of Dickerson, Brown, Curtis, and Gallagher is the power that hymns evoked at all levels of American society, and also the multiple purposes to which they were put.

Notes

1. Especially John Julian, *A Dictionary of Hymnology*, 2 vols., 2nd ed. (London: John Murray, 1907); Nicholas Temperley, ed., *The Hymn Tune Index: A Census of English-Language Hymn Tunes in Printed Sources from 1535 to 1820*, 4 vols. (Oxford: Clarendon, 1998); D. DeWitt Wesson, *Hymn Tune Index and Related Hymn Materials*, 3 vols. (Lanham, MD: Scarecrow, 1998).

2. As examples of their work, Louis F. Benson, *The English Hymn* (London: George H. Doran, 1915); Henry Wilder Foote, *Three Centuries of American Hymnody* (Cambridge, MA: Harvard University Press, 1940); Erik Routley, *Hymns and the Faith* (London: John Murray, 1955); and Paul Westermeyer, *Let Justice Sing: Hymnody and Justice* (Collegeville, MN: Liturgical Press, 1998).

3. See especially Charles W. Hughes, Albert Christ-Janer, and Carleton Sprague Smith, eds., *American Hymns: Old and New*, 2 vols. (New York: Columbia University Press, 1980); and Ian Bradley, ed., *The Penguin Book of Hymns* (New York: Penguin, 1990).

4. Highlights of this writing include many works by Donald Davie, for example, *The Eighteenth-Century Hymn in England* (New York: Cambridge University Press, 1993); M. Pauline Parker, "The Hymn as a Literary Form," *Eighteenth-Century Studies* 8 (Summer 1975): 392–419; Madeleine Forrell Marshall and Janet Todd, *English Congregational Hymns in the Eighteenth Century* (Lexington: University of Kentucky Press, 1982); Lionel Adey, *Hymns and the Christian Myth* (Vancouver: University of British Columbia Press, 1986); Adey, *Class and Idol in the English Hymn* (Vancouver: University of British Columbia Press, 1988); Richard Arnold, *The English Hymn: Studies in a Genre* (New York: Peter Lang, 1995); Ian Bradley, *Abide with Me: The World*

of Victorian Hymns (London: SCM, 1997); and J. R. Watson, The English Hymn: A Critical and Historical Study (Oxford: Clarendon Press, 1997). There is also solid treatment of hymns at many places in Horton Davies, Worship and Theology in England, 3 vols. (Grand Rapids, MI: Eerdmans, 1996 [reprinting individual volumes published in 1961, 1962, 1965, 1970, and 1975]).

5. See especially Jim Obelkevich, "Music and Religion in the Nineteenth Century," in Disciplines of Faith: Studies in Religion, Politics, and Patriarchy, ed. Jim Obelkevich, Lydal Roper, and Raphael Samuel (London: Routledge and Kegan Paul, 1987), 550–65; and Susan S. Tamke, Make a Joyful Noise unto the Lord: Hymns as a Reflection of Victorian Social Attitudes (Athens: Ohio University Press, 1978).

6. James Weldon Johnson, The Books of American Negro Spirituals (New York: Viking, 1926), which incorporate two volumes published separately in 1925 and 1926.

7. See especially Jon Michael Spencer, Black Hymnody: A Hymnological History of the African-American Church (Knoxville: University of Tennessee Press, 1992), and for Spencer's prescription of a better way, Sing a New Song: Liberating Black Hymnody (Minneapolis: Augsburg Fortress, 1995).

8. James H. Cone, The Spirituals and the Blues, 2nd ed. (Maryknoll, NY: Orbis, 1991 [1st ed. 1972]); Dena J. Epstein, Sinful Tunes and Spirituals: Black Folk Music to the Civil War (Urbana: University of Illinois Press, 1977); Wyatt Tee Walker, "Somebody's Calling My Name": Black Sacred Music and Social Change (Valley Forge, PA: Judson, 1979); Michael W. Harris, The Rise of Gospel Blues: The Music of Thomas Andrew Dorsey in the Urban Church (New York: Oxford University Press, 1992).

9. As examples, see Irene Viola Jackson, "Afro-American Gospel Music and its Social Setting with Special Attention to Roberta Martin" (PhD diss., Wesleyan University, 1974); and Alfred Adolphus Pinkston, "Lined Hymns, Spirituals, and the Associated Lifestyle of Rural Black People in the United States" (PhD diss., University of Miami, 1975).

10. See Thomas McElwain, "'The Rainbow Will Carry Me': The Language of Seneca Iroquois Christianity as Reflected in Hymns," in Religion in Native North America, ed. Christopher Vecsey (Moscow: University of Idaho Press, 1990), 83–103; Michael David McNally, "Ojibwa Singers: Evangelical Hymns and a Native Culture in Motion" (PhD diss., Harvard University, 1996); and Michael David McNally, "The Uses of Ojibwa Hymn-Singing at White Earth: Toward a History of Practice," in Lived Religion in America, ed. David D. Hall (Princeton, NJ: Princeton University Press, 1997), 133–59.

11. Sandra S. Sizer, Gospel Hymns and Social Religion (Philadelphia: Temple University Press, 1978).

12. Sizer, Gospel Hymns and Social Religion, 161–73.

13. As examples, David Joseph Smucker, "Philip Paul Bliss and the Musical, Cul-

tural and Religious Sources of the Gospel Music Tradition in the United States, 1850–1876" (PhD diss., Boston University, 1981); Esther Heidi Rothenbusch, "The Role of 'Gospel Hymns' nos. 1 to 6 (1875–1894) in American Revivalism" (PhD diss., University of Michigan, 1991); June Hadden Hobbs, "*I Sing for I Cannot Be Silent": The Feminization of American Hymnody, 1870–1920* (Pittsburgh: University of Pittsburgh Press, 1997).

14. Joanne Grayeski Weiss, "The Relationship between the 'Great Awakening' and the Transition from Psalmody to Hymnody in the New England Colonies" (DA diss., Ball State University, 1988); Mary Bhame Pope, "We Shall Meet on That Beautiful Shore: Hymns of Death in the New South, 1865–1900" (PhD diss., Emory University, 1985); Alma Elizabeth Krouse, "The Treatment of Death in Selected Nineteenth-Century Hymnals and Tunebooks from 1835 to 1870" (DMA diss., University of Missouri–Kansas City, 1990).

15. For samples from a huge volume of such writing, see Steven D. Cooley, "'And All the Silent Heaven of Love': Hymn Quotation and American Methodist Spirituality," *Methodist History* 37 (1999): 213–25; Emily R. Brink and Bert Polman, eds., *Psalter Hymnal Handbook* (Grand Rapids, MI: Christian Reformed Church Publications, 1998); William R. Lee, "Lowell Mason, Samuel A. Worcester, and the Cherokee Singing Book," *Chronicles of Oklahoma* 75 (1997): 32–51; Kenneth Logan, "Isaac Watts and 'The God of Glory': A Second-Advent Hymn Dominates Early American Publication," *Adventist Heritage* 16 (1995): 30–35; Harry Eskew and Hugh T. McElrath, *Sing with Understanding: An Introduction to Christian Hymnology*, 2nd ed. (Nashville: Church Street Press, 1995); Irvin Murrell, "Southern Ante-Bellum Baptist Hymnody," *Baptist History and Heritage* 27 (1992): 12–18; and Paul E. Dahl, "'All Is Well . . . ': The Story of 'The Hymn that Went around the World,'" *Brigham Young University Studies* 21 (1982): 515–27.

16. For Hindmarsh's own study of his author's important career, see *John Newton and the English Evangelical Tradition: Between the Conversions of Wesley and Wilberforce* (Oxford: Clarendon Press, 1996).

17. As with Hindmarsh, Tyson's study of Wesley's hymn grows out of a thorough understanding of the hymn writer himself; see Tyson, *Charles Wesley: A Reader* (New York: Oxford University Press, 1989).

18. See Mary De Jong, "'I Want to Be Like Jesus': The Self-Defining Power of Evangelical Hymnody," *Journal of the American Academy of Religion* 54 (Fall 1986): 461–93; "'With My Burden I Begin': The (Im)Personal 'I' of Nineteenth-Century Hymnody," *Studies in Puritan American Spirituality* 4 (1993): 185–223; and "'Theirs the Sweetest Songs': Women Hymn Writers in the Nineteenth-Century United States," in *A Mighty Baptism: Race, Gender, and the Creation of American Protestantism*, ed. Susan Juster and Lisa MacFarlane (Ithaca: Cornell University Press, 1996), 141–67.

19. See Samuel J. Rogal, *Guide to the Hymns and Tunes of American Methodists* (New York: Greenwood, 1986); and *Sing Glory and Hallelujah: Historical and Biographical Guide to Gospel Hymns Nos. 1 to 6 Complete* (Westport, CT: Greenwood, 1996).

20. Carol Pemberton, "An Interview with Mary Louise VanDyke," *The Hymn* 46 (July 1995): 4–10 (esp. 7–8).

21. For merest hints at a vast bibliography, see Richard Carwardine, *Evangelicals and Politics in Antebellum America* (New Haven: Yale University Press, 1993); Eugene D. Genovese, *Consuming Fire: The Fall of the Confederacy in the Mind of the White Christian South* (Athens: University of Georgia Press, 1999); C. C. Goen, *Broken Churches, Broken Nation: Denominational Schisms and the Coming of the American Civil War* (Macon, GA: Mercer University Press, 1985); Nathan O. Hatch, *The Democratization of American Christianity* (New Haven: Yale University Press, 1989); Daniel Walker Howe, *The Political Culture of the American Whigs* (Chicago: University of Chicago Press, 1997); Paul Johnson, *A Shopkeepers' Millennium: Society and Revivals in Rochester, New York, 1815–1837* (New York: Hill and Wang, 1978); Colleen McDannell, *The Christian Home in Victorian America, 1840–1900* (Bloomington: Indiana University Press, 1986); Henry F. May, *Protestant Churches and Industrial America* (New York: Harper, 1949); Mary Ryan, *Cradle of the Middle Class: The Family in Oneida County, New York, 1790–1865* (New York: Cambridge University Press, 1981); and Timothy L. Smith, *Revivalism and Social Reform: American Protestantism on the Eve of the Civil War* (New York: Harper and Row, 1957).

Sing Them Over Again to Me

I
The History in a Hymn

1
"Amazing Grace"
The History of a Hymn and a Cultural Icon
D. Bruce Hindmarsh

Swissair Flight 111 was en route from New York to Geneva on the evening of September 2, 1998, when it suddenly plummeted 2,400 meters into the Atlantic Ocean off the coast of Nova Scotia, killing all 229 people on board. The tiny tourist village of Peggy's Cove was immediately transformed into a command center for the police, Coast Guard, and other emergency-measures officials. Shocked family members arrived to look out over the waves that held their loved ones. An army chaplain went to the water's edge and offered to pray with the grieving family of a nineteen-year-old California student. He led them in prayer, and then the family started to sing a hymn in four-part harmony, and then followed this with "Amazing Grace." The chaplain noticed that the scene transfixed all the rescue workers and onlookers. He added, "Things like that were going on all day—amazing grace in the middle of incredible sorrow."[1]

It was on those same North Atlantic seas 250 years earlier that John Newton, the author of "Amazing Grace," first cried out to God for mercy in the midst of a storm that threatened to kill all on board a foundering ship bound for England. Newton wrote "Amazing Grace" some years afterward when he was settled in the English Midlands as an Anglican minister, but the hymn has endured through two and a half centuries and become today a powerful symbol for many people of hope in the midst of tragedy.

The meaning of this hymn has changed in significant ways over the centuries. Words have been changed or added, refrains appended, many different tunes sung, and it has been put to service for ends that would make John Newton shudder. According to the *Dictionary of American Hymnology,* "Amazing Grace" appears in more than a thousand hymnals in the nineteenth and twentieth centuries. This breadth of dissemination invites analysis in terms of context: What exactly did "Amazing Grace" mean to the folk who sung the hymn in so many different times and places? In what follows I will interpret the hymn first in its original context, and then outline its reception and use in American churches, before finally interpreting it again in its secular context in the late twentieth century. By thus tracing the history and interpretation of "Amazing Grace," I hope to explore how a more-or-less fixed text acquired different meanings along the way.

Didactic Biblical Theology: Amazing Grace in the English Midlands in the Eighteenth Century

John Newton (1725–1807) was a converted slave trader who went on to become one of the leading figures in the Evangelical Revival in Britain. He published an account of his own conversion in 1764, just after he entered ordained ministry, and it was this, more than anything else, that brought him to prominence. From this autobiography, it is clear that Newton had a profound sense that he had received grace and been rescued from his own wretchedness.[2]

Although his mother had given him a religious upbringing, Newton abandoned it all when he began to work in the merchant marine in late adolescence. He became an infidel, a freethinker, and a libertine, or as we would say, a convinced agnostic who began to lead an immoral life. Then in 1743 he was press-ganged into the navy. Newton attempted to desert, but he was caught, put in irons, whipped, and degraded from the office of midshipman to common seaman. As he watched the English coastline recede, he had dark thoughts of murder and suicide. Before long he was transferred to a merchant vessel in the African slave trade. He was now anonymous, and his behavior became marked by ribald and blasphemous language; he also alludes vaguely to sexual misconduct. After six months, he determined to stay on the Guinea coast of Africa to work in the onshore slave trade. Instead, during the next two years he suffered illness, starvation, exposure, and ridicule. Newton always marked this point as the nadir of his spiritual journey.

Eventually, he was rescued by an English ship. The crew returned to England along the triangular Atlantic trade route, via Brazil and Newfoundland, but encountered a severe North Atlantic storm in the winter of 1748. On March 21, Newton was awakened in the middle of the night to find that the ship was breaking apart and filling fast with water, and a man was already swept overboard. Newton muttered his first prayer for mercy in many years—and caught himself by surprise to find that he was praying at all. When the ordeal was over, he and most of the crew had survived the storm but were left with very little food or water and a ship out of repair. Newton began to read the Bible and other religious books. By the time the ship at length reached

Ireland, he considered himself no longer an "infidel." In his diary, he would always thereafter remember March 21 as the anniversary of his conversion. Indeed the very last entry he made in his diary as an eighty-year-old man was a commemoration of this event.

It is this story of Newton's conversion in the midst of near-shipwreck on the Atlantic that usually makes it into hymnal companions as an illustration of the autobiographical dimension of "Amazing Grace." In some accounts, it is made to appear as though Newton were wiping the brine from his forehead as he wrote the hymn, with the breakers still crashing over the gunwales. This was not the case. However well the hymn expresses Newton's own experience, Newton wrote it much later, in the context of his ministry as an evangelical parish priest.

Newton eventually left the sea and spent about ten years in a civil service job in Liverpool. He studied theology and became active as an evangelical layman. Then in 1764 he was ordained. For sixteen years he was the parish priest in the small market town of Olney in the English Midlands, a town of about 2,000 people. At Olney he established a variety of services and society meetings that became very popular. He also made hymns immediately a vital part of his ministry. He noted in his diary at the beginning of 1765, "We have now a fixed little company who come to my house on sabbath evening after tea. We spend an hour or more in prayer and singing, and part between six and seven."[3] A month later he was giving out hymnbooks to the children at his Thursday catechetical meetings and employing someone to teach them to sing. A part of the value of hymns in this didactic context was mnemonic. Newton had the children learn the hymns by heart, effectively catechizing them in verse.[4] During the 1770s Newton regularly wrote a hymn for the prayer meeting and often used the hymn as a basis for a small lecture. He eventually amassed a large corpus of his own compositions, which he appears to have kept in a separate notebook and numbered consecutively. This was the origin of Newton's contributions to the *Olney Hymns* (1779), a hymnbook that went into multiple editions on both sides of the Atlantic before the end of the century.[5]

The hymn-writing task was for Newton first and foremost a response to the spiritual needs of his people, and many hymns arose from very specific situations in the parish. For example, the death of parishioner Betty Abraham in February 1774 prompted Newton to write a funeral hymn.[6] However, Newton had a unique ability to write both for a particular audience and, so to speak, over their heads, for a wider public too. While the occasion of the hymns was often local, the sentiments were universal. Newton wrote in transparently simple language as the representative "I," expressing exemplary sentiments for his people. Yet at the same time he set their lives on a large eschatological canvas.[7]

"Amazing Grace" is perhaps the best example of Newton's use of simple first-person language to represent an experience of undeserved mercy shared by hymn writer and singers alike. The original title of the hymn was "Faith's Review and Expectation," and the first three stanzas reflect on a climactic evangelical conversion in the past:

> 1. Amazing grace! (how sweet the sound)
>   That sav'd a wretch like me!
>   I once was lost, but now am found,
>   Was blind, but now I see.
>
> 2. 'Twas grace that taught my heart to fear,
>   And grace my fears reliev'd;
>   How precious did that grace appear,
>   The hour I first believ'd!
>
> 3. Thro' many dangers, toils and snares,
>   I have already come;
>   'Tis grace has brought me safe thus far,
>   And grace will lead me home.[8]

The initial exclamation of "Amazing grace!" accomplishes what Pauline Parker claims a good hymn must; that is, it invites immediate congregational consent and release of emotional energy.[9] The following parenthetical response ("how sweet the sound") simply enacts the amazement just proclaimed, and focuses the whole line back upon the word "grace." Then the balance of the stanza lays out the stark contrasts that evoked the initial cry of wonder. The last two lines perfectly match cadences with the contrasting images, and the simple antitheses (lost/found, blind/see) are expressed in equally simple monosyllables. The second stanza, ringing changes on the thrice repeated "grace," harks back to the first exclamation while developing the paradox in evangelical theology that the preaching of the law, and the remorse it provokes, is itself a part of the very grace that brings powerful psychological release from the guilt of sin and the fear of damnation. The precision of "the hour I first believed" pinpoints the experience of grace as climactic in the same way the earlier dialectical images did. And by the end of the second stanza the singers have been led to express the exemplary sentiments of the amazement, sweetness, and preciousness of divine grace. Of the danger and toil of stanza three, both Newton and his poor parishioners had had much, but the last half of the stanza becomes a pivot on which the whole hymn turns, gathering the past up once more into the word "grace" and then turning with faith to face the future.

The last three stanzas trace the path of the believer through, respectively, the balance of this life, death, and the final dissolution of the elements of this world.

> 4. The Lord has promis'd good to me,
>   His word my hope secures;
>   He will my shield and portion be,
>   As long as life endures.

> 5. Yes, when this flesh and heart shall fail,
>   And mortal life shall cease;
>   I shall possess, within the vail,
>   A life of joy and peace.

> 6. The earth shall soon dissolve like snow,
>   The sun forbear to shine;
>   But God, who call'd me here below,
>   Will be for ever mine.

It is a strong final quatrain that can draw the circle from "the earth" in its final eschatological consumption to the simple reassurance of the final small word "mine."

The autobiographical significance of this hymn as a testimony to Newton's sensational conversion is well noted. William Phipps is typical of many hymnal guides and handbooks when he claims, "The first stanza of "Amazing Grace" alludes to his deliverance from the blindness that prevented his seeing the anti-Christian nature of slave trading."[10] Perhaps. But it is important to note that Newton nowhere makes this connection himself. In fact, the hymn appears in the canonical section of the Olney hymnbook, where hymns are organized according to various passages of Scripture from Genesis to Revelation. "Faith's Review and Expectation" was based on the scriptural passage 1 Chronicles 17:16–17, in which David responds in amazement to the prophet Nathan's announcement of the Davidic covenant: God's promise to maintain

David's line and his kingdom forever. David went before the Lord and said, "Who am I, O Lord God, and what is mine house, that thou hast brought me hitherto?" So we are singing a paraphrase of the words of King David when we sing "Amazing Grace." The first-person language belongs to David first, and only to us by analogy.

The passage that Newton was expounding in 1 Chronicles 17 is one of the high points in biblical theology, and the weight of accumulated Christian covenantal and typological interpretation meant that Newton would certainly have seen in this text the anticipation of Christ as that greater son of David, the one presented as the fulfillment of the divine promise to David in the genealogies of the Gospels. The typology had only to be extended to see in God's grace to David an anticipation of God's grace to Newton in his experience, as much as to the poor of Olney in theirs. The title of the hymn and the turning from past to future in stanza three suggest the kind of amazed backward and forward looking, along the line of salvation history, that David was doing in 1 Chronicles, which Newton did persistently in his own devotional life, and which Newton presented for his people as an exemplary pattern for their own piety. The force of this is even greater when it is remembered that Newton probably expounded this hymn as a part of his regular hymn discourses on Sunday evenings, making all these implicit typological connections explicit for his people. Newton held together the story of David, of Christ, of Newton himself, and of the faithful poor of Olney. In its original setting, then, "Amazing Grace" was a didactic hymn of biblical theology written for a society of believers within an evangelical Anglican parish. In the mouth of the singer, "I" and "me" and "mine" was autobiographical only within the larger context of salvation history.

The *Olney Hymns* were reprinted, and individual hymns were reissued in magazines and other hymnals in England. "Amazing Grace" was not, however, picked up by other hymn collections. The only hymnbook in England in the late eighteenth or early nineteenth century that I could find to reprint the hymn was an up-market collection by Lady Huntingdon, entitled *A Select Collection of Hymns, to Be Universally Sung in All the Countess of Huntingdon's Chapels. Collected by Her Ladyship* (London: Hughes and Walsh, 1780). But when in 1892 John Julian listed sixty-one of Newton's hymns in common usage, "Amazing Grace" was not among them.[11] Julian commented that "Amazing Grace" was "unknown to modern collections" outside of America.[12] Erik Routley has noted its increasing popularity in Britain since the 1950s, but that it did not appear in any hymnbook with its now familiar tune until 1964.[13] If we are to trace the popularity of the hymn we must turn to its reception in the United States.

From Isaac Watts to Revival Songs: Amazing Grace in Antebellum America

We cannot be certain when "Amazing Grace" was first sung in America, but the *Olney Hymns* collection was reprinted in New York as early as 1787 and then again in 1790.[14] It was also reprinted three times in Philadelphia before the end of the century. The first American hymnbook to include "Amazing Grace" was the *Psalms of David, with Hymns and Spiritual Songs . . . For the Use of the Reformed Dutch Church in North America,* printed in 1789 in New York by Hodge, Allen and Campbell—the same printers who first reissued the *Olney Hymns.* The English-speaking Dutch Reformed congregations in New York printed an English psalm book in 1767, but this was the first book to include hymns. Newton's autobiography and other works were widely available in America; many had also been translated into Dutch and were well known in the Netherlands. As a Calvinist hymn writer who stood somewhere between the sobriety of Isaac Watts and the exuberance of Charles Wesley, Newton was perhaps a trustworthy source for the immigrant church as it struggled with Americanization and made the controversial transition from psalms to hymns.

The Baptists were among the first to make full use of hymnody in their worship. In the 1790s they produced hymnbooks that began to supplement Watts's standard hymnody with selections from the English evangelicals Richard Conyers and John Rippon. These were Newton's contemporaries and their hymnbooks shared many similarities with the *Olney Hymns.* So it was that Baptists also made use of "Amazing Grace" before the end of the century. Eleazer Clay included the hymn in his *Hymns and Spiritual Songs,* published in Richmond, Virginia, in 1793. This was a period of tremendous growth for the Baptist denomination in the West and South, and their hymnody embraced a range of tastes from Watts to evangelicals such as Newton and Conyers to revival songs.

Congregationalists and Presbyterians also began to move beyond metrical psalmody and the hymns of Isaac Watts during the 1790s under the impetus of the Second Great Awakening. In 1799, Nathan Strong, a pastor from Hartford who was active in the revival, enlisted the help of another pastor and one of his deacons to compile *The Hartford Selection of Hymns.* A large number of the *Olney Hymns,* including "Amazing Grace," were adopted. The *Hartford Selection* was not an authorized hymnbook, but it was widely used in revival services, conference meetings, and new congregations. It was, according to Louis Benson, "one of the landmarks of New England Hymnody."[15] Used alongside the authorized service books by both Congregationalists and Presbyterians, it gradually modified and enriched the official psalmody.

Methodists had long had their official hymnody in various forms from John Wesley, though supplements were published before the turn of the century. But with the Western Revival and amp meetings at the turn of the century, the Methodists began to publish a series of songbooks inspired by revival. One of the earliest and most influential of these included "Amazing Grace." It was compiled by Peter D. Myers in 1829, and the title of the hymnbook says it all: *The Zion Songster: A Collection of Hymns and Spiritual Songs, Generally Sung at Camp and Prayer Meetings, and in Revivals of Religion.* It reached a ninety-fifth edition by 1854. Benson sees the aim of the camp meeting hymn as purely emotional: "It is individualistic, and deals with the rescue of a sinner: sometimes in direct appeal to 'sinners,' 'backsliders,' or 'mourners'; sometimes by reciting the terms of salvation; sometimes as a narrative of personal experience for his warning or encouragement. . . . The literary form of the Camp Meeting Hymn is that of the popular ballad or song, in plainest every-day language and of careless or incapable technique. The refrain or chorus is perhaps the predominate feature, not always connected with the subject matter of the stanza, but rather ejaculatory."[16]

In this context, then, "Amazing Grace" has been shorn of the biblical theology and didacticism of its original setting in John Newton's parish, and it has become a song of simple testimony to express and stimulate the piety of revivalism.

From this early reception among Dutch Reformed, Baptist, Congregational and Presbyterian, and Methodist denominations, it is clear that "Amazing Grace" was well adapted to function within different contexts, ranging from conservative city congregations barely moving away from Watts to emotional revival meetings on the frontier where popular "spiritual songs" predominated.

The same story could be told of the tunes to which "Amazing Grace" was sung. We do not know to what tune it was sung originally in Olney, though it was probably something somewhere between the sobriety of the old psalmody and the highly decorated Handelic melodies of Methodism and the Martin Madan circle. A tune book, *Harmonia Coelestis,* was published in America with the Congregationalist *Hartford Selection* in 1799, and it was largely in the style of Martin Madan's *Collection of Psalm and Hymn Tunes* (1769). But it was with the publication of William Walker's *Southern Harmony* in 1835 that Newton's hymn was put to the tune "New Britain" with which it is irrevocably associated today. A native of Spartanburg, South Carolina, Walker wrote down the music for a great many tunes that, he said, "I could not find in any publication, nor in manuscript."[17] His *Southern Harmony* thus fixed a number of folk musical traditions that preexisted his publication in oral form. *Southern Harmony* was an oblong tune book that used the four-shape system of notation associated with fasola singing and the Sacred Harp tradition, and which became especially popular in the South during the two decades before the Civil War. This is a musical tradition that still exists in the South, and Bill Moyers's documentary on "Amazing Grace," produced in 1982, includes recordings of "New Britain" by white singers at a Primitive Baptist Church near Bremen, Georgia, and black singers at a gathering in Ozark, Alabama. The tune was not adopted by compilers of church hymnals until the end of the nineteenth century, though it has been standard since then.

It is difficult to make judgments about musical sensibility and to relate these to cultural values, and well into the nineteenth century a common-meter hymn like "Amazing Grace" would be sung to a variety of tunes. Nonetheless, I would argue that musical shifts in the tune to which "Amazing Grace" was set represent a movement away from the didactic toward the more lyrical or even soulful. This is conjectural, but it is also precisely the kind of shift we would expect from Newton's parish to the Second Great Awakening in New England to the frontier camp meetings in the South.

The Gospel Hymn: Amazing Grace and Urban Evangelicalism in the Late Nineteenth Century

The early reception of "Amazing Grace" among five major Protestant denominations in the early Republic has been traced, but it should be stressed that "Amazing Grace" knew very few boundaries in the nineteenth century. It was reprinted, for example, in the hymnals of the Lutherans, Moravians, Universalists, Free Will Baptists, various Restorationist and Adventist churches, and the Mormons. Later in the century it was included in the songbooks of societies such as the YMCA and the Christian Endeavor Society. As so often with hymnody, "Amazing Grace" was remarkably ecumenical.

This variety applied to the new musical settings of the hymn as well. Although Walker set "Amazing Grace" to the now familiar tune "New Britain" in 1835, and the oblong tune books of the shape-note singers in the South

followed his example, upright church hymnals were slow to pick up the tune.
Bill Reynolds has traced more than twenty-four different tunes used with
"Amazing Grace" over the course of its history in the United States.[18] It was
at the end of the nineteenth century that Baptist hymn collections first made
use of the tune "New Britain." In addition to this variety of tunes, Professor
Reynolds has also traced thirty-three refrains attached to these tunes from
about the mid-nineteenth to the mid-twentieth century. These include such
rousing lines as "I'm bound for the promised land," or "O the grace, the precious grace," or "O how I love Jesus." Such refrains were typical of the gospel
hymns associated with Ira D. Sankey, and indeed Sankey reprinted "Amazing
Grace" several times to different tunes in different hymnbooks.

It was with Ira D. Sankey (1840–1908) that "Amazing Grace" found its place
among the popular gospel hymns of urban middle-class revivalism. Dwight
L. Moody (1837–1899) and Sankey became internationally renowned figures
with their evangelistic services in Britain in 1873–75. Sankey's popular singing
did much to reinforce Moody's simple preaching of God's love and the need
for conversion. In Moody's message and Sankey's hymns there was a new sen-
timentality that focused on individual salvation and private vices to the exclusion of social or political questions. "Amazing Grace" was included in
Sankey's "Sacred Songs and Solos" (1873–1903), *Gospel Hymns No. 2* (1876),
and *Gospel Hymns No. 4* (1883)—each time with a different tune.[19] But in this
new context, "Amazing Grace" was clustered with popular hymns such as
Sankey's "Ninety and Nine," that "tells of the Saviour's love as he makes his
blood-stained way through the thickets, deserts, and thunder-riven mountains to retrieve one lost sheep."[20] "Amazing Grace" becomes one more song
of exquisite feelings, with the touching contrast between a lost sinner and the
tender love of Christ.

Sankey's *Gospel Hymns* were enormously influential and epitomized the
new businesslike middle-class respectability in urban evangelicalism, since
the series represented a significant commercial enterprise. Published just after
the establishment of the Registry of Copyrights office in Washington, the series was copublished, merchandised, and promoted by the major companies,
Biglow and Main, and the John Church Company. The *Gospel Hymns* set the
tone for gospel hymns for several decades.[21]

Within this milieu, Edwin Othello Excell (1851–1921) rose to prominence
as a song leader. Like Sankey with Moody, Excell assisted Sam P. Jones (d.
1906) and Gypsy Smith in their revival meetings. Although he composed
more than 2,000 gospel songs, he left his greatest mark on gospel hymnody
as a commercial publisher and publisher's agent in Chicago. In 1900 he pub-

lished *Make His Praise Glorious,* and included an arrangement of the first four stanzas of "Amazing Grace" set to "New Britain." Ten years later he published *Coronation Hymns* and after Newton's first three stanzas, he added, "When we've been there ten thousand years, / Bright shining as the sun, / We've no less days to sing God's praise / Than when we first begun."

Bill Reynolds has recently identified the source of this final stanza as one of the more than seventy stanzas that have evolved as part of the old hymn, "Jerusalem, My Happy Home."[22] This arrangement by Excell gradually drove all other editions of the hymn from the field and became the standard form of "Amazing Grace" as most people know it today. Newton's hymn had traveled from the Dutch Reformed Congregations of New York to the emotional camp meetings of the South and the western frontier to the individualism of urban revivalism in the late nineteenth century.

A "Secular Spiritual": Amazing Grace in the Late Twentieth Century

In the postwar years of the twentieth century, "Amazing Grace" again appeared in a new context as it moved from church hymnody into the secular marketplace and commercial media. Mahalia Jackson (1911–1972) was the pioneer of twentieth-century gospel music. Her 1947 recording of "Move On Up a Little Higher" sold a million copies and launched her career as a gospel superstar. Pop music critics worked hard to find enough adjectives to describe her style: her "grainy, full-throated voice," the "syncopated bounce" to her readings of gospel classics, the "note-bending phrasing" of her Baptist upbringing, and so forth. She recorded "Amazing Grace" for Apollo Records on December 10, 1947, a few months after "Move On Up." Her soulful version of the hymn was played on the radio in the immediate postwar years and helped to move "Amazing Grace" into the popular consciousness.[23]

Jackson was a friend and supporter of Martin Luther King Jr., and she sang the hymn at rallies and marches in the civil rights movement. In the summer of 1964, Fannie Lou Hamer also sang "Amazing Grace" at rallies and voter registration drives in Mississippi. Judy Collins was at some of these rallies and she thought of the hymn as a kind of talisman. She had long left the Methodist church of her childhood behind, but she still sang the hymn. "During those days of turmoil," she writes, "I sang *Amazing Grace* as a rune to give magical protection—a charm to ward off danger, an incantation to the angels of heaven to descend. I had left the choir loft of the Methodists and was not sure the magic worked outside of church walls . . . in the open air in

Mississippi. But I wasn't taking any chances."[24] Here again is the new context for the hymn: outside of church walls in the secular and political market-place.

"Amazing Grace" featured not only in the political marketplace but also in the new therapeutic culture of the 1960s. Judy Collins had been in therapy since 1963, and in 1968 she became involved in an encounter group where members shared openly, honestly, and sometimes brutally with one another. "One night at the encounter group," she recalled, "we wanted to sing a song to end an evening that had been particularly touching to us all. The only song everyone knew all the words to was 'Amazing Grace,' and I led the singing, as I knew it well."[25] Collins went on to record the hymn as the last song on her album, *Whales and Nightingales.* The album was released in 1970 and within a few weeks "Amazing Grace" was being played on the radio. The hymn was already popular with folksingers who would often end their gatherings with everyone singing it "as a sort of prayer." But now groups of every kind were singing "Amazing Grace." On January 9, 1971, Collins's recording of the hymn made it onto *Billboard* magazine's Top 40 pop chart. It peaked at number fifteen and remained in the Top 40 for eleven weeks. Perhaps Mary Rourke's interpretation is correct. She links Judy Collins's recording of the hymn to the Vietnam War, saying, "Her version captured the melancholy and regret shared by many Americans who felt that too many lives had been lost in a war many believed the U.S. could not win."[26] Again, Collins herself described the song as "a talisman against death, against the raging war."[27]

The following year, on May 27, a recording of the same hymn on bagpipes by the Royal Scots Dragoon Guards climbed even higher on the *Billboard* Top 40, to number eleven, and charted for eight weeks. This recording had already topped the charts in mid-April in England and on the continent.[28] Perhaps the plaintive tone of the bagpipes reinforced the melancholy that Rourke as-cribed to Collins's version of the hymn. In any case, from this point forward "Amazing Grace" would be associated with bagpipes, and at countless funer-als, especially occasions of state, it would be this version of "Amazing Grace" that would be called upon. For example, on November 20, 1998, at the memo-rial service for Michel Trudeau, the son of the former prime minister of Canada Pierre Trudeau who was killed in a skiing accident, "Amazing Grace" was played on bagpipes.

Since the 1970s the hymn has been widely recorded in all genres by a variety of musical artists. The All Music Guide (www.allmusic.com) lists some two hundred albums that include the song "Amazing Grace" among their tracks. Because of this popularity the hymn has become almost a cliché, so that a book or film with a character named Grace may well be given the title, "Amazing Grace," with only the thinnest reference to the hymn.[29] But the hymn has also figured in various twentieth-century secular stories of redemption, ranging from twelve-step recovery programs to narratives of feminist or gay and lesbian emancipation.

One subtle use of the hymn was in the 1982 film *Star Trek II: The Wrath of Khan*, produced by Harve Bennett. The earlier *Star Trek: The Motion Picture* had been under the editorial control of the series creator, Gene Roddenberry, and it captured his utopian vision of the merging of humanity and technology. It was a creative and critical disaster, and with *The Wrath of Khan*, Roddenberry was pushed to the side. Bennett determined to introduce more human elements of vulnerability to the story, and so the second film is built around concerns about life and death and aging. The *Star Trek* series has always drawn broadly on philosophical and literary ideas and integrated these into its science fiction. In *The Wrath of Khan* the question is introduced quite early from Dickens's *Tale of Two Cities* of whether it is better for one man to die on behalf of the many, and this is a question to which the film returns at its climax. The story is set in the twenty-third century, and James Kirk's old nemesis Khan has stolen a top-secret device named project Genesis that has the power to create life ex nihilo in dead regions of the universe, but also to wreak havoc if used wrongly. Kirk and his crew set out to stop Khan, but the USS *Enterprise* is damaged beyond repair in battle. At the moment of crisis, Spock enters the radioactive engine room to fix the problem, but in so doing sacrifices his own life. Again, we hear the lines from Dickens about one man giving his life on behalf of the many.

In the course of the battle the Genesis device has been detonated and a beautiful new planet has been created with life evolving before everyone's eyes. There is a "funeral" for Spock, and then his casket is sent off to rest on the new Genesis planet, in a sort of burial at sea. At the climax of this "funeral" we hear "Amazing Grace" being played on bagpipes by Mr. Scott.

In the next *Star Trek* film, we find that the properties of the new Genesis planet have brought Spock back to life again. The whole film offers a picture of redemption replete with biblical allusions but reset within a secular cosmology and indeed a secular eschatology. At the center of this, "Amazing Grace" functions as a subtle quotation, and it is perfect. It is the U-shaped story of redemption carried by a tune that has already been popular in America for a decade and that has already functioned as a "secular spiritual" of psychodynamic healing and of hope in the midst of tragedy.

Yet even in secular America, "Amazing Grace" is more than a cliché. The hymn has still figured prominently at moments of intense national grieving. After the space shuttle *Challenger* burst into flames on television in 1986, the nation also heard "Amazing Grace" played at the memorial service for the astronauts. After terrorists exploded a bomb at an Oklahoma City federal building in 1995, killing 168 people, "Amazing Grace" was again carried from church services by television news programs. The memorial Mass for John F. Kennedy Jr. in July 1999 concluded with the singing of "Amazing Grace" as well. Again, immediately after the terrorist attacks on September 11, 2001, a spontaneous candlelight vigil began in Union Square in New York and people began to sing "Amazing Grace." And examples could easily be multiplied. It is, as Rourke has said, the "spiritual national anthem" of America.

Many mainline denominations have been embarrassed by Newton's use of the word "wretch" in the second line of the hymn, and have provided revisions, such as, "Amazing Grace! How sweet the sound! That saved and strengthened me!" Ironically, this objection has not surfaced in the secular use of "Amazing Grace." The fact that the hymn allows for an honest acknowledgment of wretchedness in life must certainly be part of the reason the hymn offers comfort in the midst of tragedy. Although the words of Newton's hymn express thanksgiving for grace, it has most often functioned as a prayer *for* grace as it has been sung in the midst of tragedy today.

One of the reasons why the hymn has so easily functioned in a secular context so different from the world of John Newton is that God is nowhere mentioned in the hymn except in the second to last line ("no less days to sing God's praise"). The hymn is simply a celebration of the experience of grace. At least that is how it has been received. Newton certainly intended "grace" as a metonym, where the name of an attribute stands poetically in the place of the thing (as *crown* may stand for *king*); that is, "grace" means "the God who is full of grace." But in the secular twentieth century, "grace" in Newton's hymn is often a vague personification, where an abstraction is treated as if it were a person. It is simply the experience of grace that is celebrated, the mysterious giftedness of life in the midst of death and tragedy. In many cases, and certainly in the case of Judy Collins, this is a powerful example of what M. H. Abrams in his book *Natural Supernaturalism* described as the transmutation of the Christian narrative into the wholly immanent categories of the ego, its alienation, and its reintegration.

Conclusion

Over the course of two centuries the meaning of "Amazing Grace" has changed from its original composition as a statement of biblical theology to become in nineteenth-century American evangelicalism—particularly in the frontier camp meetings at the beginning of the century and the urban revivals at its end—a testimony of wholly individual conversion. In the twentieth century the meaning of the hymn changed again to reflect its secular context, and it became a polyvalent symbol of redemption for a diverse society. It has appeared at times as an expression of hope in a vague, unspecified deity, and at other times as a therapeutic narrative of inner healing. And certainly it has continued to be sung and cherished in communities of faith.

Inevitably, I have stressed the diversity of meanings that have been wrung out of the hymn as it has been received in different contexts. But in conclusion I want to raise one other possibility. In all of these contexts the evangelical sentiment has remained that personal tragedy may be redeemed by an authentic experience of undeserved love. Perhaps, after all, the story of "Amazing Grace" is not just about communities of interpretation and reader-response hermeneutics. Perhaps, after all, the need for personal honesty and undeserved mercy is a universal anthropological reality, and not merely a culturally contingent phenomenon. Perhaps, even in secular America, John the Baptist's declaration ought to be seen as a matter of universal amazement, that the law was given through Moses, but "grace and truth came through Jesus Christ."

Notes

1. Kevin Cox, "Tidings of Comfort," *Homemaker's* (November–December 1998), 156.

2. John Newton, *Works of the Rev. John Newton*, 6 vols. (London: J. Johnson, 1808–9), 1: passim; D. Bruce Hindmarsh, *John Newton and the English Evangelical Tradition* (Oxford: Oxford University Press, 1996), 13–48.

3. Entry for Sunday, January 27, 1765, cited in Josiah Bull, *John Newton of Olney and St. Mary Woolnoth* (London: Religious Tract Society, 1868), 138.

4. John Newton, entry for June 1–7, 1767, autograph diary, written in *The Complete Pocket-Book . . . for the Year of Our Lord 1767*, Lambeth Palace Library, London.

5. On Newton's contribution to the *Olney Hymns*, see Hindmarsh, *John Newton*, 257–88.

6. John Newton, entry for February 20, 1774, ms. diary, 1773–1805, Firestone Library, Princeton University, Princeton, NJ.

7. Cf. Madeleine Forell Marshall and Janet Todd, *English Congregational Hymns in the Eighteenth Century* (Lexington: University Press of Kentucky, 1982), 88–9, 92, 102, 148.

8. John Newton and William Cowper, *Olney Hymns* (London, 1779), 1: 41.

9. M. Pauline Parker, "The Hymn as a Literary Form," *Eighteenth-Century Studies* 8 (1975): 401–2.

10. William E. Phipps, "'Amazing Grace' in the Hymnwriter's Life," *Anglican Theological Review* 72 (1990): 306.

11. John Julian, ed., *A Dictionary of Hymnology* (London: John Murray, 1892), s.v. "Newton, John."

12. Julian, ed., *Dictionary*, s.v. "Amazing Grace."

13. Erik Routley, *An English-Speaking Hymnal Guide* (Collegeville, MN: The Liturgical Press, 1979), 6.

14. Sources for hymnbook data in this section include the Research Libraries Information Network (RLIN) bibliography file; Leonard Webster Ellinwood and Elizabeth Kelly Lockwood, *Bibliography of American Hymnals Compiled from the Files of the Dictionary of American Hymnology* (New York: University Music Editions, 1983); Leonard Webster Ellinwood, *Dictionary of American Hymnology, First-Line Index* (New York: University Music Editions, 1984); and Louis F. Benson, *The English Hymn: Its Development and Use in Worship,* reprint edition (Richmond, VA: John Knox Press, 1962). I am indebted to Mary Louse VanDyke, Librarian/Coordinator of the Dictionary of American Hymnology, Oberlin College, Oberlin, OH, for her assistance in tracking down hymnal references. I am likewise indebted to William J. Reynolds, Distinguished Professor of Church Music Emeritus, Southwestern Baptist Theological College, for providing me with generous advice and with a copy of his unpublished manuscript, "'Amazing Grace': A Twentieth Century Phenomenon," text of his lecture for the 1999 Hugh T. McElrath Lecture Series, Southern Baptist Theological Seminary, October 20, 1999.

15. Benson, *English Hymn*, 374.

16. Ibid., 293.

17. William Walker, *The Southern Harmony and Musical Companion,* ed. Glenn C. Wilcox, facsimile reprint of the 1854 edition (Lexington: University Press of Kentucky, 1987), 30.

18. Reynolds, "Amazing Grace," 6.

19. Ibid., 7.

20. George Marsden, *Fundamentalism and American Culture: The Shaping of Twentieth-Century Evangelicalism* (London: Oxford University Press, 1980), 36.

21. William J. Reynolds and Milburn Price, *A Survey of Christian Hymnody* (Carol Stream, IL: Hope Publishing, 1987), 100–101.

22. Reynolds, "Amazing Grace," 13; Reynolds, "Heavens no, not John P. Rees," *The Hymn* 39 (1988): 13–15.

23. Mahalia Jackson and Evan McLeod White, *Movin' On Up* (New York: Hawthorn Books, 1966); Jules Schwerin, *Got to Tell It: Mahalia Jackson, Queen of Gospel* (New York: Oxford University Press, 1992); Mary Rourke and Emily Gwathmey, *Amazing Grace in America: Our Spiritual National Anthem* (Santa Monica, CA: Angel City Press, 1996), 112.

24. Judy Collins, Introduction to *Amazing Grace* (New York: Hyperion, 1991), 4.

25. Judy Collins, *Singing Lessons* (New York: Pocket Books, 1998), 165.

26. Rourke and Gwathmey, *Amazing Grace in America,* 116.

27. Collins, *Singing Lessons,* 166.

28. "Amazing 'Amazing Grace,' " *The Hymn* 23 (1972): 93.

29. For example, Eve Gaddy, *Amazing Grace* (New York: Bantam Love, 1998), a mass-market paperback novel—full of the usual intrigue, crime, and passion—about a character named Grace O'Malley, the sheriff of a small town in Texas.

2
The Methodist National Anthem

"O for a Thousand Tongues to Sing" and the Development of American Methodism

John R. Tyson

"O for a Thousand Tongues to Sing"
(John R. Tyson, ed., *Charles Wesley: A Reader* [New York: Oxford University Press, 1989])

1. Glory to God, and praise and love
   Be ever, ever given;
   By Saints below, and Saints above,
   The church in earth and Heaven.

2. On this glad day the glorious Sun
   Of Righteousness arose;
   On my benighted soul He shone,
   And fill'd it with repose.

3. Sudden expired the legal strife;
   'Twas then I ceased to grieve,
   My second, real living life
   I then began to live.

4. Then with my *heart* I first believed,
   Believed with faith Divine;
   Power with the Holy Ghost received
   To call the Saviour *mine.*

5. I felt my Lord's atoning blood
   Close to *my* soul applied;
   Me, me He loved—the Son of God
   For *me,* for *me,* He died!

6. I found and own'd His promise true,
   Ascertain'd of my part;
   My pardon pass'd in heaven I knew,
   When written on my heart.

7. O for a thousand tongues to sing
   My dear Redeemer's praise!
   The glories of my God and King,
   The triumphs of His grace.

8. My gracious Master, and my God,
   Assist me to proclaim
   To spread through all the earth abroad
   The honors of Thy name.

9. Jesus, the name that charms our fears,
   That bids our sorrows cease;
   'Tis music in the sinner's ears,
   'Tis life, and health, and peace!

10. He breaks the power of cancell'd sin,
    He sets the prisoner free;
    His blood can make the foulest clean,
    His blood avail'd for me.

11. His speaks; and listening to His voice,
    New life the dead receive,
    The mournful, broken hearts rejoice,
    The humble poor believe.

12. Hear Him, ye deaf; His praise, ye dumb,
    Your lossen'd tongues employ;
    Ye blind, behold your Saviour come;
    And leap, ye lame, for joy.

13. Look unto Him, ye nations, own
    Your God, ye fallen race!
    Look, and be saved through faith alone;
    But justified by grace!

14. See all you sins on Jesus laid;
    The Lamb of God was slain,
    His soul was once an offering made
    For every soul of man.

15. Harlots, and publicans, and thieves
    In holy triumph join;
    Saved is the sinner that believes
    From crimes as great as mine.

16. Murderers, and all ye hellish crew,
    Ye sons of lust and pride,
    Believe the Saviour died for you;
    For me the Saviour died.

17. Awake from guilty nature's sleep,
    And Christ shall give you light,
    Cast all your sins into the deep,
    And wash the Ethiop white.

18. With me, your chief, you then shall know,
    Shall feel your sins forgiven;
    Anticipate your heaven below,
    And own that love is heaven.

Charles Wesley's "O for a Thousand Tongues to Sing" made its American de-but in 1756 when John Wesley's 1753 collection of *Hymns and Spiritual Songs for the Use of Real Christians of All Denominations* was printed in Philadel-phia. The 1756 hymnal was not a success, and it was not reprinted. But it did provide a repository of Charles Wesley's hymns from which American hymnbook makers drew materials.[1] Wesley's 1780 *Collection of Hymns for the Use of the People Called Methodists,* commonly called "the large hymn book," quickly became available to American Methodists, but it had little influence on American hymnody till 1849.[2] In 1784, John Wesley sent the American Methodists still another hymnal, *A Collection of Psalms and Hymns for the Lord's Day (Attached to the Sunday Service of the Methodists in North America),* which he intended as the standard liturgy and collection of hymns for the American church. This collection, which Benjamin Franklin Crawford described as a "handbook on evangelism," opened with "O for a Thousand Tongues—" "a great revival hymn."[3]

American Methodists preferred a "renegade" hymnal, Robert Spence's *Collection of Hymns from Various Authors* (1781), generally known as *A Pocket Hymnbook*. John Wesley censored the *Pocket Hymnbook* because it contained hymns he considered "objectionable."[4] This began a pattern that continued through the first century of American Methodist hymnody. Hymnologist David Music observed, "[Here is] . . . one of the earliest examples of a conflict between an officially sanctioned hymnal and the tastes of the people for whom it was intended."[5] So thorough was the rejection of John Wesley's *Psalms and Hymns* that American Methodist bishops Francis Asbury and Thomas Coke took it upon themselves to develop their own version of *The Pocket Hymnbook* in 1790. This unofficial hymnbook was republished, revised, and enlarged with supplements until 1832, when the supplement was actually larger than the hymnbook itself. While gradually adding American compositions to the Wesleyan corpus (and thereby allowing the American Methodist Church to begin its own hymn tradition), the *Pocket Hymnbook* continued to carry "O for a Thousand Tongues" as its first hymn. The *Pocket Hymnbook* became a best seller among American Methodists. It went through thirty-five separate editions by 1805.[6]

In the *Pocket Hymnbook* "O for a Thousand Tongues" appears just as John Wesley presented it in his 1780 *Collection*. The hymn has ten stanzas in two parts. The first part begins with Charles's original verse seven ("O for a thousand tongues to sing") and runs through the original verse twelve ("Hear Him, ye deaf, His praise, ye dumb"). The second part begins with Charles's original verse thirteen ("Look unto Him, ye nations, own") and includes verses fourteen, seventeen, and eighteen from the original text. Verses fifteen and sixteen, which carry references to "Harlots, and publicans and thieves," as well as "Murderers, and all ye hellish crew," were judged inappropriate for public worship.

In the late eighteenth century, Wesleyan hymns first appeared in significant numbers in two non-Wesleyan American hymnals: George Strebeck's *A Collection of Evangelical Hymns* (1797) (published by the English Lutheran Church in New York) and Josiah Goddard's Baptist *A New and Beautiful Collection of Select Hymns* (1798).[7]

The Asbury Era of American Methodism

The Methodist Episcopal Church (MEC) traces its inception to the Christmas Conference of 1784, which launched the church as an independent body.

William Warren Sweet assesses correctly American Methodist hymnody: "The Methodist Episcopal Church began with a great musical tradition and possessed a hymnal from its organization, which Wesley had prepared. The hymns were so arranged as to make the hymnbook a practical manual for the teaching of Christian truth, and the hymns were, of course heavily freighted with Methodist theology."[8]

Despite the overwhelming success of the unofficial *Pocket Hymnbook,* American Methodist hymnody went off "in new and uncontrolled directions."[9] These directions were marked out by the erosion of Wesleyan liturgical standards on the one hand and the emergence of camp meetings on the other.

The Christmas Conference of 1784 evidenced some of the tensions that would persist within the Methodist Episcopal Church. The American bishops, Thomas Coke (1747–1814) and Francis Asbury (1745–1816), did what they could to implement Wesley's directions. Wesley instructed "our Helpers to read the Morning and Evening Service out of our liturgy, on the Lord's Day," and directed the preachers to "sing no hymns of [their] own composing."[10] These guidelines were intended to keep American Methodist liturgy and hymnody tied to the English Wesleyan tradition. The minutes from the Christmas Conference revealed an interest in improving singing in the Methodist Episcopal Church without moving away from its Wesleyan foundations: "How shall we reform our singing?" they asked. "Let all our preachers who have any knowledge in the notes, improve it by learning to sing true themselves and keeping close to Mr. Wesley's tunes and hymns."[11] In fact, however, John Wesley's *Sunday Service* was not often used, since Americans were "convinced that they could pray better with their books and eyes shut."[12]

Between 1784 to 1792, American Methodism rode the crest of a revival that swept the land and found expression in camp meetings.[13] For Methodists, camp meetings combined both new and familiar features.[14] John Wesley had designated "Christian Conference" as a "means of grace" in the Methodist tradition.[15] Francis Asbury's journal indicates that Methodist conferences were often large gatherings that had a revivalist tone. On November 3, 1781, for example, he noted: "We had twelve preachers and about one thousand people at quarterly meeting."[16] The quarterly conferences were occasions for preaching, prayer, testimony, the love feast, and hymns. But conferences became business sessions, while camp meetings featured the revivalist impulse.[17]

By 1802, Methodists had enthusiastically embraced camp meetings. Writing to Bishop Coke in 1811 Asbury reported: "Our camp meetings, I think, amount to between four and five hundred annually, some of which continue for a space of six or eight days. It is supposed that it is not uncommon for ten thousand persons to be present at one of those meetings."[18] Methodists collected and published the songs sung at camp meetings. An early example is *A General Selection of the Newest and Most Admired Hymns and Spiritual Songs Now in Use,* (1807) collected by Stith Mead.

The Methodist religious establishment took an ambivalent attitude toward camp meetings. Writing in 1810, Jesse Lee, an early American Methodist preacher, aptly described the situation: "these meetings have never been authorized by the Methodists, either at their General or Annual Conferences. They have been allowed of; but we, as a body of people, have never made any rules or regulations about them; we allow our presiding elders and traveling preachers to appoint them when and where they please, and to conduct them in what manner they think fit."[19]

Just as Bishop Asbury oversaw the dismantling of the Wesleyan liturgical foundations of the Methodist Episcopal Church, so also Asbury superintended the emergence of the Methodist camp meetings. Charles Ferguson reported, "Bishop Asbury combined orderliness with zeal. . . . If camp meetings were to become Methodist, they would have to become Methodistic, strict in form and reliable in plan and structure."[20] In an 1805 letter to Thomas Sargent, Asbury stressed: "My continual cry to the Presiding Elders is order, order, good order. All things must be arranged temporally and spiritually, like a well disciplined army."[21]

The quasi-official status of the Methodist camp meetings and their ambivalent relationship to the Methodist Episcopal Church's institutional structure meant that camp meeting spiritual songs were not included in official Methodist hymn books, and Methodist churches produced and used a variety of unofficial song books instead of (or in addition to) their official hymnals.

Camp Meetings and American Methodist Hymnody

"Methodist revival song books poured from the presses in the [eighteen] fifties and sixties, and nobody but the bishops [who made rules against them] seemed to pay any attention to the rules."[22] Within American Methodism a struggle between the Wesleyan hymns preferred by the denominational establishment and the popular spiritual songs featured in camp meetings soon emerged. Nathan Hatch detected a fundamental cultural undercurrent within this struggle: "Popular gospel music became a pervasive reality in Jacksonian culture because people wrested singing from churchly control. The music created a spontaneous, moving medium capable of capturing the identity of

plain people. The result was that official literary hymns had difficulty competing with lively gospel music."[23] Louis Benson described the hymnody that
resulted: "The Wesleyan hymn was . . . the inheritance: the camp meeting
hymn the most distinctive feature of American Methodist hymnody, both as
to its own practice and as to its influence on other churches. In one sense a
development of the Evangelistic hymn of the Wesleys, the camp meeting
hymn was at best a deterioration and at worst a parody."[24]

  B. St. James Fry, a nineteenth-century Methodist apologist for camp meeting songs, explained how they developed: "At the commencement of the revival those familiar hymns, known in all our orthodox congregations were
used, but it was soon felt that they gave but imperfect expression to the ardent
feelings of the worshipers. The deficiency here was principally supplied by the
preachers. Hymns or 'spiritual songs,' as they were more frequently called, to
the cultivated ear rude and bold in expression, rugged in meter, and imperfect in rhyme, and often improvised in the preaching stand, were at once accepted as more suited to their wants."[25] Benson identified the development
of the chorus or refrain as the "predominant feature" of the camp meeting
hymn. This refrain was "not always connected with the subject matter of the
stanza, but [was] rather ejaculatory."[26] Dickson Bruce described it as follows:
"The minister initiated a song and then was joined by the congregation, and
this pattern was further reflected in the verse-chorus structure of the camp-
meeting spiritual songs. The verse, usually based on a regular church hymn,
demanded some prior knowledge to be sung in a setting where either there
were no books or it would have been too dark to use a book anyway. But the
choruses were simple and redundant and were sung several times during a
song; therefore every one present could quickly learn the words and join in
singing."[27] Such spiritual songs were, in Fry's words, "quickly committed to
memory, and to considerable extent usurped the place of the older and more
worthy hymns."[28]

  Just as simplicity of text and tune accounts for the success of camp meeting "spiritual songs," so also it explains the emotional tone of the meetings.
Spiritual songs reshaped the role of Methodist hymnody. The Wesleys, as
evident in John Wesley's famous Preface to the 1780 *Collection of Hymns*, concerned themselves with the teaching role of their hymns. John Wesley frequently cited or appended hymns to his published sermons as didactic, doctrinal pieces.[29] But with the advent of the camp meeting, the emphasis upon
the didactic role of hymns gave way to an interest in the emotional tone the
hymns employed. Fry, writing in 1859, represented this transition well: "The

hymns of the church are not primarily designed to afford instruction in doctrine, but to open a channel for the expression of feeling."[30]

Camp meetings shaped the form (verse-chorus), literary and musical style (crude and popular), and emotional texture of spiritual songs and also set their theological focus. As Bruce observed: "Just as conversion was the core of the camp meeting, so was it the foundation upon which the spiritual choruses were built."[31] "O for a Thousand Tongues to Sing" is a classic conversion hymn, which fits well with the theological agenda of the spiritual song. "O for a Thousand Tongues to Sing" shared the personal language and evocative descriptions of conversion with the typical spiritual songs. Yet, "O for a Thousand Tongues to Sing" does not appear frequently in revival songbooks of this era. In the antebellum period, it is generally found only in official denominational hymnals.[32]

In some instances, though, camp meetings used hymns as "mother-hymns" from which spiritual songs were produced. Jane Ellen Lorenz described a "mother-hymn" as: "the words of a 'standard' hymn in part or whole (usually set to a folk-hymn tune), to which has been attached a camp meeting chorus."[33] "O for a Thousand Tongues" took at least four different forms as a "mother-hymn." The most common revivalist adaptation married it to the gospel song "Blessed Be the Name." The Wesleyan text functions as a "mother-hymn," and "Blessed Be the Name" provides the repeating chorus. This version of the hymn uses only the first two lines of three verses of the original (seven, nine, and ten) along with a new couplet: "I never shall forget that day / . . . When Jesus washed my sins away." The repeating chorus: "Blessed be the name of the Lord!" is sung between the two lines of the couplets, and again twice as a longer chorus after each verse. Hymnologist William J. Reynolds attributes this alteration to Ralph E. Hudson who published it in *Songs for the Ransomed* (1887).[34] This version of the hymn became popular in Southern Baptist Churches and is still carried in the *Baptist Hymnal*. A common tune tradition, which weds "O for a Thousand Tongues" to the tune "Blessed Be the Name" without adapting a chorus to it, may also have its basis in Hudson's adaptation.[35]

D. B. Turner's *Hymns New and Old* (1891) includes another adaptation. Charles Wesley's original verses seven through ten become the verses of the new hymn, and a new chorus is added: "O, matchless Christ / O, Wondrous King! / O Lamb for sinners slain; / Let all the earth Thy praises sing / While angels join the strain." A third adaptation is in *Billows of Song* (1895), where verses seven–ten of Charles Wesley's text were married to a new chorus: "I've been redeemed, and I am singing / Eternal praise to Him I'm bringing / The triumphs of His grace proclaiming; / Hallelujah! To the Savior King."[36] The hymn is set to a tune called "Bryant." A final adaptation of "O for a Thousand Tongues" is attested in *Jewels in Song,* published in 1925. In this version Wesley's verses seven through nine were combined with two new verses: "Jesus, the name to sinners dear; / The name to sinners given! / It scatters all their guilty fear; / It turns their hell to heaven." And: "O that the world might taste and see / The riches of His grace! / The arms of love that compass me / Would all the world embrace."[37] The chorus appended to this song is an adaptation of Wesley's tenth verse: "He breaks the power of cancell'd sin / He sets the prisoner free."

The camp meeting was primarily an event of "the plain folk" of the American frontier: it allowed them to express themselves in ways that were not dictated by "their European Protestant heritage or by some governing body foreign to them."[38] Methodists gradually turned away from the traditional Wesleyan hymnody born in the eighteenth-century English revival in favor of the cruder spiritual songs born in nineteenth-century camp meetings. While there is some evidence that Wesleyan texts like "O for a Thousand Tongues to Sing" functioned as "mother-hymns" from which revival songs developed, the main stream flowing out of the revivalist movement took American Methodism away from its European Wesleyan roots toward a more populist American identity.

Nathan Bangs and the Beginnings of Consolidation

If the Asbury era of American Methodism was characterized by adaptations associated with camp meetings, the next period—epitomized by the career of Nathan Bangs (1778–1862)—represents the transformation of the Methodist movement into a national church. Bangs assumed leadership of Methodism in New York City in 1810. During his fifty-year tenure, he saw membership grow from 2,000 to more than 17,000. Two or three humble buildings became a network of more than sixty churches, "with some of them," he admitted, "ranking among the best ecclesiastical edifices of the nation."[39] Like Asbury and the Wesleys, Nathan Bangs did not oppose "experimental Christianity," but he did oppose the emotional excesses that prompted Philip Schaff to describe Methodism as "barbarous Christianity."[40] He put an end to emotional displays in the churches under his immediate direction and gradually set the tone for a more stately liturgical form of Methodist worship better suited to the urban environment and the rising social status of the membership. As part of his program of bringing propriety and middle-class legitimacy to American Methodism, Bangs opposed camp meetings and the spiritual songs associated with them. These he described as "ditties," which "possessed little of the spirit of poetry [paraphrasing John Wesley's 1780 Preface] and therefore added nothing to true intellectual taste."[41] Contrasting the respective roles and postures of Asbury and Bangs, Nathan Hatch concluded: "Bangs envisioned Methodism as a popular establishment, faithful to the movement's original fire but tempered with virtues of middle-class propriety and urbane congeniality. If Asbury's career represented Methodism's triumph as a populist movement, with control at the cultural periphery, then Bangs' career illustrates the centripetal tug of respectable culture."[42]

Within American Methodism, the process of consolidation and development of denominational identity influenced the production of the Methodist Episcopal Church's first standard hymnbook in 1836. An official hymnbook would (presumably) end the deluge of unofficial songbooks popular in Methodist churches. Ironically, the first official American Methodist hymnbook was composed entirely of hymns of European origin. It was, as Crawford described it, "a veritable hand book of Methodist revivalism," but it was a compilation of *English* Methodist revivalism.[43] The 1836, *Methodist Hymn Book* (MHB) carried 429 Wesleyan hymns, and "O for a Thousand Tongues" was the first hymn in the collection. The Wesleyan identity of the 1836 hymnal could hardly be more complete. But camp meeting favorites were conspicuous by their absence.

Denominational hymnbooks are one of the venues in which churches claim their historical identity and chart their theological direction. Following the "revivalist" hymnbook of 1836, each successive official hymnal evidenced increased institutionalism. As Crawford noted: "There is a marked trend after the first hymn book [1836] toward an interest in religious institutions, emphasizing their functional aspects, such as the church, the sabbath, the Scriptures, the Sacraments, the keeping of special days, commemorations, thanksgivings, schools, and colleges."[44]

The *Methodist Quarterly Review* gives ample evidence of the struggle that ensued within the MEC over the direction of the church's hymnody. An 1844 editorial by George Peck voiced support for the establishment's apparent attempt to exclude camp meeting songs from official hymn books: "As the *halt* and *maimed* were unfit for sacrifice, so the medium through which praise is offered to the Most High should be *without blemish*. Common-place thought, feeble expressions, unmeaning expletives cost nothing. When tortured, for the service of the sanctuary, into limping doggerel, and slip-shod jingling, they become an abomination."[45] A later article by Fry, written in 1859, admitted the crude lyrics and style of some of the spiritual songs, but also argued that some compilations, like *The Pilgrim Songster,* had validity as authentic conveyors of American Methodist tradition, "a relic of the days of Bishops Asbury, McKendree, Burke, Wilkinson, Sale, Lakin, Taylor, and many others, long since resting from their labors."[46]

The second official MEC hymnbook was published in 1849. It was much larger than the 1836 edition, offering a total of 1,148 hymns. The 1849 *Methodist Hymn Book* included an increased number (558) of Wesleyan hymns; "O for a Thousand Tongues" continued in its place of prominence, at the head of the *Methodist Hymn Book.* Equally significant, the 1849 hymnal also included fifty hymns of American composition. This suggests that the committee tried to compromise between traditionalists who wanted a Wesleyan hymnbook and revivalists who lobbied for the inclusion of indigenous American songs. Dissatisfaction with the 1849 hymnal resulted in the publication of several unofficial hymnals, which were commonly called "social hymnbooks."

Social hymnbooks "were intended for use in the prayer service and conference meeting. They were a compromise between the churchly hymn book and the camp meeting song book."[47] Because of their mediating position, these semiofficial books modified, preserved, and improved the camp meeting songs as they brought them into contact with the church and churchly functions. Reverends McDonald and Hubbard compiled *The Wesleyan Sacred Harp* (1856) by combining the best spiritual songs with hymns from the official Methodist hymnbook. "O for a Thousand Tongues" appears in *The Wesleyan Sacred Harp* as a cento based on verses seven through eleven. It is carried as well as a hymn and set to the (fuging) tune "Coronation." *The Methodist Church School Hymnal* (n.d.) of the same period offers a longer version of "O for a Thousand Tongues" set to a statelier tune called "St. Magnus." *Heart and Voice,* an 1865 publication of the MEC, and *Songs of Zion,* an 1864 imprint of the MEC South, both carry "O for a Thousand Tongues" (and other authorized hymns) along with a large selection of gospel songs; both books set "O for a Thousand Tongues" to the tune "Antioch." Hymnbooks designed specifically for use in the MEC also appeared in this period without "O for a Thousand Tongues to Sing."[48]

During this same period, "O for a Thousand Tongues" appeared more frequently in hymnbooks published by other American Protestant churches. Its use in non-Wesleyan contexts brought about interesting textual alterations. One of the earliest in the Free Will Baptist hymnbook, *Hymns for Christian*

Melody, (1843) introduced a subtle repudiation of the Wesleyan doctrine of Christian Perfection. Charles Wesley had penned "full salvation" into the first two lines of (the original) verse ten: "He breaks the power of cancell'd sin, / He sets the prisoner free." Perhaps that message was too optimistic for non-Methodists, and those lines were often amended to: "He breaks the power of *reigning* sin; / He sets the prisoner free." Many Baptist hymnbooks, such as *The Psalmist, with Music* (1860), 1864 *Devotional Hymn Book* of the American Baptist Church, and *The Baptist Hymn and Tune Book* (1871), *The Baptist Hymnal* (1896) carried "O for a Thousand Tongues" with this alteration. It also appeared in nondenominational revivalist songbooks influenced by the Baptist tradition, for example: *The Vestry Harp* (1862), *The Clarion* (1867), *The Apples of Gold* (1867), *Gospel Light* (1895) and in Reformed and Presbyterian hymnals.[49] This theological alteration appears as well in a few MEC social hymnbooks. One instance is *Songs of Zion* (1864), an unofficial publication of the MEC South. This suggests something the Wesleyan and Free Methodist Churches already knew: American Methodism was becoming uncomfortable with its traditional doctrine of entire sanctification.[50]

A second alteration of roughly the same period also had theological significance. It first occurs in the Free Will Baptist *Hymns for Christian Melody* (1841). It also appears in Presbyterian *Psalms and Hymns* (1843) and *Songs of the Church* (1862).[51] "O for a Thousand Tongues" is carried as a cento comprised of Wesley's original verses number seven through ten and eighteen. The last verse is altered from the original: "With me, your chief, you then shall know, / Shall feel your sins forgiven; / Anticipate your heaven below, / And own that love is heaven," to *"Let us obey,* we then shall know / Shall feel our sins forgiven; / Anticipate in our heaven below, / And own that love is heaven."[52] The omission of Charles Wesley's original verse seventeen, which provided the context for the first line of this stanza, may have made verse eighteen sound strange to the editor's ear. But the alteration changed the theology of the hymn by turning a doxological prayer for perfect love into a charge to obey God in order to gain a foretaste of heaven. This seems to take significant steps toward the legalism that began infecting conservative Protestantism during this period. This alteration appears with considerable frequency in hymnals published between 1847 and 1901.[53]

Episcopalians who embraced "O for a Thousand Tongues" changed none of Charles Wesley's words. They simply reshuffled the order of Wesley's original stanzas. The earliest example occurs in *The Book of Common Praise* (1868), a companion to the *Book of Common Prayer.* A relatively long version of Wesley's text (verses seven, nine, eleven, twelve, eight) is set to the tune "Boston."[54] Wesley's original verse eight moves to the end of the hymn. The revised hymn ends with these words: "My Gracious Master, and my God, / Assist me to proclaim / To spread through all the earth abroad / The honors of Thy name." Where Charles Wesley's original version leaves the singer contemplating an infusion of God's love as "heaven below," the Anglican revision concludes with a mandate to evangelism. Not all American Episcopalian hymnals used this alteration. The Protestant Episcopal *Hymnal with Tunes* (1872) for example, does not. By 1893, however, American Episcopalians joined their Anglican cohorts in using the altered version. It appears in *The Hymnal of the Protestant Episcopal Church* of that year and continues thereafter.[55] This version subsequently found its way into hymnals of some non-Episcopalian denominations.[56]

New Methodist Denominations

During the antebellum period, the MEC experienced five significant schisms. Each reacted to the growing institutionalization of the MEC and its embrace of the values of mainstream American culture.

The people who founded the African Methodist Episcopal (AME) Church in 1816 and the AME Zion Church in 1821 expected the Methodist church to stand against the racist views of the dominant culture. Those who established the Methodist Protestant church wanted more democracy than the Methodist episcopacy was willing to give them. The Wesleyans and the Free Methodists lamented the loss of revival fire as well as of many earlier values, practices and emphases. The MEC South resisted the attempts of the MEC to keep it in the larger orbit of the national church. The 1844 North-South schism foreshadowed the division that would soon plunge the nation into the Civil War. Each of these bodies left the MEC and took with it a repository of Wesleyan hymnody as an authentic part of its historical heritage and theological tradition.

The earliest AME hymnal, *A Collection of Hymns and Spiritual Songs* (1801), edited by Bishop Richard Allen, carries several of Charles Wesley's hymns, but not "O for a Thousand Tongues to Sing." The hymn did appear in the *Collection of Hymns* (1843), where it is near the front of the collection and again in the *African Methodist Episcopal Church Hymn Book* (1868). The use of the hymn signals the AME connection to the heritage and theology of the Wesleyan tradition.[57] There is reason to believe that "O for a Thousand Tongues" was sung in a distinctive manner by the African American Methodists.[58]

The Collection of Hymns (1851) published by the newly formed Wesleyan Methodist Connection, carried "O for a Thousand Tongues," though not as the first hymn. With the appearance of the *Hymnal of the Wesleyan Methodist Church* (1884) the hymn took its place of honor at the head of the Wesleyan hymnal, and the text was set to the same tune that was championed by the MEC, "Azmon." The Wesleyan Church's *Sacred Hymns and Tunes* (1895) also carried "O for a Thousand Tongues" number one. The earliest Free Methodist hymnbook about which I have information was the *Free Methodist Hymnal* (1910), which Benson describes as a joint project with Wesleyan Methodists; apparently one book was marketed with two titles.[59] "O for a Thousand Tongues" is the first hymn in this hymnal. This may imply that the dissenting churches of the Wesleyan tradition wanted to signal their continuity with the historical roots of the tradition. While the book includes two hundred Wesleyan hymns among 730, gospel songs clearly predominate.

Concerted Consolidation in the Post–Civil War Era

After the Civil War, the MEC took steps toward corporate consolidation; as Crawford put it: "What was in the beginning a revival movement had become a church."[60] The shelf life of the 1849 official MEC North hymnbook had been enhanced significantly by the production of *The Lesser Hymnal* (1875). The Book Committee officially sanctioned this book, and its appearance indicated their recognition that the 1849 *Methodist Hymn Book* had not successfully bridged the gap between the institutional church and the church-going public who were purchasing unofficial social hymnbooks and gospel songbooks in ever increasing numbers. *The Lesser Hymnal* was, as the title implies, a significant abridgement of the bulky official hymnbook, and it attempted to placate the singers of spiritual songs by including "enough lighter hymns to make it more competitive, especially for Sunday-Schools, youth groups, and social gatherings."[61]

The 1876 MEC North General Conference ordered the production of a third standard hymnbook. It is appropriate to see this development in the context of the process of consolidation already underway at various levels in the church; this assessment is certainly borne out by the contents of the new hymnbook when it appeared in 1878. A minor revision of the title of the 1878 book suggested a significant change of direction. Where the previous MEC books had been called *The Methodist Hymn Book*, this one was *The Methodist Hymnal*; the churchly title described a more liturgical book. "O for a Thousand Tongues" was "the flagship" hymn in the MEC *Hymnal* (1878). It is carried in a relatively long, unaltered version made up of Charles Wesley's (original) verses seven through twelve. The book broke new ground in moving away from the traditional text-only format and printing lyrics and music on the same page. This procedure has particular significance for "O for a Thousand Tongues," since this is the first time that an official Methodist hymnbook marries Charles Wesley's lyrics to Lowell Mason's arrangement of Carl Gläser's tune "Azmon."

The chasm between official Methodist hymnals and nondenominational social hymnbooks seems to have widened during the last third of the nineteenth century. This growing distance was demonstrated in the unofficial, revivalist songbooks by their willingness to develop their own text traditions for "O for a Thousand Tongues to Sing." These amounted to wholesale revisions of the Wesleyan shape of the hymn. The most common of these, as noted above, turned it into a gospel song by adding the repeating chorus: "Blessed Be the Name." Several other interesting alterations began appearing in the 1870s. One of these appeared in *Christian Hymns and Tune Book* (1870).[62] The hymn is set to the tune "Mason's Chant" and presented as a cento composed of Wesley's original verses seven through nine, as well as a new verse: "Hosanna to the Lord be given / In loudest, noblest strains! / Hosanna in the highest heaven! / Our great Redeemer reigns!" The new verse adds nothing to the theology of the hymn except the sort of "pious ejaculations" the editors of standard Methodist hymnals were determined to avoid.

A revision that had more lasting impact as a text tradition appeared in *Songs for the Ransomed* (1887).[63] Here the chorus: "I never shall forget the day, / When Jesus washed my sins away," has been added to the Wesleyan text. Although metaphors of "washing" one's sins away were not foreign to Charles Wesley's poetical texts, his version of the hymn used categories associated with sacrifice and pardon. This particular text pattern lived on in nondenominational hymnbooks; in most instances the altered text is set to the tune of "Blessed Be the Name" in a way that turns the Wesleyan hymn into a gospel song.[64]

The most extensive textual alteration of "O for a Thousand Tongues" in this era appears in *Sought Out Songs* (1887), where three stanzas of unknown origin are interpolated.

From Consolidation Toward Unification

This marriage of text and tune (Azmon) and the placement of "O for a Thousand Tongues" at the head of the official *Methodist Hymnal* played a part in the process of defining and consolidating the American Methodist tradition and laid a foundation for denominational reunion. Writing in 1899, for example, C. F. M'Kown identified the hymnbook as one of the fundamental "Unifying Factors in Methodism."[65] M'Kown located the unifying power of the Methodist hymnals in the hymns' conveyance of authentic Methodist theology: "Our hymnology is part and parcel of our theology. It is one of the strong bonds of union."[66] On this basis, then, the writer thanked the authorities for providing the denomination with standard hymnals and urged their use: "Let us make more of our *Hymnal* as a bond of union!"[67] The fact that the author argues so strongly for the adoption and application of official Methodist hymnals suggests, of course, that this practice was not as uniform as many within the MEC preferred. That the *Methodist Hymnal* (1878) did not succeed in unifying the worship of the church and ending the use of unofficial hymnbooks is illustrated by the publication of *The Epworth Hymnal* (1885).

Developed under the leadership of Bishop John H. Vincent, *The Epworth Hymnal* was published under the authority of the MEC General Conference primarily for use in Sunday schools and other social occasions. Emory Bucke noted "a suggestion of defensiveness" in the editors' Preface. The book included "popular songs" in which "the severest criticisms might point out slight defects" that "although sufficient to exclude them from the classic lists, do not justify their omission in a book 'for the people.' "[68] "O for a Thousand Tongues to Sing" was the first hymn in the *Epworth Hymnal*. It was set to "Azmon" and shortened (slightly) to verses seven, eight, nine, ten, and twelve of the original. This traditional Methodist hymn was becoming increasingly "popular" as well. As "O for a Thousand Tongues to Sing" became emblematic of Methodist denominational identity and organizational unity it began to disappear from social hymnbooks.

The *Methodist Hymnal* (1905) was a joint effort by a commission authorized by the MEC North, and the MEC South. It reflected interests, which reached back to the 1886 General Conference of the MEC South, for the development of a "a pan-Methodistic hymnal."[69] C. T. Winchester's article in the *Methodist Quarterly Review,* which heralded the appearance of the 1905 *Hymnal,* voiced the aspirations behind its publication: "The publication of a new hymnal for use by the two Methodist Episcopal Churches of America is, for various reasons, an event of deep interest, perhaps hardly anything could tend more powerfully to draw these two great bodies into closer sympathy and hasten the time that reunion, which, to some Methodists at all events, seems a consummation devoutly to be wished."[70] The *Hymnal* was a smaller book than its predecessors, and it carried only 121 of Charles Wesley's texts (a decrease of 187 from the 1878 edition). These were replaced, in part, by more hymns of American composition and a musical style that was "more popular and less Anglican."[71] "O for a Thousand Tongues to Sing" continued as number one in the 1905 *Methodist Hymnal*. It was set to "Azmon," by now the "standard tune" (at least among Methodists), and was composed of six verses (original seven, eight, nine, ten, eleven, and twelve).

Where the 1905 *Hymnal* had been perceived as being "more southern than northern, more rural than urban,"[72] the *Methodist Hymnal* (1935) reached for more inclusiveness. Crawford viewed it as reflecting "the trend toward a more stately worship, a matter of no little importance to the Church of this day."[73] An obvious example of this can be seen in the fact that "O for a Thousand Tongues to Sing," which had been the first hymn in all of the official Methodist hymnals that preceded the 1935 edition, was replaced by "Holy, Holy, Holy! Lord God Almighty," at the head of the hymnal. "O for a Thousand Tongues to Sing" appeared as number 162, in about the same location as in the *United Brethren Hymnal* (number 168) of the same year. The placement of "O for a Thousand Tongues" in the 1935 *Methodist Hymnal* makes sense if one accepts Crawford's theory that the book intended to move away from those hymns that "promote an evangelistic atmosphere."[74] "O for a Thousand Tongues to Sing," born in the conversion of Charles Wesley, carries connotations of individualism and revival. After thoroughly analyzing the contents of the 1935 hymnal, Crawford concluded: "the new hymnology has broadened its interest from that of saving souls from the depravity of sin to that of promoting the total meaning of life expressed in Christ's idea of a Kingdom of God."[75] Seen in this light, the *Methodist Hymnal* (1935) reflected larger doctrinal concerns.[76]

The appearance of *The Book of Hymns: Official Hymnal of the United Methodist Church* (1964), marked the next step toward American Methodist consolidation and unification. The 1964 *Book of Hymns* gave much more attention to the Wesleyan heritage than had its predecessor. In explaining its process, the hymnal committee referred to John Wesley's 1780 Preface to *A Collection of Hymns for the Use of the People Called Methodists*. Wesley's "Directions for Singing" (which he had published in his Preface to *Sacred Melody* [1761]) appeared for the first time in an American Methodist hymnal.[77] The liturgical revisions begun in the 1878 *Book of Hymns* continued; an "Order of Worship" preceded the hymns; and a Psalter, along with other "Aids for the Ordering of Worship" and "The Ritual" followed. The number of Charles Wesley's compositions increased to seventy-five (from the fifty-six of the 1935 edition), and "O for a Thousand Tongues" returned to its historically significant place at the head of the hymnal.

But the 1964 *Book of Hymns* did not meet the response hoped for. The 1968 merger with the Evangelical United Brethren Church (EUB) left the new body with two standard hymnals—the Methodist 1964 *Book of Hymns,* and the EUB *Hymnal* of 1957. Further, the rapidly changing theological landscape made sensitivity toward religious language and inclusion of hymnody from various Christian traditions increasingly important.[78] A series of officially sanctioned supplementary hymnbooks signaled that the regional, traditional (EUB, MEC), and rural-urban tensions within the American Methodist tradition had not yet been resolved: *Songs of Zion* (1981), *Supplement to the Book of Hymns* (1982), *Hymns from the Four Winds* (1983). The appearance of *Celeberemos I* and *II* (1992) and *Voices: Native American Hymns and Worship Resources* (1992) illustrated the United Methodist Church's (UMC's) growing concern for ethnic diversity within her communion.

The 1989 UMC hymnal was developed with these concerns in mind. As its Preface states: "The United Methodist Hymnal . . . embodies our former Methodist and former Evangelical United Brethren traditions, yet it is the first substantial revision of content and format since the 1870s. It has more singable qualities and contains a broader base of musical styles than any of its predecessors. Its contents reflect our Wesleyan heritage and witness: evangelical and ecumenical."[79] The 1989 UMC *Hymnal* includes fifty-one hymn texts composed by Charles Wesley (a decline of twenty-four from the 1964 *Book of Hymns* and of 368 from the first official American *Methodist Hymn Book* [1835]). The edition followed a pattern established in 1849, which began jettisoning little-used Wesleyan hymns in favor of more popular contemporary ones. "O for a Thousand Tongues" appears as the flagship hymn in the 1989 *Hymnal.* "O for a Thousand Tongues to Sing" carries more weight as a conveyor of the Wesleyan tradition in this hymnal, as indicated by the unusual attention given it. It is preceded, on the facing page, by an extensive introductory note that sets the hymn in its historical and theological context, and the next page reprints seventeen verses of Wesley's original text set out in poetical form.[80] This is the first time since 1740 that the full text of the hymn was published in a Methodist hymnbook. The special treatment accorded "O for a Thousand Tongues" in the recent UMC *Book of Hymns* indicates that it has come to symbolize the American Methodist tradition in a particular way, and that it serves as a rallying point for the diverse constituencies within the Church. It has become the national anthem of the American Methodist tradition.[81]

But difficulties may lie ahead for the hymn as United Methodists and other American Protestants work to develop hymnbooks that unify. Wesley's original seventeenth verse was omitted from the poetical presentation of text in the 1989 *Book of Hymns* because of its description of Christ's light allowing one to "Cast all your sins into the deep. / And wash the Ethiop white." This adjustment was made, almost certainly, with African American singers in mind. Similarly, the *Book of Hymns* carries an asterisk at verse six, reminding the singer that this verse—which carries Wesley's metaphorical references to the "deaf, dumb, blind, and lame"—"May be omitted."[82]

While the application of "O for a Thousand Tongues to Sing" within the United Methodist Church signals a sensitivity to all people, the church also attempts to convey the Wesleyan revivalist tradition of the hymn. Other American hymnals use this hymn differently. Where among Methodists "O for a Thousand Tongues" is felt to convey "our theology," among other American Protestants its words are more readily altered to fit into standard theology.

"O for a Thousand Tongues" provides a useful vantage point from which to view the development of American Methodism. Throughout growth and change, "O for a Thousand Tongues" remained an important link to Methodism's Wesleyan revivalist heritage. Its welcome into the hymnbooks of other Protestant churches illustrates Methodism's success in finding a place of prominence within the American Protestant tradition. The alterations the hymn received evidenced how other American Protestants reacted to distinctive elements of Wesleyan theology. This hymn has functioned as a conduit of Wesleyan tradition, a rallying point when Methodists needed one, and a distinctive expression of Methodist theology over the theologies of other Protestant traditions.

Notes

1. David W. Music, "Wesley Hymns in Early American Hymnals and Tunebooks," *The Hymn*, 39 (1988): 39. Several Wesleyan hymnbooks preceded *Hymns and Spiritual Songs'* appearance in America, but these did not carry the hymn in question.

2. Emory S. Bucke, ed., *The History of American Methodism* (Nashville: Abingdon Press, 1964), 3: 631–32.

3. Benjamin Franklin Crawford, *Theological Trends in Methodist Hymnody* (Carnegie, PA: Carnegie Church Press, 1939), 15.

4. Louis Benson, *The English Hymn: Its Development and Use in Worship* (Richmond, VA: John Knox Press, 1962), 287.

5. Music, "Wesley Hymns in Early American Hymnals," 41.

6. Benson, *English Hymn,* 297.

7. The Lutheran hymnal carried nineteen Wesley hymns, whereas the Baptist book carried twenty.

8. William Warren Sweet, *Methodism in American History* (New York: Methodist Book Concern, 1933), 151.

9. Nathan Hatch, *The Democratization of American Christianity* (New Haven: Yale University Press, 1989), 150.

10. Benson, *English Hymn,* 283.

11. Ibid., 285. Methodist Episcopal Church, *Minutes,* 1795, 71.

12. James White, *Companion to the Book of Liturgy* (Nashville: Abingdon Press, 1970), 16.

13. Sweet, *Methodism in American History,* 119–20.

14. Russell Richey, *Early American Methodism* (Bloomington: Indiana University Press, 1991), 21.

15. Thomas Jackson, ed., *The Works of John Wesley A.M.,* (London: The Wesleyan Conference, 1872), 8: 322–24. "The Large Minutes," of 1746.

16. Francis Asbury, *The Journal and Letters of Francis Asbury,* ed. Elmer T. Clark (Nashville: Abingdon Press, 1958), 1: 413.

17. Richey, *Early American Methodism,* 30.

18. Asbury, *Journal and Letters,* 3: 455.

19. Jesse Lee, *A Short History of the Methodists* (Baltimore: Magill and Clime, 1810), 367.

20. Charles W. Ferguson, *Organizing to Beat the Devil: Methodists and the Making of America* (Garden City, NY: Doubleday, 1971), 142.

21. Asbury, *Journal and Letters,* 3: 333.

22. Hatch, *Democratization of American Christianity,* 151.

23. Ibid., 153.

24. Benson, *English Hymn,* 311.

25. B. St. James Fry, "The Early Camp Meeting Song Writers," *Methodist Quarterly Review* 41 (1859): 407.

26. Benson, *English Hymn,* 293.

27. Dickson Bruce, *And They All Sang Hallelujah: Plain-Folk Camp-Meeting Religion,* (Knoxville: University of Tennessee Press, 1974), 84–85.

28. Fry, "Camp Meeting Song Writers," 407.

29. Albert Outler, ed., *Works of John Wesley: Sermons* (Nashville: Abingdon Press, 1987), 1: 224, 245, 290, 292, 296, 312, 323, 329, 348, 351, 352, 456, 459, 482, 484, 498, 545, 589–91; *Sermons,* 2: 16, 17, 80, 122–24, 128, 169, 255, 313, 315, 340, 346–47, 361, 365, 366, 369, 412, 430, 432, 433, 447, 465, 469, 495, 542, 544, 548, 554, 599, etc.

30. Fry, "Camp Meeting Song Writers," 405.

31. Bruce, *And They All Sang Hallelujah*, 97.

32. This assessment is based on my study of the "Data Base," and the Hymn Book collection housed at the Billy Graham Center, Wheaton College, Wheaton, IL.

33. Ellen Jane Lorenz, *Glory Hallelujah! The Story of the Campmeeting Spiritual* (Nashville: Abingdon Press, 1980), 132.

34. William J. Reynolds, *Companion to the Baptist Hymnal* (Nashville: Broadman Press, 1976), 156–57.

35. This form is found in *Songs for the Ransomed* (Alliance, OH: R. E. Hudson, 1887), 67; *Bells of Heaven* (Waco, TX: John C. F. Kyger, 1896), 143; and *Pentecostal Hymns, No. 1* (Chicago: Hope Publishing, 1894), 87.

36. *Billows of Song* (Cincinnati: S. P. Creasinger, 1893), 9.

37. *Jewels in Song* (New York: H. L. Stephens, 1925), 44.

38. Bruce, *And They All Sang Hallelujah*, 60.

39. John H. Wigger, *Taking Heaven by Storm: Methodism and the Rise of Popular Christianity in America* (New York: Oxford University Press, 1998), 189.

40. William Nast, "Dr. Schaff and Methodism," *Methodist Quarterly Review* 31 (July 1857): 431.

41. Nathan Bangs, *A History of the Methodist Episcopal Church* (1840–53), 2: 105. Cited in Hatch, *Democratization of American Christianity*, 202.

42. Hatch, *Democratization of American Christianity*, 202.

43. Crawford, *Theological Trends*, 162.

44. *Ibid.*, 165.

45. George Peck, "The Methodist Hymn Book," *Methodist Quarterly Review* 26 (1844): 165.

46. Fry, "Camp Meeting Song Writers," 401.

47. James Sallee, *A History of Evangelistic Hymnody* (Grand Rapids, MI: Baker Book House, 1979), 46.

48. *Hymns for the Use of the Methodist Episcopal Church* (Cincinnati: Poe and Hitchcock, 1866); *A Warmth* (Nashville: Methodist Episcopal Church Publishing House, 1871); *Gems of Praise* (Philadelphia: Methodist Episcopal Book Room, 1873); *Living Songs* (Nashville: Methodist Episcopal Church Publishing House, 1892).

49. *The Church Hymnal* (New York: The Centenary Co., 1916), no. 189; *The Reformed Church Hymnal* (New York: Board of Publications and Bible School Work of the Reformed Church, 1928), no. 215.

50. Wigger, *Taking Heaven by Storm*, 20, 184; A. Gregory Schneider, *The Way of the Cross Leads Home: The Domestication of American Methodism* (Bloomington: Indiana University Press, 1993), xxviii.

51. *Psalms and Hymns* (Philadelphia: Presbyterian Board of Publications, 1843), no. 231.

52. *Hymns for Christian Melody* (Dover, MA: Trustees of the Free Will Baptist Connection, 1841), no. 141; and *Songs of the Church* (New York: A. S. Barnes and Burr, 1862), no. 62.

53. *Hymns for Christian Melody* (1847), *A Pastor's Selection* (1859), *Songs of the Church* (1862), *The Presbyterian Hymnal* (1874), *Psalms, Hymns and Spiritual Songs* (1875), *A Selection of Spiritual Songs* (1875), *A Calvary Selection of Hymns* (1881), *Select Songs for Sunday Schools* (1884), *Songs of the Church* (1886), *Select Songs, Nos. 1 and 2* (1888), *Hymns of the Ages* (1891), and *New Psalms and Hymns* (1901).

54. *Book of Common Praise* (New York: A. S. Barnes, 1868), no. 127.

55. See *The Hymnal of the Protestant Episcopal Church* (1894), *Hymnal of the Church* (1897), *The Hymnal of the Protestant Episcopal Church* (1904), *Book of Common Praise* (1907), *Mission Hymnal* (1911, 1914), and *Hymnal Supplement* (1976).

56. In 1899, for example, it was carried in the official *Hymnal of the Evangelical Church* (no. 637). It was carried in nondenominational collections like *Church Hymns and Tunes* (1906), *Christian Hymns* (1908), and the *Grace Church Hymnal* (1909). It soon began appearing in hymnbooks of the Congregational Church, *The Hymnal* of the Church of the Brethren (1943), several Presbyterian hymnals, the *Bible Baptist Hymnal* (1951), and *The Churches of God Hymnal* (1953).

57. For a careful examination of the hymnological heritage of African American Methodists see Jon Michael Spencer, *Black Hymnody: A Hymnological History of the African American Church* (Knoxville: University of Tennessee Press, 1992), 3–73.

58. Melva Wilson Costen, *African American Christian Worship* (Nashville: Abingdon Press, 1993), 50–55; Willis J. King, "The Negro Membership of the (Former) Methodist Church in the (New) United Methodist Church," *Methodist History* 7 (April 1969): 32–43; Wendell P. Walum, "Black Hymnody," *Review and Expositor* 70 (1973): 341–55.

59. Benson, *English Hymn*, 310.

60. Crawford, *Theological Trends*, 162.

61. William Rice, "A Century of Methodist Music, 1850–1950" (PhD diss., University of Iowa, 1953), 45.

62. *Christian Hymn and Tune Book* (Chicago: Root and Cady, 1870), no. 47.

63. *Songs for the Ransomed*, no. 67.

64. *Songs of Zion* (1908), *Christian Gospel Hymns* (1909), *Evangel Hymns* (1909) of the American Baptist Church, *Make Christ the King* (1912), *Harvest of Light* (1913), *Worship and Service Hymns* (1916), *King of Glory* (1916), *Songs of Salvation and Service* (1919), *Songs of Redemption* (1920) of the Southern Baptist Church, *Jesus Only Songs, #1* (1925), *Voice of His Praise* (1925), *Precious Hymns* (1938), *Songs of Inspiration* (1955).

65. C. F. M'Kown, "Unifying Factors in Methodism," *Methodist Quarterly Review* 81 (1899): 732–37.

66. M'Kown, "Unifying Factors," 732.

67. Ibid., 734.

68. Bucke, ed., *History of American Methodism*, II: 633–34.

69. Benson, *English Hymn*, 304.

70. C. T. Winchester, "The New Methodist Hymnal—The Hymns," *Methodist Quarterly Review* 87 (1905): 681.

71. Benson, *English Hymn*, 304.

72. Carlton R. Young, *Companion* to the United Methodist Hymnal (Nashville: Abingdon Press, 1993), 113, citing Walter Vernon, *The History of United Methodist Publishing* (Nashville: United Methodist Publishing House, 1988), 2: 200.

73. Crawford, *Theological Trends*, 165.

74. Ibid., 61–62.

75. Ibid., 132.

76. Robert Chiles, *Theological Transitions in American Methodism, 1790–1935* (Nashville: Abingdon Press, 1965), 61–76, 180–83.

77. Preface, *The Book of Hymns*, viii. Cf. Young, *Companion*, 117.

78. For a thorough study of the concerns that led to the development of the 1989 *United Methodist Hymnal* see Carlton Young's treatment in *Companion*, 123–80.

79. Carlton Young, ed., *The United Methodist Hymnal* (Nashville: United Methodist Publishing House, 1989), Preface, v.

80. Verse seventeen, with its reference to "Wash the Ethiop white," was not printed, probably because of its (apparently) negative reference to African people. Wesley's allusion, of course, was not an indication of racial prejudice, but an awareness of the biblical text of Jeremiah 13:23.

81. Dian Sanchez, ed., *The Hymns of the United Methodist Hymnal: Introductions to the Hymns, Canticles, and Acts of Worship* (Nashville: Abingdon Press, 1989), 37; and Gabriel Fackre, "Christian Teaching and Inclusive Language Hymnody," *The Hymn* 50 (April 1999): 30.

82. Young, ed., *United Methodist Hymnal*, 57.

3

"All Hail the Power of Jesus' Name"

Significant Variations on a Significant Theme

Mark A. Noll

"On the Resurrection, the Lord is King"
Edward Perronet (1779/1780)

P1. All hail! the power of Jesu's Name;
    Let angels prostrate fall;
    Bring forth the Royal Diadem,
    To crown him Lord of all.

P2. Let highborn seraphs tune the lyre,
    And as they tune it, fall
    Before His face who tunes their choir,
    And crown Him Lord of all.

P3. Crown Him ye morning stars of light,
    Who fix'd this floating ball;
    Now hail the strength of Israel's might,
    And crown Him Lord of all.

P4. Crown Him, ye martyrs of your God,
    Who from His altar call;
    Extol the stem of Jesse's rod,
    And crown Him Lord of all.

P5. Ye seed of Israel's chosen race,
    Ye ransom'd of the fall,
    Hail Him Who saves you by His grace,
    And crown Him Lord of all.

P6. Hail Him, ye heirs of David's line,
    Whom David Lord did call;

The God incarnate, man Divine,
And crown Him Lord of all.

P7. Sinners! whose love can ne'er forget
The wormwood and the gall,
Go—spread your trophies at His feet,
And crown Him Lord of all.

P8. Let every tribe and every tongue
That bound creation's call,
Now shout in universal song,
The crownéd Lord of all.

"The Spiritual Coronation, Cant. Iii.11"

John Rippon (1787)

R1. All-hail, the power of *Jesus'* name!
Let angels prostrate fall:
Bring forth the royal diadem,
And crown Him Lord of all.

R2. Crown Him, ye martyrs of our God,
Who from His altar call;
Extol the Stem of Jesse's rod,
And crown Him Lord of all.

R3. Ye *chosen seed of Israel's* race,
A remnant weak and small;
Hail Him, who saves you by His grace,
And crown Him Lord of all.

R4. *Ye Gentile sinners,* ne'er forget
The wormwood and the gall;
Go—spread your trophies at His feet,
And crown Him Lord of all.

R5. Babes, men, and sires, who know His love,
Who feel your sin and thrall,
Now joy with all the hosts above,
And crown Him Lord of all.

R6. Let every *kindred, every tribe,*
   On this terrestrial ball,
   To Him all majesty ascribe,
   And crown Him Lord of all.

R7. Oh that, with yonder sacred throng,
   We at His feet may fall;
   We'll join the everlasting song,
   And crown Him Lord of all.

In the Preface to his much-reprinted *A Selection of Hymns from the Best Authors. Intended to be an Appendix to Dr. Watts's Psalms and Hymns,* the English Baptist pastor, publisher, and general factotum, John Rippon, defended at length the need for new hymns. Rippon, who published the first edition of his *Selection* in 1787, acknowledged the enduring usefulness of Isaac Watts, whose hymnbook at that time reigned supreme among English Nonconformists. But Rippon then went on to suggest that, as good as Watts was, he provided very few hymns on important Christian subjects like "the Character of Christ—the Work of the Spirit—the Christian Graces and Tempers," and also hardly any for baptisms, ordinations, prayer meetings, and special services for youth. What Rippon hoped to provide with his new book was a greater number of hymns for a more diverse set of Christian doctrines and a broader range of Christian worship. "Too great a Variety," in Rippon's opinion, was "scarcely to be conceived of." And so he had perused more than ninety books of hymns, sacred verse, and paraphrased psalms—"all the Collections I could obtain in this Country and from America"—in search of "truly evangelical" hymns that could supplement Watts. Rippon closed the Preface by expressing his special satisfaction at being able to present hymns from both well-known Calvinists (like Augustus Toplady) and leading Arminians (like Charles Wesley), from both Anglicans and Dissenters, and from both England and America. His hope, in making such an ecumenical section available, was that all sorts of believers might join their voices in songs of praise, especially with "Christ . . . the Subject of the Song." As befitted a collection of hymns, Rippon concluded by setting his hopes into a Common Meter quatrain: "*Europe* and *Asia* shall resound, / With *Africa,* his Fame; / And now, *America,* in Songs, / Redeeming Love proclaim."[1]

Several themes in Rippon's Preface forecast, as it were prophetically, the American career of what would become the most popular new hymn in his

Selection. "All Hail the Power of Jesus' Name" did not originate with John Rippon, but his substantially rewritten version of that hymn became the predominate text in later American hymnals. Because American editors put freely to use both the original from which Rippon worked and Rippon's own version—and because they also freely exercised their own editorial initiative—tremendous variety came to characterize the shape of this one hymn in American imprints. It is the purpose of this chapter to chart some of the most significant variations in the American publishing history of this hymn as well as to speculate on what the evolution of a single, if complex, hymn text reveals about American religious history more generally. But because the pre-American history of the hymn was so important for what happened on these shores, it is necessary to begin the story in Britain.

The Hymn Takes Shape

The text of "All Hail" was multiform even before it migrated across the Atlantic. The famous opening stanza, very nearly in the form that would later be most widely circulated, was published by Edward Perronet in the *Gospel Magazine* of November 1779. Significantly, William Shrubsole's bracing tune, "Miles Lane," was published alongside this single verse in its first appearance and would remain closely associated with the British publication of the hymn. Perronet (1726–1792), a descendent of Huguenot refugees to England, was the son of a leading Anglican supporter of John and Charles Wesley. With his brother Charles, Edward Perronet also worked diligently for the early Methodist movement. But an independent spirit and a refusal to temper his criticism of midcentury Anglicanism eventually alienated Perronet from the Wesleys. After leaving the Methodists behind, Perronet for a brief period in the early 1770s served one of the Countess of Huntingdon's chapels at Canterbury, but his cast of mind—"intermittently rebellious and violent" in the words of a detractor—soon led to estrangement from Lady Huntingdon's connection. For most of the last years of his life Perronet ministered to a small Congregational chapel in Canterbury. He published several volumes of sacred verse, but "All Hail the Power of Jesu's Name" was his only enduring poem.[2]

For his part, William Shrubsole (1760–1806) followed Perronet at least part way as an ecclesiastical pilgrim. Shrubsole was only nineteen and a chorister of Canterbury Cathedral when he wrote the tune, "Miles Lane." Later he was appointed the organist of Bangor Cathedral but then lost that position by becoming too friendly with the Methodists and other Dissenters. Ralph

Vaughan Williams once singled out Shrubsole's repetitions on "crown him" for special commendation and passed along with approbation Edward Elgar's opinion that "Miles Lane" was "the finest [tune] in English hymnody."[3]

Five months after the original publication in the *Gospel Magazine* the same periodical brought out seven additional stanzas under the title, "On the Resurrection, the Lord is King." These eight verses constituted Edward Perronet's "All Hail the Power of Jesu's Name," which in America was never as popular as John Rippon's version but that did return over time to exert a continuing influence on American reprintings.

John Rippon (1751–1836) was one of the most significant individuals moving the English Baptists of the late eighteenth century from the sectarian confines of hyper-Calvinism to a broader, more evangelical Calvinist Nonconformity.[4] His education at Tiverton and the Baptist's Bristol Academy was based more on the evangelical Independent Philip Doddridge, himself a notable hymn-writer, than the consistent Calvinism of Baptist leader John Gill. During his more than six decades (1772–1836) as pastor of the Carter Lane Baptist Church in Southwark, London, Rippon promoted the kind of evangelical theology encouraged among the Baptists by Andrew Fuller, who was also a channel transmitting the perspectives of Jonathan Edwards to an English constituency. In an age of evangelical and Dissenting innovation, Rippon was a master networker. From 1790 to 1812 he edited the *Baptist Annual Register*, which, by publishing theology, moral exhortation, and news from at home and abroad, aimed to unite the efforts of Baptists in Britain and the new United States. He was an indefatigable historian of Baptist worthies and associations. In 1812 he became the first chairman of the Baptist Union. He was a major force behind the Baptist Missionary Society that sent William Carey to India in 1793. For Baptists throughout the English-speaking world, his pulpit in London was a nearly universal point of mediation.

Yet none of Rippon's labors meant so much as his work in encouraging a broader, more popular hymnody. His *Selection* to augment Watts, his *Selection of Psalm and Hymn Tunes* (first published 1791), and his topical *Arrangement of the Psalms, Hymns and Spiritual Songs of the Rev. Isaac Watts* (first published 1801) all passed rapidly through multiple editions, some of which he oversaw with great personal diligence and some of which appeared without his approval from piratical Americans.[5] Within two years of the 1787 publication of his *Selection*, half the Baptist churches in England were using the book. By 1792, at least 15,000 copies were in print. Of the hymns in the first edition, almost 150 were previously unpublished, while about three hundred had been published but not yet included in any previous general collection.[6] Besides "All Hail the Power," Rippon's *Selection* included thirty-three other hymns from the *Gospel Magazine.*

As an editor, Rippon followed the activist pattern of his age, nowhere better exemplified than by John Wesley who was a compulsive fiddler with the hymn texts, including his brother's, that he published in so many editions for the Methodists. Rippon's handiest editorial device was the ax with which he abridged many of his hymns. But he also sometimes rearranged verse order, altered meter, rhymes, and pluralizations, and very occasionally did a little theological reconstruction. For twenty hymns, he added verses or made other radical alterations. "All Hail the Power" was among this select group. According to Kenneth Manley, who has provided the best account of this editorial work, "All Hail the Power" offers "perhaps the outstanding illustration of Rippon's facility for improving a hymn."[7]

Whether or not Rippon's work on Perronet's original improved the hymn, it manifestly reflected a pattern of alteration that spurred its later popularity in America. Rippon's "All Hail the Power" was, first, a much simpler hymn. Two of the four Perronet stanzas he either dropped or extensively revised contained expressions requiring singers to sustain a thought across several poetic lines: P2—"Let highborn seraphs tune the lyre, / And as they tune it, fall / Before His face"; P6—"Hail Him, ye heirs of David's line, / Whom David's Lord did call." In Rippon's version, by contrast, every line was a self-contained thought. A third stanza (P8) was entirely rewritten (R7) in order to replace an incomprehensible line in Perronet's original ("That bound creations call"). Rippon's simplifications also included altering the hymn's first line from Perronet's latinate "Jesu" to the much more ordinary "Jesus." Simplification extended as well to intellectual concepts. The cosmology of P3 is complexly Newtonian: "Crown Him ye morning stars of light, / Who fix'd this floating ball." But in R6, though Rippon has borrowed Perronet's "ball" as a term for the earth, his use of the image requires a much less sophisticated natural theology.[8]

Although it was a change that did not survive for long in later reprintings, Rippon's anchoring of the hymn to a direct biblical text may also have eased its way in America.[9] One of Rippon's main purposes in publishing the *Selection* was to provide Baptist ministers with a fuller range of hymns for use after sermons. To further that end he supplied each of his hymns with a title and a biblical text. Thus it was that Perronet's "On the Resurrection, the Lord is King" became "The Spiritual Coronation, Cant. iii.11," with the biblical reference plying the era's standard christological interpretation of the Song of

Solomon and perhaps providing some of the material for Rippon's Jewish-Gentile permutations: "Go forth, O ye daughters of Zion, and behold king Solomon with the crown wherewith his mother crowned him in the day of his espousals, and in the day of the gladness of his heart." The biblical linkage was important because "All Hail the Power" crossed the Atlantic precisely when American concern to set aside tradition-encrusted creeds in favor of "the Bible alone" was at its height.[10]

A further set of changes that have endured in America reworked Perronet's verses in order to engage singers much more directly. Thus, "ye martyrs of *your* God" (P4) became "ye martyrs of *our* God" (R2). The electing choice for Israel was shifted from the abstract "race" to the more personal "seed"—from "Ye seed of Israel's chosen race" to "Ye chosen seed of Israel's race."[11] Rippon's triumphant concluding stanza (R7), with its double evocation of the singing saints as "we," personalized the hymn in a way that Perronet's concluding general exhortation (P8) did not. Significantly, Rippon's final stanza has been reprinted almost universally, even with some texts based otherwise on Perronet.

In sum, Rippon's "All Hail the Power of Jesus' Name" was a shorter, simpler, more personally direct hymn than the Perronet original from which he worked. Even before examining the actual record of republication, these changes suggest a revealing tendency about the hymn's later history. While it is possible to make too much of stereotypes contrasting American and English religious styles, there are nonetheless solid reasons for thinking of English religion as somewhat more cerebral, somewhat more reserved, and somewhat more elitist than the more direct, personal, and democratic religious idiom in the United States.[12] If this contrast is granted, it is not surprising that the Perronet text of "All Hail the Power" retained a stronger presence in British (and not just English) hymnody than in the United States where from the first Rippon's version was always the majority to Perronet's minority text.[13]

The Hymn Arrives in the United States

"All Hail the Power" was first printed in America in 1791, only four years after the appearance of Rippon's *Selection*. The text was a nearly exact copy of the full seven-stanza Rippon. The editor was Joshua Smith, who in 1784 had brought out the first edition of his *Divine Hymns or Spiritual Songs* in Norwich, New Hampshire. The third edition, published in Exeter, New Hampshire, contained the hymn with only three slight variants, all of which could have been typographical mistakes: "the alter" for "His altar" in R2, "week" for "weak" in R3, and "sirs" for "sires" in R5.[14] The fact that Smith simplified the title to "The Coronation of Christ" may speak for his broader intentions, for he was an energetic populist publisher who has been identified by Nathan Hatch as one of the era's eager promoters of a people's religion opposed to the hierarchical tendencies that lingered in American culture after the War for Independence.[15]

As in Britain, the hymn was almost from the start associated with a popular tune. On this side of the Atlantic that tune was "Coronation," published by Oliver Holden (1765–1844), a multitalented patriot, artisan, sailor, farmer, legislator, and singing master from Charlestown, Massachusetts.[16] Between 1792 and 1803, Holden published seven tune collections as composer or editor including *The Union Harmony* of 1793 that contained the tune soon wedded to "All Hail the Power." Before 1820, "Coronation" was reprinted at least eighty-two times, each time as the tune for this hymn.[17]

Rippon's "All Hail the Power" immediately established a strong presence. After its initial appearance in 1791 this version was reprinted independently at least fourteen times in its first American decade. This same version was also conveyed to an even broader audience through American printings of Rippon's *Selection*. From the first, John Rippon hoped that his hymnbook would be a force for uniting American and British Baptists, and so he made provisions to send relatively large quantities of the book to Baptist ministers for resale in Philadelphia, Providence, and Charleston. Eight hundred of the first 6,000 copies printed in England were dispatched to America as part of this scheme.[18]

Not for the only time, however, intellectual larceny proved simpler than a well-regulated trans-Atlantic trade. Already by the turn of the century, a parishioner from the Carter Lane chapel who had immigrated to Philadelphia was telling Rippon about the casual American approach to intellectual property. The parishioner, John Bowen, did report on a small amount of business he had been able to transact on behalf of Rippon's books, but then was compelled to reveal that there were a lot more of the hymnbooks circulating in the new world than Rippon had sent over himself. About this situation the parishioner waxed philosophical: "Thus you see the English Labors and the American enjoys the sweets of their Labor with little trouble, it is so with every new Publication that is likely to sell, that comes over."[19] It has been estimated that by 1828 there were more than 100,000 copies of Rippon's *Selection* circulating in America, but only a tiny fraction of that number had come from Rippon.[20]

Unauthorized printings of Rippon's *Selection* began in 1792 and were a major factor in the general spread of evangelical hymnody among the American populace. Including the first two editions in 1792, a total of eighteen American "Rippon's" were issued within the next thirty years. It is significant that the American editions of the *Selection* came from population centers in the middle states where the most rapid expansion of Christian churches and religious voluntary societies was taking place in the early republic—six from Philadelphia, four from Baltimore, three from Wilmington, two from New York, and one each from Elizabeth-Town, New Jersey, Burlington, New Jersey, and Chillicothe, Ohio.[21] Whether in independently issued hymnbooks or in reprintings of Rippon's *Selection,* the revised version of "All Hail the Power" was off to a fast start in the new world.

Yet Rippon's version did not exist by itself for long. In 1799 a trio of Connecticut Congregational ministers published *The Hartford Selection of Hymns, From the Most Approved Authors* in which "All Hail the Power" appeared under yet a new title, "Christ Crowned as Lord of All." The Connecticut Congregationalists reported that "the demand for books of this kind [had] been very great of late, owing to the happy revival of religion in many towns in New-England." Their hymns—taken mostly from Newton, Cowper, Doddridge, and Rippon—were intended for "the use of Christians in their closets, families, and private religious meetings." Profits from their sale were to support missionaries in the new western settlements.[22] The editors— including Nathan Strong and Abel Flint, the pastors of Hartford's two most prominent churches—were zealous New Light evangelicals, but also leaders of the new para-church voluntary societies that supported the periodicals, missionary work, and other collective activities that so disconcerted the era's more radical evangelicals.[23] Their text was Perronet's, with one stanza slightly revised.

The first American appearance of Perronet's "All Hail the Power" is important for several reasons. In the first instance it established a pattern that has prevailed to the present. Hymnbooks from more traditional denominations and hymnals edited by committees of learned clerics and academics have shown a disposition in favor of Perronet's somewhat more complex text. By contrast, the early purveyors of Rippon's version were Baptists or members of other nonelite denominations. Unlike the Connecticut Congregationalists, who were still uneasy about using nonbiblical hymnody in regular ecclesiastical worship, this latter group of compilers definitely wanted "All Hail the Power" and the other new hymns they provided to be sung in church. The contrast is clear from a comparison of those who reprinted each version. Perronet's version was published most often by the more elite Congregational

leaders of voluntary societies. Rippon's "All Hail the Power" was reprinted by
Baptists, by independent (and independent-minded) single redactors, and by
Universalists (who were in this period radically biblicist as well as radically
populist).[24] After Joshua Smith, the most frequent early American publisher
of Rippon's text was Elias Smith, a democratic activist who battled for the
religious rights of the people just as colorfully as he assaulted the lingering
bastions of religious privilege.[25]

One other harbinger of the American career of "All Hail the Power" is
found in the 1799 publication from the Connecticut Congregationalists. For
the original last stanza these editors replaced Perronet's baffling second line
with "Let every tribe and every tongue / That *hear the Savior's call* / Now
shout . . . " This alteration was minor, but it anticipated a flood of later editorial revisions that would ultimately produce several hundred different variations in the text of this one hymn. Even before it had been in America for
even a decade, in other words, "All Hail the Power" was proving to be an indispensable *American* hymn, but also a hymn of great potential plasticity in
responding to the convictions, whims, idiosyncrasies, prejudices, and literary
tastes of American editors.

An Extraordinarily Popular Hymn

The main business of the chapter is to show how varied appearances of the
hymn text tracked important changes in American popular Protestantism,
but this exercise will mean more if at least some documentation is provided
for the unusually broad reach of the hymn. Easy enough to accumulate are
the rapturous superlatives: "one of the greatest of hymns," "the greatest hymn
of praise in the English language," or "the most inspiring hymn in the English
language."[26]

Since the enduring popularity of the hymn in Britain was bound to exert
an influence across the Atlantic, it is worth recording that this hymn has been
a source of inspiration for even more new hymn tunes there than in America,
where the text has been more widely reprinted than in Britain.[27] The central
place of the hymn's theme in the expanding world of eighteenth-century
British evangelicalism is indicated by the fact that it was sung at the founding
meeting of the London Missionary Society in 1795.[28] It enjoyed a secure place
in the flourishing world of Victorian hymnody.[29] It was a favorite of the pious
high-church prime minister W. E. Gladstone.[30] In the mid-twentieth century
it was described by Erik Routley as one of only fifty-two hymns making up
the "basic canon" of English hymnody, "hymns which the ordinary English-

man knows, whose tunes he can immediately place, and which have a place in his common life more assured perhaps than any other religious literature, the Bible not excluded."[31] Several decades later, Ian Bradley included the hymn in his authoritative *Penguin Book of Hymns*.[32] It is also recorded in Britain with some frequency.[33]

From Britain the hymn has been carried around the world. It has been translated multiple times into languages as predictable as Spanish or German and as unexpected as Latin.[34] Like the countless reprintings in Britain and America, translators indicate by which versions they use and how much of each one they translate something about religious sensibilities outside the English-language domains of the hymn's origin.

The exalted status of the hymn is also suggested by the myths, legends, and stories that sprang up around it. One of the most often repeated has a missionary to India, E. P. Scott, rescued from hostile indigenous peoples by playing the hymn on his violin.[35] Another has a dying person—variously reported as a pious lady visiting Paris for "the great exhibition," "a good man," and a once "happy Christian" who became an infidel[36]—stammering out "bring, bring," and after some confusion finally getting auditors to realize that the reference was to "bring[ing] forth the royal diadem" of P1 or R1. A more recent account relates the story of an indigenous tribe discovered on Okinawa by a war correspondent toward the end of World War II where, with almost no previous Western contact, a flourishing Christian society had developed. The secret was a missionary who years before had left a Bible and taught the Okinawans two hymns, "Fairest Lord Jesus" and "All Hail the Power of Jesus' Name."[37]

As popular as the hymn has been in other venues, its greatest popularity has always been in the United States. Accounting for this popularity must include consideration of the pleasing variety of its tunes, for editors have been able to supplement the always popular "Coronation" with many editions of "Miles Lane" as well as many printings since the mid-nineteenth century of "Diadem." The latter tune was composed in 1838 for the anniversary of the Wesleyan Sunday School in the Droylsdon region of Manchester, England, by an eighteen-year-old hatter, John Ellor (1819–1899).[38] It soon migrated to the United States, as did its composer. In America this tune's vigorous melody and a bracing, repetitive chorus soon made it more popular than it would ever become in Britain. Linked with this tune, "All Hail the Power" was also poised for transition to the gospel era of the late nineteenth century when rhythmic vigor and racing choruses became the sine qua non for popular hymns.[39]

In whatever musical dress, "All Hail the Power" has never been out of fashion since its first introduction. American worshipers through the decades have responded with enthusiasm to the same features that made it instantly popular among the first Protestants who sang it.[40] For a people immersed in Scripture, the hymn's manifold biblical allusions were an immediate point of contact—for example, the angels falling prostrate in P1/R1 (from Hebrews 1:6 and Deuteronomy 32:43), the praise from "every tribe" in R6 (from Revelation 5), or "the wormwood and the gall" in P7/R4 (from Lamentations 3:19). The hymn's evocative power no doubt also arose from its straightforward, objective assertion of Christian doctrines that were propounded much more ponderously in innumerable sermons. It also was a succinct, singable evocation of time-honored Christian injunctions to render due praise to Jesus as the one who fulfills the divine purpose for humanity.

With this sharply realized, but also generic, Christian affirmation, the hymn has built bridges among a very wide circle of denominations. Moving out from its original base among Baptists, Congregationalists, and populist independents, it rapidly became a tremendous force for grass-roots ecumenicity. It was picked up as early as 1806 by Lutherans, 1816 by Dunkers, 1822 by Methodists, 1823 by Presbyterians, 1832 by Seventh-Day Baptists and Disciples of Christ, 1841 by the Mormons, 1842 by General Six Principle Baptists, 1845 by Episcopalians and Unitarians, 1849 by Adventists, 1862 by Dutch Reformed, 1863 by Roman Catholics, and on into increasingly wider circles.[41]

Widespread use in and among the denominations made the hymn ubiquitous. Timothy Dwight, the Yale College president widely recognized as the most effective handler of elite young men in the early national period, was an enthusiastic booster of the hymn.[42] In late 1864, troops of the Fourth Massachusetts Regiment sang it as they marched into battle.[43] It was a favorite at the holiness camp meetings that began to spring up in the late 1860s, so much so that when a group of holiness advocates toured Washington, D.C., in the summer of 1870 or 1871, they sang the hymn together "under the high dome of the Capitol."[44] The hymn has been a favorite of African American believers since before the Civil War. It was quoted at the climax of a moving missionary sermon at the annual meeting of the African Methodist Episcopal Church in 1902.[45] Only a few years later it was sung at the dedication service of the doubtless all-white First Baptist Church of Charlotte, North Carolina, when on May 2, 1909, its grand new church was dedicated with a sermon by the president of the Southern Baptist Convention, E. Y. Mullins.[46] In 1881, it was invoked by Kate and Sue McBeth, intrepid Baptist missionaries to the Nez Perce, at a moment of potentially dangerous strife in their Indian community.[47] On November 4, 1956, Martin Luther King Jr. offered a letter as if written from the Apostle Paul to Americans at the Dexter Avenue Baptist Church in Montgomery, Alabama, in which he asked his hearers to consider "the tragic fact that when you stand at 11:00 on Sunday morning to sing 'All Hail the Power of Jesus' Name' and 'Dear Lord and Father of all Mankind,' you stand in the most segregated hour of Christian America."[48] Even more recently the hymn has been a featured cut on a cassette called "Christian Power Walking 5."[49] And for years "and crown him Lord of all" has been sung as the fade-out on Billy Graham's widely broadcast "Hour of Decision" weekly radio program.

"All Hail the Power" is such a fixture in American religious life that it has become a useful tool for innovators or polemicists to adapt to their own purposes. On September 5, 1939, Father Divine preached a sermon to loyal followers in Philadelphia in which, after quoting R1 from the hymn, he then adapted it to himself: "All hail the power of Father's name, / Let angels prostrate fall."[50] The hymn has been altered to fit the needs of revival in the Pentecostal Assemblies of Canada.[51] The same thing happened in the Churches of Christ during a dispute over the Second Coming in the 1940s and 1950s. Two different editors, to avoid the supposed support provided by traditional versions of the hymn to premillennial views, offered new verses where the offending "Lord of all" in one instance became "Judge of all," and in another was jettisoned altogether: "Ye ransomed in the Christian race, / Keep e'er your hope aflame; / Hail Him who saves you by His grace, / And praise His wondrous name."[52]

In a word, it is difficult to find a venue related to the history of Protestants in the United States that has not been touched by the presence of this hymn.

Revelations from a Complicated Publishing History

The question of the general popularity of "All Hail the Power" is not, however, the same question as to what ordinary worshipers actually sang when they opened their hymn books or what they recalled by memory from the singing in church, Sunday school, or special-purpose rally. To answer that more complicated question, it is necessary to look individually at the texts that have been printed and reprinted in American hymnals. Study of variants—especially for a popular hymn that began with multiple base texts—is extraordinarily fruitful. While one can never be quite sure that what is printed in hymnals expresses the religious convictions or the theological preferences of the ones who sing the hymn, careful attention to the actual content of popular hymns still may come as close to ascertaining the lived religious convictions of ordinary men and women as it is humanly possible to come.[53]

The analysis that follows draws on the text of "All Hail the Power" as recorded in about 1,300 American printings from 1791 to the mid-1990s, with more particular attention to about 410 appearances of the hymn in the periods 1791–1811, 1840–59, 1880–99, and 1970–95. The assumption is that important continuities as well as important discontinuities will be revealed by noting the frequency with which various stanzas from the original versions are reprinted, by recording the number of stanzas commonly found, by paying close attention to patterns of abridgment, and by examining the material that editors add to the hymn. Answering the question of who is doing the editing and why they are doing it would require extraordinarily extensive research, but even on that complex issue it is sometimes possible to offer speculative conclusions.[54]

1791–1811

The early American history of "All Hail the Power" was marked by unusual editorial restraint. Compared to what came later, American editors in this early period were mostly content simply to reproduce copies of the Rippon or Perronet versions.

Editorial conservatism lasted, however, for only a short period. In a new edition of Joshua Smith's *Divine Hymns* from 1802 (Smith had died in 1795), a reviser changed Rippon's cumbersome "Babes, men, and sires" (R5) to "Young men and old."[55] Three years later Joshua Spaulding modified Rippon's last stanza to read "Let all creation join their tongues / At once before him fall, / And shout, in universal songs, / The crownéd Lord of All."[56] What would rapidly become the more common way of altering Rippon had begun at least by 1808, when two different but paired hymnals deleted R2, a practice soon followed by an editor in 1810 who deleted R5.[57] The latter deletion would soon become nearly universal. Still, for the most part the hymn as printed in America continued to be the hymn that was first published in England.

There were, however, two exceptions. One of the 1808 hymnals, with no editors named on the title page, systematically changed all six of the Rippon verses it reprinted from "And *crown* him Lord of all" to "And *own* him Lord of all."[58] In 1808 tensions were again rising with monarchical Great Britain, and a national debate was taking place over President Thomas Jefferson's effort to influence European nations by means of a boycott on trade from America. This tension was felt with special force in trading centers like Boston where this version was published. Under these circumstances one can presume that talk of "crowning," even if directed at Jesus, had become, at least for some, politically incorrect.

Less presumption is needed to explain the first full recasting of the hymn. It appeared in 1811 in *The New Hymn-Book for . . . the Free Church,* published by Abel Morgan Sarjent. Sarjent was, like Elias Smith, a populist firebrand dedicated to extirpating privilege and hierarchy from American society. As an example of his radicalism, Sarjent in 1807 wrote of how "the poor have but a dull chance to obtain Justice in carnal courts," since such venues were so often "under the dominion of the beast" where "the power and influence of money and false Agency over-balanced equity and right."[59] Sarjent's new version of the hymn was brought out in New York but advertised on the title page as also available from "ministers of the Halcyon Church on the waters of the Ohio," a liberated denomination that he himself had founded. In a hard-hitting preface, Sarjent expatiated at length on the stark differences between, on the one hand, "what is generally called theology, revealed religion, and Christianity"—to Sarjent a "counterfeit" marred by "manifest corruptions"—and, on the other hand, "the plain dealings of Jesus Christ." The title he gave his new hymn expressed unequivocally Sarjent's rejection of earthly human sovereignty, "Jesus Christ the Universal and only lawful Potentate." It retained many of Perronet's and Rippon's rhymes, but its appeal to "All creatures," "angels," "spirits," and "Ye grov'ling worms" was an entirely new rendition.[60]

The hymn that Perronet wrote and Rippon revised was spreading out rapidly in America, presumably because it so successfully expressed Christ-centered, biblical themes of praise. Already in this editorially conservative period, however, the hymn was beginning to migrate—impatience with old-world diction was leading to abridgment or alteration, the resonance of a victorious Christ was being applied to American events in an American idiom, the multifaceted process of textual evolution had begun.[61]

1840–59

By midcentury expanding editorial license in an increasingly uncoordinated religious landscape meant that the pace of textual change accelerated. From an admittedly small sample for these years, only one of thirty-two hymnals with "All Hail the Power" reprinted Rippon's entire version, and none came even close to republishing all of Perronet.

Abridgment was now the rule, with Rippon's awkward R5 almost gone and with rapidly vanishing sentiment for the martyrs of R2, the "remnant weak and small" of R3, and "Ye Gentile sinners" of R4. The combination of R3 ("Ye

Table 3.1
1791–1811

		Rippon stanzas	Peronnet stanzas	Other stanzas
No. of hymnals	36	R1—26	P1—5	revP8—6
No. of printings	36	R2—24	P2—7	W—2
Avg. no. of stanzas	6.9	R3—26	P3—7	B—3
No. of new hymns	1	R4—26	P4—6	mR3P5—1
		R5—24	P5—7	new—6
		R6—25	P6—7	
		R7—25	P7—7	
		P8—2		

rev = substantial revision of a stanza
W = Wilks's 1798 revision
B = Burder's 1784 revisions
m = mixed stanzas
new = entirely new verses

chosen seed of Israel's race") and P5, often as modified by Burden ("Ye ransomed of [or from] the fall") was well on its way to canonical status, as was also Perronet's "Sinners!" (P7). More favor existed for Wilks's variation on the hymn's first line than ever before or since in American hymnody. The use of Perronet's third verse ("Crown Him ye morning stars of light") was largely restricted to a more upscale constituency—for example, *The Church Psalmist*, a collection edited by the Congregationalist reformer George B. Cheever, and the hymnal produced at Henry Ward Beecher's fashionable Plymouth Church in Brooklyn.[62] Interestingly, the thoughtfully edited new *Baptist Hymn and Tune Book* of 1859 sat lightly to the Rippon text by returning not only to P3 but also to the by then rarely published P6 ("Hail Him, ye heirs of David's line").

Of creative new renditions, one survived for at least fifteen years. It offers an example of another kind of adaptation to American environment, this time not so much ideological as practical. The text was associated with the American Sunday School Union and was provided for those whom the Union sought to equip and inspire: "Teachers, who surely know His love, / Who feel your sin and thrall, / Now join with all the hosts above / And crown Him Lord of all."[63] The story told by the textual evolution of "All Hail the Power" is not yet a dramatic one. Certainly the American run of R5 is almost finished, although it is doubtful if ideology led to its demise. The spondees wrecking the first line's iambic cadence and the awkwardness of "thrall" in the second line were probably sufficient, on poetic grounds alone, to bring about its exclusion.

It is likewise hard to find an interesting reason for the relative frequency of Wilks's opening line, except that it might have reflected a new, more professional approach to church music associated with the Boston Academy of Music and its director, Lowell Mason, who became in 1827 the first American to embark on a full-time career as a professional church musician.[64] Two of the versions with the Wilks opening also revised R2 in order to introduce the theme of salvation by Christ's blood, a prominent theme in the era's evangelical religion but not one that ever gained a foothold in this hymn.[65]

The period's other textual alterations may be more revealing. Although it is precarious to draw too much from acts of abridgments, it could be significant that the Rippon stanzas appearing much less frequently in these years all emphasized the paltriness of the singer. The 1840s and 1850s constituted an era of surging national prosperity and unprecedented refinement of church life. In retrospect, modern observers know that these years were hastening toward a shattering Civil War, but those who lived in that period did not. To speak, even at worship, of martyrdom (R2), of being "a remnant weak and small" (R3), or of "Gentile" alienation (R4) may have subtly jarred against the rising aspirations of the American nation and its mainstream Protestant churches. The retention of P7 ("Sinners!") kept the hymn from becoming excessively triumphalistic, but the era's canonical version still contained more single-minded affirmation and less consciousness of chastened insignificance than either of the two originals. In this era the hymn had essentially become the following:

1. All hail, the power of Jesus' name
   Let angels prostrate fall:
   Bring forth the royal diadem,
   And crown him Lord of all

2. Ye chosen seed of Israel's race,
   Ye ransomed from the fall,
   Hail Him, who saves you by His grace,
   And crown him Lord of all

3. Sinners! whose love can ne'er forget
   The wormwood and the gall;

Go—spread your trophies at His feet,
And crown Him Lord of all

4. Let every kindred, every tribe
   On this terrestrial ball,
   To Him all majesty ascribe,
   And crown him Lord of all

5. Oh that, with yonder sacred throng,
   We at his feet may fall;
   We'll join the everlasting song,
   And crown Him Lord of all.

1880–99

The great age of popular American hymnody was also the great age for "All Hail the Power of Jesus' Name." In the decades between the Civil War and World War I, hymnbooks tumbled from American presses in ever-rising numbers, propelled both by the growing self-consciousness of the denominations and by the manifest success of evangelistic troubadours like Ira D. Sankey, the musical partner of D. L. Moody.[66] Most of these multiplying numbers of hymnbooks seem to have contained "All Hail the Power." For the thirty-seven years from 1875 to 1912, the compilations prepared for *The Dictionary of American Hymnology* record a staggering 901 reprintings of the hymn, 266 from denominational hymnals and 635 from independently published books.

While patterns can be seen for these years in the history of the text, so many individual variations had come to exist that it is no longer possible to canvass them comprehensively. The most obvious development was the emergence of another important distinction to overlay the difference in use between the Perronet and Rippon versions. The new polarity was between renditions geared to the populist world of the gospel song and renditions edited for use in more formal church settings. The gospel variant appeared most often in a very popular three-stanza version. It was promoted in Sankey's many hymnbooks and their many imitators; it often was garnished with a new tune or a new chorus.

By contrast, more historically conscious editors were offering churches and denominations several versions of six-stanza, or even seven- and eight-stanza, versions of the hymn. They appeared in books with titles like *The Epworth Hymnal* (1885), *Carmina Sanctorum* (1886), *The Church Praise Book* (1888), *Laudes Domini* (1889), and *The Book of Praise* (1893). About the same number of such versions appeared (ninety-one) in these years as the number of three-stanza gospel abridgments (ninety). It is, however, harder to categorize these longer versions since editors were deploying the full range of options offered by the Perronet and Rippon versions as well as intervening editorial revisions. Although a wealth of minor variations differentiate these longer versions from each other, they mostly reprise the Perronet and Rippon texts as slightly modified by earlier British and American editors. What had clearly emerged with this one inherited text was a distinction between "learned" and "popular" hymns.[67]

The most significant mark of the era's editorial creativity was not texts but tunes. Editors on both sides of the Atlantic eagerly joined different versions of "All Hail the Power" to newly written music as well as to older tunes not heretofore put to use with this hymn. Of the 288 American reprintings with tunes, 78 percent stuck to "Coronation," and another 11 percent imported "Miles Lane" (or "Shrubsole"). But that left thirty-two printings that used twenty different tunes for this one text. British musical exuberance rose even higher. Of thirty-eight British reprintings with tunes in this sample, 50 percent used "Miles Lane," 8 percent borrowed "Coronation" from the Americans, but then seventeen other reprintings put twelve different tunes to use. Of these tunes newly printed with "All Hail the Power," only "Diadem" would reappear later with any frequency in America and only "Ladywell" in Britain. Nonetheless, the burst of new music indicated at least two things: it was an era of rapid religious change where a premium was being placed on new expressions of Christian faith, but it was also an era in which retaining the religious expressions of a previous age remained important.

Significant editorial revisions of the period pointed not only to diverging "popular" and "learned" traditions but also to significant British and American differences. The hymn presented in British hymnals differed from the American one by retaining more of Perronet and Rippon originals and by including more verses.[68] There was, in other words, less gospelizing of British hymnody in this era than in America.

In addition, during this period at least, British editors were more likely to attempt radical alterations of the hymn than American editors. In Britain there appeared interesting minor variations from compilers whose fame long antedated their activity as hymn editors. Sir Arthur Sullivan's version of "All Hail the Power" revised R2 to read: "Crown Him ye martyrs of our God . . . ; Praise Him whose blood-stained path ye trod . . . "[69] William Booth's rendition of 1889 took off from Burder's revision of P5 to create a virtually new stanza: "Ye sinners lost, of Adam's race, / Partakers of the fall, / Come and be saved by Jesus' grace, / And crown Him Lord of all!"[70] The era's most radical version came from Paisley, Scotland, where the enterprising editor of *The Gospel Choir* not only solicited a tune from Frances Ridley Havergal but also substantially rewrote most of the six verses, as illustrated by an entirely new fourth stanza: "Ye realms of every tongue and name— / Nations and Islands all— / The mighty Savior's praise proclaim, / And Crown Him Lord of all."[71]

In the United States, editorial innovation was restricted to the construction of new choruses, none of which were particularly interesting as religious verse, but all of which testified to the adaptability of the hymn. In every case, the new choruses were appended to three-stanza abridgments. And in every case the end in view was not so much literary ramification as emotional effect.[72]

The appearance of "All Hail the Power" during the 1880s and 1890s reflected the religious innovations of the period. An American Protestantism that had never been particularly unified was now dividing even more clearly between a populist strand stressing a simple gospel faith and a more respectable variety concerned about intellectual propriety. It would be wrong to think that the appearance of populist and learned versions of this hymn presaged the later fundamentalist-modernist battles within American Protestantism, since the abridged gospel versions with bouncy new choruses were the ones that dropped consideration of "sin" and other traditional emphases retained in the longer church versions. The clear distinction between versions of the same hymn does, however, underscore the fact that when ecclesiastical and theological differences did lead to a Protestant schism between fundamentalist and modernist camps, there had already come to exist in the religious lives of American believers a polarity in styles of worship that would reinforce the intellectual fissure. The divide in "All Hail the Power" also reinforces a conclusion drawn by Martin Marty that the kind of religion heading toward fundamentalism was "modernist" in the sense of eagerly innovating in its moods, expressions, and delivery of religious material.[73] To set "All Hail the Power" to "Arlington," "Amazon," "Avon," "Cressy," "Crown Him Lord of All," "Jesus Is All," "Lowe," "McGranahan," "McHose," "McIntosh," and "Newbold," as American editors did in this period, was to evince a remarkable flexibility toward religious tradition.

As testified by the reprinted texts of "All Hail the Power," American Protestantism into the 1880s and 1890s was still distinctly conservative. During this period more radical textual variants came from Britain than the United States. American revision of the text, when it occurred at all, featured abridgment more than revision. But the abridgments found in some American

Table 3.2
1880–1900

		Rippon stanzas	*Peronnet stanzas*	*Other stanzas*
No. hymnals	280 (US 250, UK 30)	R1—298	P1—4	mR3P5—106
No. printings	334 (US 294, UK 40)	R2—38	P2—11	revP8—8
Avg. no. stanzas	4.6 (US 4.5, UK 5.6)	R3—14	P3—52	revR6—4
No. new hymns	1	R4—19	P4—23	mP8R6—4
		R5—0	P5—47	revW—2
		R6—253	P6—30	revR2—2
		R7—258	P7—153	new—3
			P8—9	

rev = substantial revision of a stanza
W = Wilks's 1798 revision
m = mixed stanzas
new = entirely new verses
Note: Stanza counts tally only one set of texts per book, unless (as happened with some frequency) hymnals included not only two tunes but also two versions of the text.

quarters—as also the movement in other quarters toward longer, more self-consciously historical versions of the hymn—bespoke defining characteristics as surely as the greater textual liberties of earlier and later periods.

1970–95

A relatively small sampling of recent hymnbooks testifies to the enduring popularity of "All Hail the Power," as also to the fact that earlier trends have continued to the present. The British use more verses (an average of 5.6 per printing) than the Americans (4.6). Independently produced hymnals with titles like *Hymns of Truth and Praise* (1971) and *Hymns of Faith* (1980) usually present shorter versions, although in the modern period several of the denominational hymnals have also reduced the number of stanzas. Where, however, six- or seven-stanza versions exist, they are more likely to come from official sponsorship, as *The New Catholic Hymnal* (1971), *The Lutheran Book of Worship* (1978), the Episcopalians *Hymnbook 1982*, the *Trinity Hymnal* (1990 ed.) of the Presbyterian Church in America and the Orthodox Presbyterian Church, the *United Methodist Hymnal* (1994 [orig. 1989]), and *Hymns for To-day's Church* (1982) edited by an Anglican bishop. New tunes continue to be written, but not nearly as often as a century ago (only two new tunes with three appearances out of sixty-four printings sampled). The British continue to prefer "Miles Lane" (three out of seven sampled) and Americans "Coronation" (twenty-five out of fifty-seven), but on both sides of the Atlantic "Diadem" is popular. It has become de rigueur in American hymnbooks to print the hymn with at least two tunes (twenty-two out of twenty-nine books), with "Miles Lane" and "Diadem" about equally popular as the second (or third) tune after "Coronation."

In the United States a four-stanza version has become the majority practice (thirty-five out of fifty-eight printings), with over two-thirds of these printings presenting R1, revR3-P5 ("Ye chosen seed of Israel's race, / Ye ransomed of [from] the fall"), R6, R7. Otherwise the text is all over the map. Of Perronet's original stanzas, only P5 as modified by Rippon and Burden remains current and, somewhat less commonly, P7 ("Sinners! whose love . . ."). Learned denominational hymnbooks occasionally retrieve P3 ("Crown Him ye morning stars of light") or P6 ("Hail Him, ye heirs of David's line"), but these stanzas are otherwise almost extinct. Rippon's "Gentile sinners" (R4) have joined his "Babes, men, and sires" (R5) in the liturgical lumber room, while his "martyrs" (R2) clings to a marginal life.

Editors now regularly offer minor changes on the inherited texts. A long-standing nervousness about "the stem of Jesse's rod" (R2) has given way to at least two modern variations: "Extol him in whose path ye trod" and "Praise him whose way of pain ye trod."[74] For reasons that may be mostly literary, the Lutherans and Christian Reformed have tinkered with the already much-revised opening lines of R3/P5 to produce, "O seed of Israel's chosen race / Now ransomed from the fall."[75]

Extensive alterations in this era are rare, but unlike the period 1880–89 they are more likely to be found in the text than in the tunes. The 1979 version of *The Brethren Hymnal* creatively merged a "Miles Lane" rendition of R1 with two verses of Thomas Kelly's "The head that once was crowned with thorns."[76] Under the oversight of Bishop Michael Baughen, Anglicans produced a substantially new text for an entirely new tune. The name of the tune, "Jubilate," reflected a desire to express the sentiments of the old song in fresh phrases, but also in phrases that did not alter the originals' evangelical sentiments. Its last two stanzas reflected that intent: "4. Let all who trust in Christ exclaim / In wonder, to recall / The one who bore your sin and shame, / And crown him Lord of all / 5. Then in that final judgment hour / When all rebellions fall, / We'll rise in his triumphant power, / And crown him Lord of all."[77]

Different agendas were at work among American Roman Catholics and Congregationalists who provided their substantially new versions. The editors of *The New Catholic Hymnal* seemed to have returned to Rippon's original spirit by trying to add another category of beings to the chorus of praise: "You prophets who our freedom won, / Disciples great and small; / By whom the work of truth is done, / Now crown him Lord of all." In addition, to provide an even number of stanzas for a very rare American appearance of Ferguson's "Ladywell," with its doubled Common Meter, the editors inserted this new stanza: "Adore him as our God and King / Who lay within a stall, / Unceasingly his praises sing, / And crown him Lord of all."

The revision offered by the United Church of Christ's *New Century Hymnal* of 1995 is the most obvious bending to intellectual fashion since the Boston hymnbook of 1808 substituted "own him Lord" for "crown him Lord." Now it is Lordship itself that has become the problem, so Christ becomes "servant of all," "bearer of all," "teacher of all," and "savior of all."[78]

In general, however, reprintings of "All Hail the Power" in the modern period are mostly conservative. The hymn is now shorter and usually simpler. Great affection seems to cling to Christ as "Lord of all," although the path of martyrdom and the naming of sin have joined an emphasis on Jewish-Gentile categories as subjects not often mentioned in polite religious society. "All Hail the Power" remains a historical landmark important enough in some circles to be extensively adjusted to meet the sensibilities of the moment. But in most hymnals it is now a cherished but relatively unthreatening remnant of bygone days, distinguished more by its plurality of tunes than by the bite of its text.

Conclusion

The constantly evolving form of "All Hail the Power of Jesus' Name" has been a revealing index of several important features of American religious life. How it is sung has been a marker of class, first between populist singers of the Rippon original and establishmentarian singers of Perronet, and then between populist singers of stripped down abridgments and learned denominational singers of historically faithful versions.[79] The gradual shrinking in the number of verses marked a decline in both biblical knowledge and worshipping intelligence, since the stanzas from both Perronet and Rippon that vanished were both more complicated rhetorically and more allusive biblically. The stanzas that have dropped away also reveal a growing skittishness about the more realistic aspects of traditional Christian teaching, since stan-

Table 3.3
1970–1995

		Rippon reprints	Peronnet reprints	Others
No. hymnals	34 (US 30, UK 4)	R1—34	P1—0	mR3P5—16
No. printings	65 (US 58, UK 7)	R2—9	P2—0	new—7
Avg. no. stanzas	4.7 (US 4.6, UK 5.6)	R3—3	P3—2	revR2—4
No. new hymns	1	R4—1	P4—2	
		R5—0	P5—16	
		R6—31	P6—5	
		R7—34	P7—11	
			P8—1	

rev = substantial revision of a stanza
m = mixed stanzas
new = entirely new verses
Note: Again, stanza counts tally only one set of texts per book; in this period multiple tunes almost always are used for the same text.

zas featuring "martyrdom" and "sinners" have both steadily declined. Use of the hymn also reveals the continuing cultural influence of Britain in America, since many of the alterations found in the hymnbooks of mature American denominations have been picked up from historical retrievals advanced by the British. Finally, the nearly universal enjoyment of the hymn has made it a prime target for extensive textual revision as well as for the composition of new tunes. In both cases, "All Hail the Power" has exerted a power too strong to resist and yet also to leave alone.

In the American evolution of "All Hail the Power" most of the variations have been sterile sports. That there have been so many testifies to the evocative fecundity of the poem's master image of the once-despised Jesus now adored by the hosts of all the earth. That these variations have almost never been reproduced widely—that most of them in fact appeared only once or only in successive printings of a single editor's work—testifies to the original skill of Perronet and Rippon in communicating the master image.

The extraordinarily diverse history of "All Hail the Power of Jesus' Name," has more than fulfilled John Rippon's desire for a various hymnody with Christ as the focus of song. A great mass of detail is required even to introduce the publishing history of this hymn, but that welter of particulars should not be allowed to obscure the central, overriding reality of its history: in all its myriad variations, "All Hail the Power of Jesus' Name" has been popular because it depicts so effectively the triumphant rule of Jesus Christ.

Notes

I am pleased at the outset to acknowledge with gratitude the very substantial help I have received in preparing this chapter: Jonathan Blumhofer, Joel Moore, Mary Louise VanDyke, Maggie Noll, Sue Miles.

1. John Rippon, *A Selection of Hymns from the Best Authors. Intended to be an Appendix to Dr. Watts's Psalms and Hymns* (sold by the author, and at his vestry, Carter-Lane [London], at [specifically named printers in] London, Bristol, Leeds, and Edinburgh, and "by the Baptist ministers" in Philadelphia, Boston, and New York: ca. 1793), iii–vii. The Preface is quoted here from an undated but early edition in the Regent's Park College Library, Oxford.

2. Nehemiah Curnock, ed., *The Journal of the Rev. John Wesley* (London: Epworth, 1909–16), 3: 277n2. On Perronet, see Luke Tyerman, *The Life and Times of the Rev. John Wesley, M.A., Founder of the Methodists*, 3rd ed. (London: Hodder and Stoughton, 1876), 2: 57, 84–85, 200, 241–44, 253–55; J. Vincent Higginson, "Edward Perronet," *The Hymn* 18 (1967): 105–13; A. Skevington Wood, "Edward Perronet," *Dictionary of Evangelical Biography, 1730–1860*, ed. Donald M. Lewis, 2 vols. (Oxford: Blackwell, 1995), 2: 876; and *Dictionary of National Biography*, 15: 904–5.

3. R. Vaughan Williams, "Shrubsole: From an article . . . in the *Manchester Guardian*," *Bulletin of the Hymn Society of Great Britain and Ireland* 25 (October 1943): 1–2.

4. Kenneth Manley, "John Rippon," is the essential source for the life, but see also Manley's informative brief article in *Dictionary of Evangelical Biography*, 2: 941.

5. Rippon brought out at least twenty-seven editions of his *Selection*, with the twenty-seventh in 1828 being the third major expansion of this hymnal. Manley, "John Rippon," 146.

6. Ibid., 153–54.

7. Ibid., 158, with 157–62 on Rippon's work as editor of hymn texts.

8. Lionel Adey, *Hymns and the Christian "Myth"* (Vancouver: University of British Columbia Press, 1986), 130.

9. Several of the early American printings of Rippon's *Selections* did retain Rippon's full title, with scripture text.

10. See Nathan O. Hatch, "*Sola Scriptura* and *Novus Ordo Seclorum*," in *The Bible in America*, ed. Hatch and Mark A. Noll (New York: Oxford University Press, 1982), 59–78.

11. In light of the pattern of editorial changes made by Rippon, it is likely that he

altered this line in order to heighten the directness of its appeal as well as to provide his version with a verse for converted Jews (R3) followed by a verse for believing Gentiles (R4).

12. David W. Bebbington, "Evangelicalism in Modern Britain and America: A Comparison," in *Amazing Grace: Evangelicalism in Australia, Britain, Canada, and the United States,* eds. George A. Rawlyk and Mark A. Noll (Grand Rapids, MI: Baker; and Montreal/Kingston: McGill-Queen's University Press, 1994), 183–212; David W. Bebbington, "Canadian Evangelicalism: A View from Britain," in *Aspects of the Canadian Evangelical Experience,* ed. G. A. Rawlyk (Montreal/Kingston: McGill-Queen's University Press, 1997), 38–54.

13. In 1798, Matthew Wilks altered the first line to read "All Hail! the great Immanuel's name." This variation would turn up occasionally in American printings. See John Julian, ed., *A Dictionary of Hymnology* (London: John Murray, 1892), 42.

14. My thanks to Mary Louise VanDyke for help in spotting these variants.

15. Nathan O. Hatch, *The Democratization of American Christianity* (New Haven: Yale University Press, 1989), 148.

16. On Holden, see especially Ralph T. Daniel, *The Anthem in New England before 1800* (Evanston, IL: Northwestern University Press, 1966), 129–33.

17. Nicholas Temperley, ed., *The Hymn Tune Index: A Census of English-Language Hymn Tunes in Printed Sources from 1535 to 1820,* 4 vols. (Oxford: Clarendon, 1998), 4: 123, 287.

18. Manley, "John Rippon," 190.

19. Comments from August 15, 1801, reprinted here verbatim from "Letter to Dr. Rippon from New York," *Transactions of the Baptist Historical Society* 1 (1908–9): 69–76, quotation 72.

20. Manley, "John Rippon," 192. That quantity in 1828 would equal something like 2.2 million copies if sold in proportionate numbers to the American public ca. 2000.

21. Ralph R. Shaw and Richard H. Shoemaker, *American Bibliography: A Preliminary Checklist, 1801–19* (New York: Scarecrow Press, 1958), passim.

22. "Preface," *The Hartford Selection of Hymns, From the Most Approved Authors. To which are added a number never before published* (Hartford, CT: J. Babcock, 1799), "All Hail the Power," no. 87 (quotation from preface, iii).

23. On Strong and Flint, see William B. Sprague, *Annals of the American Pulpit* (New York: R. Carter, 1857–69), 2: 34–38, 273–75.

24. Stephen A. Marini, *Radical Sects of Rural New England* (Cambridge, MA: Harvard University Press, 1982), 68–75 and passim.

25. Smith published Rippon's "All Hail the Power" in at least twenty hymnals printed between 1804 and 1817. On Smith as radical biblical populist, see Michael G.

Kenny, *The Perfect Law of Liberty: Elias Smith and the Providential History of America* (Washington, DC: Smithsonian Institution Press, 1994); and Hatch, *Democratization,* 57, 68–76, 134–35, and on his hymn books, 148.

26. Amos R. Wells, *A Treasury of Hymn Stories* (Grand Rapids, MI: Baker, 1945), 12; Terry L. Lindsay, *Devotionals from Famous Hymn Stories* (Grand Rapids, MI: Baker, 1974), 28; Louis Albert Banks, *Immortal Hymns and Their Story* (Cleveland: Burrows Brothers, 1898), 308. The last phrase appears in almost identical wording in Duncan Morrison, *The Great Hymns of the Church* (Toronto: Hart and Co., 1890), 154.

27. By 1820, "All Hail the Power" had been printed with at least ten different tunes or significant tune variations. The majority of these tunes came from Britain. Temperley, *Hymn Tune Index,* 3: 679–80; 4: 52, 123, 287, 414, 538, 601, 608, 637.

28. Erik Routley, *Hymns and Human Life,* 2nd ed. (London: John Murray, 1959), 267.

29. See Ian Bradley, *Abide with Me: The World of Victorian Hymns* (London: SCM, 1997), 194–95, where the hymn is placed in the second tier of most popular English hymns. This ranking confirms Lionel Adey's earlier finding that "All Hail the Power" belonged in the middle rank of British hymns; Adey tallied it as the forty-ninth most reprinted hymn in a large selection of hymnbooks studied for his *Class and Idol in the English Hymn* (Vancouver: University of British Columbia Press, 1988), 257.

30. W. T. Keeler, *The Romantic Origins of Some Favourite Hymns* (London: Lutterworth, 1947), 24.

31. Routley, *Hymns and Human Life,* 288–89.

32. Ian Bradley, *Penguin Book of Hymns* (London/New York: Viking, 1989), 19–21, with the text presented as Perronet's original with the exception of revision in P8.

33. For example, Maddy Prior with the Carnival Band, *Sing Lustily & with Good Courage: Gallery Hymns of the 18th and Early 19th Centuries* (Chipping Manor, England: Saydisc Records, 1990), track 11. The text in this very lively rendition, which intersperses other well-known evangelical hymns of the era as interludes between the verses, is a typical modern mongrel: R1, revR2, P5, P7, revP8, R7.

34. Spanish, for example, "Loores dad a Christo Rey," *El nuevo himnario evangélico, para el uso del iglesias evangélicas de habla española en todo el mundo* (New York: Sociedad American de Tratados, 1914), no. 105; and a somewhat altered printing of the same translation in *Celebramos su gloria* (Dallas: Celebremos/Libros Alianza, 1992), no. 241. German, "Preis sei dem Namen Jesu Christ," in Ira Sankey and Walter Rauschenbusch, *Evangeliumslieder 1–2* (Chicago: Bigelow and Main, 1897), no. 13. Latin, "Salve, Nomen potestatis!" in Richard Bingham, *Hymnologia Christiana Latina* (London: Baillière, Tindal, and Cox, 1871), 188–91; and "Jesu! prepotens Nomen," in Duncan Morrison, *The Great Hymns of the Church* (Toronto: Hart and Co., 1890), 152–53.

35. The earliest version of the story I have found is in Morrison, *Great Hymns of the Church,* 157, which cites Williams Reynolds of Peoria, Illinois, "the well known Sunday school worker," as the source of the story.

36. M. Guthrie Clark, *Sing Them Again: A Companion to "Sunday Half-Hour"* (London: Henry E. Walter, 1955), 49–50; I. Doricott and T. Collins, *Lyric Studies: A Hymnal Guide* (London: T. Danks, n.d. [early 1900s]), 139; Ira D. Sankey, *My Life and the Story of the Gospel Hymns* (New York: Harper and Bros., 1906), 319–20.

37. The story appeared in Clarence W. Hall, *Together Magazine,* October 1960; reprinted in *Australia's Fair Dinkum E-Zine and Magazine,* issue 53, wysiwyg://107/ http://members.iweb.net.au/~dinkum/dink53.htm (April 20, 2000).

38. On Ellor, see Charles Albert Boyd, *Stories of Hymns for Creative Living* (Philadelphia: Judson, 1938), 22.

39. Frances A. Mosher, "Toward Singing with the Understanding: A Discussion of the Gospel Hymn—Part I," *Journal of the Grace Evangelical Society* 5: 1, www.faithalone. org/journal/index.html (Spring 1992).

40. Frank Colquhoun, *Hymns that Live: Their Meaning and Message* (London: Hodder and Stoughton, 1980), 124–31; Clark, *Sing Them Again,* 50–51; Morrison, *Great Hymns of the Church,* 156–57; and Erik Routley, *Hymns and the Faith* (London: John Murray, 1955), 276–79.

41. From information collected for *The Dictionary of American Hymnology* and kindly made available by Mary Louise VanDyke.

42. Theron Brown and Hezekiah Butterworth, *The Story of the Hymns and Tunes* (New York: American Tract Society, 1906), 29; citing a note in the old *Carmina Sacra.*

43. R. Don Kersley, "Some Thoughts and Facts about Music," *The Ladies' Repository* (March 1865): 174.

44. George Hughes, *Days of Power in the Forest Temple: A Review of the Wonderful Work of God at Fourteen National Camp-Meetings, from 1867 to 1872* (Boston: John Bent, 1874), 259–60.

45. "Report of Fraternal Delegates," *African Methodist Episcopal Church Review* 19, 1 (July 1902): 432, http://dbs.ohiohistory.org/africanam/page.cfm?ID=2276&Current=P441 (April 20, 2000).

46. http://www.charweb.org/charlotte/walktour/wlksec17.htm (April 13, 2000).

47. "Kate and Sue McBeth, Missionary Teachers to the Nez Perce," http://menolly. lib.uidaha.edu/McBeth/index.htm (April 24, 2000).

48. From Clayborne Carson and Peter Holloran, eds., *A Knock at Midnight: Inspiration from the Great Sermons of Reverend Martin Luther King, Jr.* (New York: Warner, 1998), from http://www.stanford.edu/group/king/sermons/contents.htm (April 24, 2000).

49. http://www.sportsmusic.com/christp.html (April 13, 2000).

50. Father Divine, "How Can We Expect to Express Our American Independence Unless We Get Away from Soliciting, Borrowing and Begging?" http://www.libertynet.org/fdipmm/word1/39090519.html (April 13, 2000).

51. Lewis Gary Massarelli, "A Study of the Music of the Pentecostal Assemblies of Canada and How It Changes in Time of Revival" (master's thesis, California State University–Dominguez Hills, 1998), figure 1; from http://ephbc.edu/music/Thesis.htm (April 10, 2000).

52. Jim Mankin and Jason Fikes, "'When Shall I Reach That Happy Place?' Apocalyptic Themes in the Hymns of the Stone-Campbell Movement," *Restoration Quarterly* 38 (1996): 25–26.

53. Stephen Marini, "Evangelical Hymns and Popular Belief," in *Music and the Public Sphere, 1600–1900,* ed. Peter Benes (Boston: Boston University, 1998); Bradley, *Abide with Me,* xi–xiv; John Wolffe, "Praise to the Highest Hymns and Church Music," in *Religion in Victorian Britain, Vol. V: Culture and Empire,* ed. John Wolffe (Manchester: Manchester University Press, 1997), 59–99, esp. 62–66; and, with attention to literary questions, J. R. Watson, *The English Hymn: A Critical and Historical Study* (Oxford: Clarendon, 1997), 4–8 ("The power of hymns").

54. Biases in what follows arise from the nature of the texts consulted.

55. Joshua Smith and Samuel Ogun, *Divine Hymns, or Spiritual Songs* (Wilkes-Barre, PA: Asher and Charles Miner, 1802), no. 107.

56. Joshua Spaulding, *The Lord's Songs* (Salem, MA: Cushing, 1805), no. 139.

57. *Psalms, Hymns, and Spiritual Songs: Selected . . . for the Church Universal* (Boston: Monroe, Francis and Parker, 1808), no. 131; *Psalms, Hymns, and Spiritual Songs . . . for the Use of the Independent Christian Church of Gloucester* (Boston: Monroe, Francis and Parker, 1808), no. 173; *Hymns Chiefly Selected for Public and Social Worship* (Salisbury, NC: Easton, 1810), no. 20.

58. *Psalms . . . for the Church Universal,* no. 131.

59. Quoted in Hatch, *Democratization,* 76, where he appears as "Sargent."

60. Abel Morgan Sarjent, *The New Hymn-Book for the Use of the Free Church* (New York: for A. M. Sarjent, 1811), no. 40, preface quoted from iv–v.

61. Most of these early printings were without music. Where a tune was either present or specified, it was usually "Coronation," although "Miles Lane" was already showing up in a few printings, though the tune name is given as "Marlborough."

62. *The Church Psalmist* (New York: Mark H. Newman, 1847), no. 186; George B. Cheever and J. E. Sweetser, *Christian Melodies: A Collection of Hymns and Tunes* (New York: H. S. Barnes, 1851), no. 61; R. S. Thomas and G. W. Wood, *Plymouth Collection of Hymns and Tunes for the Use of Christian Congregations* (New York: A. S. Barnes, 1855), no. 174. On Cheever, see *American National Bibliography,* 4: 768–70.

63. Found, for example, in *Union Hymns* (Philadelphia: American Sunday School

Union, 1845), no. 419; *The Union Singing Book* (New York: Anson D. F. Randolph, 1845), no. 23; and William B. Bradbury, *Oriola, a New and Complete Hymn and Tune Book* (Cincinnati: Moore, Wilstach, Keys; New York: Ivison and Phinney, 1859), no. 135.

64. The return of Wilks's opening, "All Hail the great Immanuel's name," bespeaks both research and pretense. It is found, for example, in *The Boston Academy's Collection of Church Music* (Boston: J. H. Wilkins and R. B. Carter, 1840), no. 128; Lowell Mason, *Carmina Sacra* (Boston: J. H. Wilkins and R. B. Carter, 1841), no. 112; Lowell Mason, *Church Psalmody* (Boston: T. R. Marvin, 1847 [early ed. 1831]), no. 139; D. Storrs Willis, *Church Chorales and Choir Studies* (New York: Clark, Austin and Smith, 1850), no. 100; and J. L. Tracy, *The American School Manual* (Cincinnati: H. W. Derby, 1856), no. 99. One hymnal reproducing the Wilks opening that does not seem associated with the new musical professionalism of the period was *Hymns for Christian Melody* (Dover, [NH?]: Free-Will Baptist Connection, 1841), no. 118.

65. Mason, *Church Psalmody*, no. 139: "Crown Him, ye martyrs of our God . . . ; Praise Him who shed for you his blood . . . "; Willis, *Church Chorales*, no. 100: "Crown Him, ye martyrs of our God . . . ; Praise Him who saves you by his blood . . . "

66. Sandra S. Sizer, *Gospel Hymns and Social Religion: The Rhetoric of Nineteenth-Century Revivalism* (Philadelphia: Temple University, 1978).

67. Adey, *Class and Idol*, 21–92.

68. By this time, however, considerable cross-fertilization is evident in hymn publication. As examples, Sankey's *Gospel Songs* were being regularly reprinted in London, while more American editors were returning to versions of Perronet's text than were the British (who before this period had been the main sustainers of distinctively Perronet versions).

69. Sir Arthur Sullivan, *Church Hymns with Tunes* (London: Society for Promoting Christian Knowledge, 1896 [ca. 1872]), no. 330.

70. William Booth, *Salvation Army Music* (London: John Snow, 1889), no. 285.

71. R. Stewart, *The Gospel Choir* (Paisley, Scotland: J. and R. Parlance, 1892), no. 381.

72. John B. Shaw and C. A. Shaw, *Beautiful Offerings of Sacred Song* (Chicago: Shaw Brothers, 1894), no. 73; O. S. Grinnell, Levi White, et al., *Gospel Melodies* (Cleveland: W. R. Smellie, 1885), no. 7.

73. Martin E. Marty, *Modern American Religion, Vol. 1: The Irony of It All, 1893–1919* (Chicago: University of Chicago Press, 1986), 194, 208–9, 219–20.

74. The first from *The Church Hymnary*, 3rd ed., produced for the Church of Scotland and the Presbyterian churches of England, Scotland, and Wales (London: Oxford University Press, 1973), no. 382; the second from the *Hymnal 1982: According to the Use of the Episcopal Church* (New York: Church Publishing, 1982), 450.

75. *Lutheran Book of Worship* (Minneapolis: Augsburg, 1978), nos. 328, 329; Emily Brink, *Psalter Hymnal* (Grand Rapids, MI: CRC Publications, 1987), nos. 470, 471.

76. *The Brethren Hymnal* (Elgin, IL: Brethren Press, 1979 [revised from 1951]), no. 103.

77. Anthony Petti and Geoffrey Laycock, *The New Catholic Hymnal* (New York: St. Martin's Press, 1971), nos. 4, 5.

78. Arthur G. Clyde, *The New Century Hymnal* (Cleveland: Pilgrim Press, 1995), no. 304.

79. In Britain, by contrast, "All Hail the Power" has indicated class more by the tune with which it is accompanied—"Miles Lane" for the establishment, "Diadem" for the proles; see Bradley, *Abide with Me,* 18.

II
Hymns and Hymnbooks
as Cultural Icons

4
Textual Editing and the "Making" of Hymns in Nineteenth-Century America

Mary De Jong

SUNG AND RECITED from memory at all manner of public and private occasions, hymns permeated nineteenth-century thought, private writings, and conversation. Americans interpreted and expressed their experiences in terms of a hymnic language at once authoritative and familiar. The expressive power of that language is articulated in a letter that Ann Hasseltine Judson wrote in 1823 to her missionary husband in Burma: "Your last letter lies before me, and Winchell's Collection [of Psalms and hymns also; open at the hymn 'Blest be the tie that binds.'] Not that I cannot repeat it without the book, but I wish to refresh myself with a view of the very words. How exactly suited to our case! How it describes the manner in which we have lived together, . . . the pain which we feel in being parted, and the glorious hopes and prospects before us!"[1]

Judson's respect for "the very words" on the page reflects the unexamined ideal of the hymn as an authoritative, permanent text: it was "true" to Christian experience and therefore seemed timeless, fixed like verses from the King James Bible. Accordingly, phrases from hymns were engraved on believers' tombstones. Yet anyone who read hymnbooks carefully or listened to hymn singing would notice that hymn texts were not actually fixed in the sense of being unchangeable.

Hymnologists defined the genuine hymn as "true"—scriptural, doctrinally sound, and based in Christian experience. Clergymen and other commentators who reviewed hymnbooks and sought to influence editors' work identified additional criteria for the hymn suitable for congregational performance. It must be "singable"; commentators therefore advocated formal regularity; pleasing, preferably exact rhyme; rhythmic fluency; "refinement of poetic taste"; and freedom from irreverent associations.[2] Many writers asserted that a hymn should not be conspicuously or merely didactic. (There must be no dogmatic "pills of doggerel," stipulated one clergyman.)[3] Yet reviewers would praise hymnals that possessed "doctrinal wealth" and censure books "without doctrine."[4]

The Second Great Awakening of 1790–1835 kindled interest in evangelical hymnody.[5] Hymnbooks offering to rejuvenate congregational singing proliferated by midcentury in such numbers that many reviewers remarked on their number and the competition among them.[6] Selecting promising lyrics from other hymnbooks and periodicals, and soliciting new hymns from devout poets, editors proceeded to make the hymns they wanted by changing words and phrases, recasting and deleting entire stanzas, and occasionally inserting new ones. They also accepted texts that had been made by previous editors, often because they were unable or unwilling to locate the poets' original lyrics. The century was well advanced before accurate attributions and authentic texts even of some well-known hymns were established. Most nineteenth-century editors did not mark even texts they had substantially revised as "alt."

In 1850 at least two secular periodicals reported an incident that illustrates both the common conviction that there is just one authentic text of a favorite hymn and the reality of editorial alteration. Eminent clergyman George Washington Bethune, himself a hymnist, became incensed while giving out "There is a fountain filled with blood" in Boston's Park Street (Congregational) Church. At the fifth stanza he "rather suddenly" stopped reading and "startled" the audience by declaring, "This last stanza is not as Cowper wrote it! As he wrote it, it runs thus." Laying down the hymnal, Bethune recited the hymn he knew by heart. "I should like to know," he continued, "who has had the audacity to alter Cowper's poetry! The choir will sing only the first four stanzas of the hymn."[7] Ironically, the gentleman himself was altering a printed text on the spot, as many eighteenth-century clergymen and song leaders had done.

Isaac Watts (1674–1748) stated in the preface to his *Hymns and Spiritual Songs* (2nd ed., 1709) that persons in charge of singing were free to alter his texts as they saw fit.[8] Nevertheless, the idea of the text as fixed became ingrained over time. By the early nineteenth century, Watts's own paraphrases of the Psalms and his original hymns had near-biblical authority for many American evangelicals, especially in churches with Calvinist roots.[9] John Wesley (1703–1791) contributed to the idea of a fixed text by directing future hymnbook makers not to alter the lyrics in his *Collection of Hymns for the Use of the People Called Methodists* (1780).[10] British hymnist James Montgomery (1771–1854), who had rewritten hundreds of hymns by other poets, asked future editors not to revise his. Yet he acknowledged that after his death, his "hymns [would], no doubt, be altered to suit the taste of appropriators; for it is astonishing how really religious persons will sometimes feel scruples about a turn or a term." Quoting Montgomery's plea, the authors of *Hymns and Choirs* noted that his prediction was accurate. They demonstrated the prevalence of textual alteration and devoted most of their 160-page second chapter to defending the practice as necessary.[11] Lowell Mason, music editor of the *Sabbath Hymn and Tune Book* (1859), wrote Edwards Amasa Park, textual editor of that volume, after reading the proof sheets of *Hymns and Choirs*: "The question of alteration is surely settled," he exulted, "and no one will cry out more for original copies," meaning poets' original texts.[12] He underestimated his clerical contemporaries' investments in "turns" and "terms."

Although an occasional article for a wide readership addressed the issue of textual alteration, I have seen little evidence in print or in published letters that laypeople paid much attention to textual variants of hymns.[13] (Poets whose lyrics were accepted or appropriated as hymns did respond to editors' alterations of their work.)[14] But denominational journals and other religious periodicals published numerous statements and articles about textual editing, many of them critical of "tinkers," also ironically called "menders" and "improvers." Alterations deemed unjustifiable were called "mutilations."[15]

Anticipating harsh criticism but hoping to win favorable reviews, many mid- and late-century hymnbook editors wrote prefaces that articulated their positions on textual alteration (a term that covered the gamut from changing a few words to rewriting entire stanzas) and "remodeling" (an early nineteenth-century term that indicated substantial revision). Several editors considerate of hymn-lovers' sensibilities or wary of their wrath stated that they had taken all possible steps to "restore" original texts. Henry Ward Beecher took that path affirming, "No language can well replace that which the original inspiration of the author suggested."[16] Eventually, there was general agreement that editors should use poets' original texts—unless these were objectionable on legitimate grounds or altered versions had been "sanctioned" by wide use.[17] An editor who introduced an alteration should note that fact.[18]

Aware, then, that their knowledge, competence, and taste—and, as we shall see, even their piety and moral purity—might be questioned, nineteenth-century editors nevertheless altered lyrics to achieve doctrinal, ideological, prosodic, and grammatical "correctness." To disarm critics, they usually explained their purposes and rationales in prefatory statements. Some asked friends to write reviews supportive of their work.[19] Others used their positions as editors of and regular contributors to periodicals to legitimate and promote their hymnbooks.[20] Even so, some of the textual variants that editors created or propagated are not readily explicable by any of the commonly stated criteria for excellent hymns.

Textual emendations are worthy of study as evidence of the meanings evangelicals attached to hymns—especially by clergymen, who were in positions to influence many singers' exposure to and experience of hymns, and who assumed that hymns attach meanings to evangelicals. Editing reveals not only which doctrines mattered but also which beliefs about self and society and what kind of verbal expression churchmen considered appropriate for a mass audience.

The following observations are based on my analysis of variants of twelve well-known hymns originally published between 1707 and 1865. The texts examined appear in a sample of seventeen hymnbooks published in the United States between 1824 and 1895 and representative of the major evangelical denominations. The purposes and significance of variants are assessed in light of other documents: (1) editorial prefaces in several dozen hymnals dating from Watts's *Hymns and Spiritual Songs* to the early 1900s, (2) critical commentary on hymns, hymnbooks, hymn editing, and hymn singing published in nineteenth-century American denominational journals; religious magazines; popular, predominantly secular magazines; and hymnological studies, and (3) hymnbook editors' correspondence. Some variants are interpreted in light of recent historical, hymnological, and gender studies scholarship.[21]

Hymn editors and critics insisted on orthodoxy, and some textual variants do reflect theological issues. The vocabulary used for God and Jesus reflects fundamental beliefs about the nature of deity and the divine plan for humankind. In an 1854 sermon Unitarian clergyman G. W. Burnap stated that few hymns portray "a Trinity of persons in God." Yet most churches' hymnbooks deliberately assert that doctrine "in a sort of appendix . . . in the form of a doxology."[22] Scrupulously consistent Unitarians declined, even while singing, to attribute supernatural powers to Jesus; hymns that did so were adapted or rejected. In lines about divine prerogatives, editors typically replaced "Jesus" with "Father" or with "God," in the latter case adding another syllable somewhere in the same line.[23]

Unitarians' alterations were of course a sore point for evangelical Protestants. The *Methodist Quarterly Review*'s notice of *The Sabbath Hymn Book* (1858), a collection edited by Congregationalist theologians, challenged many of their textual alterations. In particular, the reviewer charged, it sometimes appeared "as if the compilers had been seeking to gratify Unitarians" by "obliterat[ing] the name of Jesus [in a hymn] and substitut[ing] for it God." He also singled out an alteration in Charles Wesley's "God of My Life, Whose

Gracious Power": "my loving Saviour's breast" had been "barbarously, we were going to say sacrilegiously," changed to "my loving Father's breast." From this writer's trinitarian and Arminian perspectives, the Calvinist hymnbook-makers offended by deliberately obscuring the Wesleyan doctrine of Christ's full atonement for sin.[24]

Significant doctrinal differences also affected some editors' and hymnologists' treatment of "Nearer, My God, to Thee" (1841). Its author, Englishwoman Sarah Flower Adams (1805–1848) had lived with the family of W. J. Fox, a prominent liberal man of letters and Unitarian minister, after her parents died. Apparently uncomfortable with the poet's Unitarianism, some nineteenth-century British editors printed altered texts that introduce references to Christ and the "Almighty Trinity."[25] In the United States, the editors of the 1889 Protestant Episcopal hymnal inserted in Adams's lyric—which addresses only God—two stanzas that appeal to "Christ" and the "Spirit."[26] A commentator in the Episcopalians' own *Church Review* protested that the interpolated lines "do not add to either the sense or the beauty of the hymn."[27] Nine of the fourteen hymnals in my sample published after 1841 include "Nearer, My God, to Thee." All made minor changes such as altering a subjunctive and replacing "send'st to me" with "sendest me," changes probably calculated to make the poem more idiomatic, accessible, and singable. Only a few evangelicals commented explicitly on the doctrinal orientation of "Nearer, My God, to Thee," or rather, its author. To one critic it was "a purely Unitarian hymn, . . . wholly destitute of Christian experience."[28] Making a case for interdenominational Christian unity—a prominent theme in late nineteenth-century hymnology—Baptist clergyman William H. Parker remarked in 1889 that Adams "no longer doubts the divinity of her Lord," thus reminding readers of a doctrinal difference that still mattered, though not enough to evoke explicit criticism of the poem or poet.[29]

Variants of Isaac Watts's "Alas! And Did My Saviour Bleed" (1707) likewise reflect hymnists' and editors' concern about the proper names for and understanding of God. Watts's third stanza insists on the stunning fact that humans had crucified a divine being: "Well might the sun in darkness hide, / And shut his glories in, / When God, the mighty Maker, died / For man the creature's sin."

Many nineteenth-century editors changed "God" to "Christ," for it was the divine-yet-human Jesus who was crucified, and, as one hymnologist remarked, "It is said to be unscriptural, as well as revolting, to speak of the death of God."[30] But "Christ, the mighty Maker" was also objectionable, for Jesus was not understood to be the Creator of the world. *Church Psalmody*

(1831), widely used by Congregationalists and Presbyterians, made two alterations, producing "Christ th'almighty Saviour," perhaps to reinforce the trinitarian doctrine that Jesus was both divine and human.[31] The *Congregational
Hymn and Tune Book* (1856) substituted "Christ, the Lord of glory." The textual editor of the *Presbyterian Hymnal* (1895), scrupulous about following
original texts or indicating that the versions he printed had been altered, supplied "He, the mighty Maker" and footnotes specifying which line he had
changed. This awkward alteration by a scholarly clergyman testifies to the
perceived importance of changing Watts's "God, the mighty Maker."

Doctrinal differences and denominational loyalty influenced the editing
and criticism of other classic hymns. A contested line in Charles Wesley's
"Love Divine, All Loves Excelling" (1747) reads, "Let us find that second
rest"—meaning sanctification, commonly known within the Holiness movement as the "second blessing." Although embraced by thousands of non-
Methodists, the doctrine of immediate sanctification by faith was controversial, even among Methodists, throughout the nineteenth century.[32] Of the
fifteen hymnbooks in my sample that included "Love Divine," only three reproduced the Wesleyan phrase "second rest": the official Methodist Episcopal
hymnbooks for 1849 and 1878 plus an 1857 collection for Congregationalists.
Over time, many American hymn singers accepted "Let us find the promised
rest"—an altered version of Wesley's problematic line—as authoritative.[33]

A greater diversity of views among mainline evangelical Protestants is
reflected in emendations and criticism of "Rock of Ages, Cleft for Me" (1776).
Anglican clergyman Augustus M. Toplady's best-known hymn, a decidedly
Calvinistic portrayal of human inability to overcome sin, is built on the doctrines of justification and atonement through Jesus's blood.[34] Half of the
hymnbooks in my sample printed variously altered versions of these lines in
the initial stanza: "Let the water and the blood, / From thy riven side which
flowed, / Be of sin the double cure, / Cleanse me from its guilt and power."
The fourth of these lines was reworded in half the hymnbooks, thus achiev-
ing an exact rhyme by placing "pure" at the end. But rhyme was not the
editors' only consideration, as further alterations of the hymn attest. Most
hymnals eliminated "riven," a semantic parallel with "cleft," from the second
line of the quoted passage. Some replaced it with "wounded"; others substituted "a healing flood," thereby creating a rhyme with "blood." "Riven" may
have been cut as an archaism that does not appear in the King James Bible or
as an image reminiscent of Moravian hymns that evoked the "side-hole" of
the crucified Christ. Its removal has the effects of reducing the emphasis on
Christ's suffering while stressing his blood's efficacy for the believer. Most

texts also combined the second and third of Toplady's four six-line stanzas (though the hymn was not excessively long by nineteenth-century standards), in the process decreasing the poet's emphasis on human helplessness.

Of the fourteen texts of "Rock of Ages" in my sample, no two are identical; two hymnals from the 1870s printed two distinct versions. Explaining the impossibility of all churches and editors agreeing on a single text, the Congregationalist hymnbook editor who also coauthored *Hymns and Choirs* expressed regret in 1860 at "the multiplicity of changes that have hopelessly ingratiated themselves into the favor of some admirers" of this classic.[35] A Baptist critic agreed with a Presbyterian that the doctrinal rigor of Toplady's hymn had been weakened by unjustified alterations. The Baptist clergyman angrily objected, "All the Rock [was] taken out of it."[36] Ironically, both of these commentators quoted as Toplady's original verse some lines that had been altered. A Unitarian sided with his evangelical cousins in deploring the extensive alteration of "Rock of Ages," but his point was that remodeling violated the principle of authorship: it was dishonest and disrespectful of a Unitarian editor to print as a Calvinist's hymn a poem that was not his, a revision in which "a very prominent orthodoxy has been softened quite out of sight."[37]

A case can be made that the alterations of "Rock of Ages" were not prompted exclusively or even primarily by reactions against Toplady's conspicuous Calvinism, but rather by concern for decorum. His poem is a horrifying portrayal of suffering. Its fourth stanza begins, "While I draw this fleeting breath, / When my eye-strings break in death . . ."[38] The hymnals in my sample printed several variants; none restored that excruciating line. Editors' cutting of stanzas and rearrangement of lines can be interpreted, as we have seen, as efforts to soften the poem's doctrinal rigor. Despite the Arminian tendency of evangelical Protestantism, however, most nineteenth-century versions of "Rock of Ages" strongly convey that sinners are helpless to effect their own salvation. Editors may have reduced Toplady's depiction of Christ's agony and the sinner's mortality not to de-emphasize human guilt but to reduce the depiction of gore and pain they considered indecorous for public performance.

Editorial practices and hymnological discourse reflect contemporary standards of linguistic propriety and related ideologies of class and gender. There was overall agreement on the necessity for decorum. Yet some writers charged that contemporary "supercritics," also known as "hypercritics," were overly concerned with mere propriety; to avoid embarrassment and discomfort, they compromised hymnody's emotional power. The traditional metaphor of

Christ as Lover and Bridegroom derives from the Song of Solomon (permeated by Lover imagery, which commentators insisted on interpreting as symbolic of Christ), passages in Old Testament prophetic books that portray Israel as God's wife (Jeremiah 3:20, Hosea 2:19–20), and various New Testament verses (2 Corinthians 11:2, Ephesians 5:22–23) that envision Christ coming to wed the faithful. These metaphors have been meaningful for centuries because they characterize Christ as desiring and seeking union, the Christian as beloved. This metaphor of intimate relation evokes and interacts with social roles; it can function as a model of selfhood and a guide for proper human interaction. As anthropologist James W. Fernandez observes, "the metaphoric assertions men make about themselves or about others influence their behavior." [39] Editors' and critics' responses to "Jesus, Lover of My Soul" as a hymn for public performance register contemporary views of the proper understanding and presentation of intimacy. Hymnological commentary that overtly appeals to linguistic propriety reflects contemporary attitudes about eroticism, gender, and class.

The use of and critical response to Lover and Bridegroom imagery in hymnbooks is best understood within the context of the development of psalmody and hymnody in America. European colonists who were familiar with the Bible brought the Lover-Bridegroom imagery to the New World. In early seventeenth-century New England, portrayal of Christ as Bridegroom and the individual believer as his beloved Bride was common in public as well as private expression. Both Anne Hutchinson and her antagonist John Winthrop so described themselves. [40] The spousal metaphor was also applied to the church. Puritan sermons regularly figured Christ as the Bridegroom until 1700, when, according to Michael P. Winship, "this imagery grew far more constrained in expression and constricted in use" in response to "post-Restoration assumptions about the nature of legitimate religious language, imagery, and experience." [41] Only versified psalms were sung in early American congregational worship, so the Lover and Bridegroom imagery was not used in the sanctuary. In private writings and in hymns, which were sung and read aloud as well as silently in private settings, the imagery of love and espousal persisted through the eighteenth century, especially but not exclusively among mystics, Methodists, and women. [42]

During the Great Awakening of the 1730s and 1740s, new lyrics—most notably, the works of Isaac Watts—came into general use throughout the colonies. His hymns, spiritual songs, and verse paraphrases of the Psalms were used and virtually canonized by 1800 in many churches (Congregational,

Baptist, and Presbyterian) with Calvinist roots. Clergymen as well as lay-people called for collections of psalms and hymns that preserved "Watts Entire." Watts's lyrics were resisted also by "the most traditional constituencies in each communion" and "attacked" by antirevivalist groups.[43]

Watts's lyrics based on the Song of Solomon portrayed Jesus as Lover. Hymns in the Bridegroom tradition by John Wesley, Charles Wesley (1707–1788), and contemporary European and American evangelicals became popular as new hymnbooks proliferated. In one of John Wesley's hymns, the speaker-singer, characterized as "betrothed to Christ," anticipates "His coming from the sky, / To wed my happy soul."[44] Many of the lyrics of Charles Wesley portray the ardent mutual love of Christ and the believer. Still, such imagery was not universally acceptable, as John Wesley realized. While editing—sometimes, substantially remodeling—his brother Charles's lyrics, he toned down some of the arguably "amatory" lyrics representative of Charles's own sensibility and influenced by Moravian hymnody; John did not include "Jesus, Lover of My Soul" in a selective hymnbook he published in 1748.[45]

It is likely that churchmen reacted against effusive "fondling" speech and lyrics in part because they were associated with the familiar addresses to deity and the enthusiastic expressions characteristic of frontier camp meetings led by Methodist, Baptist, and Presbyterian preachers. Evangelists, European tourists, advocates of rational religion, and other observers of camp meetings described physical displays and other markedly unconventional behaviors and behavior. Many commented on the assembled masses' ecstatic singing of hymns and spiritual songs.[46] Like other collections of lyrics used in frontier meetings, *The Camp Meeting Chorister* (Philadelphia, 1830) collected anonymous songs of recent composition along with venerated texts. Several lyrics in this book address Christ as "Love," a usage that would be discontinued in congregational hymnals.[47]

The growth of active evangelism had immediate and long-term implications for hymn singing, hymnbook-making, and hymn criticism. Most authorities carefully differentiated congregational singing in the sanctuary from singing at revivals and in other situations such as Sunday schools, meetings of missionary and temperance societies, and domestic devotions. As nineteenth-century poets, editors, and publishers produced different hymns for different purposes, relatively inexpensive "social hymnbooks" flourished. Although such collections included classic hymns, they featured a distinctive style of texts and tunes that came to be known as gospel hymns. Late-century hymnologists insisted on the difference—in the same way as commentators of the early 1800s had set camp meeting spirituals and revival songs apart from hymns for the sanctuary, and for the same reasons. Throughout the nineteenth century, group singing was regarded as an important means of expressing religious feeling. Writers on the subject of hymns accepted the prevailing tradition that lyric poetry, especially when sung, voices emotion. Group singing was also firmly linked with emotion because of a general awareness of the enthusiastic singing characteristic of camp meetings and undisciplined revivals.

Like contemporary literary critics, commentators on nineteenth-century hymnody claimed that they lived in a "refined" age. Some hymnological writings deprecated the hymnody of the previous century as crude, even "vulgar."[48] Certain of Watts's lyrics, particularly those based on the Song of Solomon, were deemed inappropriate for congregational singing. As early as 1819, a Wesleyan Methodist layman warned his denominational kin against indiscriminate enthusiastic singing of Watts: "Dedicated to divine love, they are too amorous; and fitter to be addressed by a lover to his fellow mortal than by a sinner to the most high God."[49] This book reflects an emergent conscious of different and unequally decorous styles of religious expression.

Much more influential among hymn editors, clergymen, and other commentators on hymnody was a pronouncement about inappropriately intimate language and excessive emotionalism by musician Lowell Mason and clergyman David Greene in the 1831 preface to *Church Psalmody,* the hymnbook they coedited: "All familiar and fondling epithets, or forms of expression, applied to either person of the Godhead, should be avoided, as bringing with them associations highly unfavorable to pure devotional feeling." Furthermore, hymns that distract sinners from thoughts of their own "guilt" by evoking "a high state of agreeable sympathetic excitement" are unlikely to produce repentance; many "revival hymns" have that fault.[50] In the same period, as evangelicals' experiences continued to be influenced by the Second Great Awakening, Mason made another move to counter the style of hymnody associated with frontier evangelism. In 1832, in collaboration with Thomas Hastings, he published *Songs for Social Worship,* a hymnbook designed for subdued revival services; it was calculated to compete with Joshua Leavitt's *The Christian Lyre* (1830), a collection that includes folk hymns and further reflects frontier revivalism by using popular secular tunes. Both collections were initially serialized in periodicals edited by Hastings and Leavitt. Mason and Hastings took their stand against Leavitt's (and others') use of tunes "reeking . . . with impure associations."[51] A respected leader among reformers who advocated proper texts sung to proper tunes, Mason exerted great influence on the editing and performance of hymns, for he was a composer of hymn tunes, a reformer of church music, and an advocate of music instruction in public schools.[52]

Editorial treatments of Charles Wesley's "Jesus, Lover of My Soul" (1740)— as well as hymn critics' commentary on textual alterations and restorations of this classic hymn—register nineteenth-century views of the proper presentation of the believer's engagement with Christ. Only a few antebellum editors were sufficiently uncomfortable with Wesley's language to substitute "saviour" for "lover." But one of these was Mason, whose *Church Psalmody* (1831) sold about 150,000 copies. Used by many New England Congregationalists and by New School Presbyterians in New York State, it was reprinted as late as 1866.[53] Mason insisted that the hymn text is primary, the tune secondary. His work was part of a widespread nineteenth-century movement to reform congregational singing. According to the reformers who co-edited *Hymns and Choirs*, Professor Ebenezer Porter of Andover Theological Seminary had "insisted on modifying" all "erotic expressions in hymns, even such as have their parallel in the inspired word"; he "once remarked, that the line 'Jesus Saviour of my soul,' was 'infinitely better'" than Wesley's original.[54] "Jesus, Lover of my soul" was a site for contesting views of linguistic propriety.

One hymnologist who castigated the "mutilators" of sacred poetry cited offenses against Wesley's widely popular lyric, sarcastically expressing pity at the wretched "taste" of the editor who scratched down this new opening couplet: "Jesus, refuge of my soul, / Let me to thy mercy fly."[55] A contributor to the *Christian Examiner* focused on the same hymn as he questioned the common Unitarian practice of altering texts. Arguing that a Unitarian editor's double alteration of Wesley's opening line to read "Father, refuge of my soul" was an aesthetic offense, he demonstrated that the two changes in the opening lines make the imagery in the poem as a whole inconsistent. This critic's thesis was that editors wrong poets by attributing to them texts that they did not write.[56] As decades passed, poets' rights were acknowledged in some hymnal prefaces and hymnological writings. But others implicitly or explicitly dismissed the concept of authorship as insignificant— because hymns belong to everyone.[57] Still other commentators, taking no interest in the aesthetic or ethical dimensions of textual alteration, voiced concern for the believers' spiritual health. In some statements of this kind the careful reader may detect defensiveness about these writers' own histories, practices in worship, and investments in traditions and language hallowed by habit and memory—but now subject to criticism as unrefined.[58] Commentators' often vague and sometimes angry remarks about "taste" and "refinement" mask concerns deeper than decorum in the sense of politeness.

Some nineteenth-century writers pointed out that the imagery of deity's "breast," "bosom," and "arms" is biblical. Like the occasional explosive pronouncement, closely reasoned distinctions reflect commentators' efforts to discriminate between appropriate and indecorous indications of emotional and physical intimacy. Apparently there was no objection to imagining a Christian held in God's strong, supportive arms—probably because the expression "everlasting arms" was both scriptural (Deuteronomy 33:27) and so widely familiar as to be considered a fixture of the language. (The image of God's arms frequently appeared in published and private writings.) Furthermore, God was, for many nineteenth-century evangelical Protestants, a paternal figure. For most ordinary people, scriptural authority and common evangelical usage would rule out erotic readings of deity's "bosom," "arms," and embrace. But hymn editors and hymn critics manifested some discomfort with the embrace or "arms" of Jesus, a figure with a human history.

Singers and readers were expected—sometimes, explicitly instructed—to identify with the expressed or implicit "I" of the hymn text. The "voice" of the genuine hymn was regarded as an ideal model of Christian identity and selfhood.[59] Editors and critics therefore paid close attention to personal pronouns, sometimes debating whether "I" should be replaced by "we" in general and in particular texts.[60] Editors tinkered with language that placed the performer in intimate relation to Jesus, especially if the believer was characterized as female or "feminine."[61]

Treatments of John Newton's "How Sweet the Name of Jesus Sounds" confirm that attention was paid to the textual gendering of the soul. This hymn with seven four-line stanzas begins: "How sweet the name of Jesus sounds / In a believer's ear! / It soothes his sorrows, heals his wounds, / And drives away his fear." Gender-inclusive language was not prized during the nineteenth century, perhaps not conceivable. None of the twenty-five nineteenth-century versions of this hymn I have examined altered the masculine pronouns in this stanza. But other gender-related changes were made. In the fifth stanza of Newton's lyric—and of the poem as printed in all three eighteenth-century American editions (1790, 1791, 1795) of Newton's *Olney Hymns* (London, 1779)—the speaker addresses Jesus as "my Shepherd, Husband, Friend, / My Prophet, Priest and King." Among the fifteen books in my sample that included "How Sweet the Name," eleven either omitted the stanza cataloging Christ's roles or replaced "Husband" with another word: "Saviour," "Guardian," or "Brother." Evidently, male editors preferred not to cast the "believer" of stanza one as a wife. The now-standard fifth stanza typically addresses Jesus as "shepherd, savior, friend" while the opening stanza retains masculine pronouns for the performer. A few defenders of original texts deplored the "emasculation" of hymns, as if the texts themselves were alive and male.[62]

Scholars interpreting hymnologists' "Amens!" and silences should recall that most editors and critics were males and that they tended to think of the voice of the text—especially of hymns that mattered to them—as male. Many editors and critics rejected "fondness" and familiarity to avoid the enthusiastic language associated with camp meetings, undisciplined revivalism, and excitement that could be interpreted as fanatical, sensuous, or vulgar. At deeper psychosexual levels they wanted to be rid of childishness and the kind of vulnerability or weakness commonly associated with femininity. All these considerations and anxieties, conscious or unconscious, could motivate rejection of some occurrences of Lover and Bridegroom imagery. Editors who excised "Love" as an address to Jesus sometimes substituted "Lord," a word indicative of male authority and power rather than warm affection and spiritual intimacy. Meanwhile, the imagery of loving attachment and marital union was common in the writings of women, especially women in the Holiness movement.[63]

Still, there were critics who expressed incredulity or resentment at others' capacity to perceive Lover-Beloved imagery as improper. Stating that most people loved "Jesus, Lover of My Soul" and saw nothing wrong with it, a Southern Presbyterian clergyman went on to suggest the eroticism scented in such hymns actually luxuriated within the carpers themselves.[64] A Methodist minister in Ohio framed the issues—believers' relationship with deity and the forms used to characterize that bond—differently. He asserted that only persons devoid of "experimental" religion could fault "Jesus, Lover of My Soul" as "too sensuous." Ardent experimental hymns "jar upon sensibilities made delicate by mere art culture, but they defy age and criticism," he argued—because they express genuine experience.[65] He may have used "delicate" to imply that advocates of refinement were effete. From this perspective, persons who elevated "propriety" and "taste" over testimonies to the presence of God in human lives were, to put it bluntly, unspiritual and snobbish, cold as the clay. This Ohioan confronted a fact rarely acknowledged in hymnological discourse about itself: it reflects the views of privileged (white) men.

Some commentators who did not oppose the Lover metaphor were troubled by certain hymnic uses of "bosom," "breast," and other bodily imagery. A clergyman who defended "Jesus, Lover of My Soul"—arguing that its allegedly erotic content was "redeemed" by scriptural precedent and religious context—found other representations of intimacy with deity too "sensual." He cited as "offensively amatory" one lyric that anticipates a time when Christ "may caress thee, / And call thee His bride."[66] An associate editor of the *Presbyterian Quarterly Review* protested two hymnals' alterations of the following couplet about Christ: "His heart is made of tenderness, / His bowels melt with love." One mangler, he exclaimed with an air of disbelief, had replaced "bowels" with "bosom"; another made the second line read "And overflows with love." Expressing no objection to "bosom" in this context, the Presbyterian called it "a false delicacy" to eschew the traditional image of the bowels as the seat of compassion.[67] The usage is biblical; it occurs in John Bunyan's *The Pilgrim's Progress* and many other religious works revered by nineteenth-century Americans; and the 1859 revised edition of Noah Webster's *An American Dictionary of the English Language* indicates that "bowels" was used to represent "tenderness" and "compassion."[68]

But other nineteenth-century hymn critics turned up their noses at bowel imagery. The previously cited Southern Presbyterian who would proscribe "vulgar" language in hymnody complained that the following line addressed to God—"Let us in Thy Bowels sound"—was "nauseous."[69] A like-minded reviewer of the latest Methodist Episcopal hymnal listed among texts inappropriate for public performance those that used "expressions repugnant to good taste and objectionable to judicious criticism." He pronounced unacceptable a graphic hymn that describes a bloody, weeping sinner who addresses these words to the pitying savior: "Thy bowels yearn'd, and sounded,—Live!" That hymn, our critic remarked, "has been repeatedly adduced as a glaring example of bad taste."[70]

Social standards that affected hymnody became more "refined" during the nineteenth century with rising literacy, increasing interest in middle-class respectability, and a growing demand for an educated ministry. Criteria for expressive yet properly "impressive" (formative) hymnody were, as the Ohio advocate of "experimental" hymns realized, influenced by "art culture." But much editorial behavior and critical commentary cannot be accounted for in terms of refinement as promoted by the privileged classes. Social constructions of gender, the body, and sexual behavior changed markedly—for many Americans, frighteningly—during the century.[71] Developments in church history (notably, the ascendance of Methodism and general acceptance of revivalism) and the social changes mentioned above made certain hymns favored by earlier generations unsingable—some because they now seemed vulgar or amatory (perhaps specifically homoerotic), others because they "feminized" deity or the believer or both.

Alteration and criticism were motivated in part by men's psychosexual issues. Nineteenth-century editorial practice and hymn criticism offer glimpses of men's, especially clergymen's, ideals of and struggles with the meanings of "taste," propriety, intimacy, eroticism, and gender. Symptomatic of anxiety about Christian manhood are remarks about the weakening and "emasculation" of old hymns. The same concern may have motivated one commentator's ridicule of his own denomination's hymnal committee for accepting a certain text whose "palty bustle" suggested to him "some girls' game."[72]

During the nineteenth century, evangelical Protestants became increasingly concerned about men's relative indifference to organized religion. Clergymen were held responsible for this problem (as were mothers: it was proverbial that prayers, hymns, morals, and patriotism are learned at Mother's knee). Late-century social hymnbooks explicitly pressed for a manly Christianity.[73] Hymn editors would not have worked so hard, argued so intensely, or risked so much criticism if they had not been convinced of the expressive and formative powers of hymnody. One clergyman spoke for many evangelicals when he affirmed, "The hymn-book is next to the Bible among religious books in its influence over mind and heart."[74]

Notes

1. Judson to Adoniram Judson, *American Baptist Magazine* 4 (March 1823): 57, quoted in Joan Jacobs Brumberg, *Mission for Life: The Story of the Family of Adoniram Judson . . .* (New York: Free Press, 1980), 60.

2. Austin Phelps, Edwards A. Park, and Daniel L. Furber, *Hymns and Choirs: Or, the Matter and the Manner of the Service of Song in the House of the Lord* (Andover, MA: Warren F. Draper, 1860), 5–6, quotation from p. 6; "Church Poetry and Music," *Presbyterian Quarterly Review* 6 (1857): 488–520, especially 497–511; "Hymns from Compilers' Hands," *American Quarterly Church Review and Ecclesiastical Register* 14 (1861): 34–62; "The Revised Methodist Hymnal," *Methodist Quarterly Review* 61 (1879): 522–45; A. F. Dickson, "Hymn-Book Making," *[Southern] Presbyterian Review* 15 (1862): 61–78; Mary De Jong, "'Theirs the Sweetest Songs': Women Hymn Writers in the Nineteenth-Century United States," in *A Mighty Baptism: Race, Gender, and the Creation of American Protestantism*, ed. Susan Juster and Lisa MacFarlane (Ithaca, NY: Cornell University Press, 1996), 149, 155.

3. Dickson, "Hymn Book Making," 70.

4. *A Selection of Hymns*, *Biblical Repertory and Princeton Review* 33 (1861): 172; *The Sabbath Hymn Book*, *Congregational Quarterly* 1 (1859): 91.

5. Louis F. Benson, *The English Hymn: Its Development and Use in Worship* (Richmond, VA: John Knox Press, 1962 [1915]), 358–434.

6. *North American Review* 88 (1859): 266; "Another New Hymn Book," *Methodist Quarterly Review* 43 (1861): 49; *Congregational Quarterly* 13 (1871): 348; *Baptist Review* 2, no. 6 (1880): 284; *Presbyterian Quarterly and Princeton Review* N.S. 4 (1875): 566.

7. "Altering the Hymns," *Home Journal*, March 23, 1850, n.p. This item was copied from New York's *Literary World*.

8. Selma Bishop, ed., *Isaac Watts: Hymns and Spiritual Songs, 1707–1748: A Study in Early Eighteenth-Century Language* (London: Faith Press, 1962), lii.

9. Harry Escott, *Isaac Watts, Hymnographer: A Study of the Beginnings, Development and Philosophy of the English Hymn* (London: Independent Press Ltd., 1962), 248.

10. Franz Hildebrandt and Oliver A. Beckerlegge, eds., with the assistance of James Dale, *The Works of John Wesley* (New York: Oxford University Press, 1983), 7: 75.

11. Montgomery quoted in Phelps et al., *Hymns and Choirs*, 146, hereafter cited as *Hymns and Choirs*.

12. Mason to Park, May 1, 1860, Boston Public Library, Ch. E. 2.11–2.12.

13. D. Curry, "Our Hymns—Amended and Mangled," *The Ladies' Repository* 13 (1853): 548–50.

14. Samuel Johnson's protest is noted in Benson, *English Hymn*, 467.

15. "Church Poetry and Music," 506, 507; S. W. Christophers, *Hymn-Writers and Their Hymns* (New York: Anson D. F. Randolph, 1867), 196; Q. Q., "Pure Hymns," *Guide to Holiness* 65 (January 1874): 21.

16. Beecher, "Introduction," *Plymouth Collection of Hymns and Tunes* (New York: A. S. Barnes, 1855), iv; Elias Nason, "Preface," *Congregational Hymn Book* (Boston: John P. Jewett, 1957), 4.

17. Quotation from "Preface," *Book of Praise* (Hartford: Hamersley and Co., 1869), iii.

18. "Preface," *The Hymnal of the Presbyterian Church in the U.S.A.*, ed. Louis F. Benson (Philadelphia: Presbyterian Board of Publications and Sabbath School Work, 1895), iii.

19. Phoebe Cary to Henry W. Bellows, November 9, 1869, Massachusetts Historical Society; Lowell Mason to Edwards A. Park, August 15, 1859, Boston Public Library, Ch. E. 2.11–1.12; Cyrus Brewer to Elias Nason, June 15, 1857, Nason Papers, American Antiquarian Society, box 4, folder 2.

20. Thomas Hastings, who co-edited *Spiritual Songs for Social Worship* (1832) with

Lowell Mason, initially serialized the collection in the *Western Recorder,* a religious weekly that he edited. Hastings also used the Recorder to discredit competitor Joshua Leavitt's *The Christian Lyre* (1831), which Leavitt serialized and defended in his *New York Evangelist.* On this matter, see Michael Broyles, *"Music of the Highest Class": Elitism and Populism in Antebellum Boston* (New Haven: Yale University Press, 1992), 75–80. Edwards A. Park and Austin Phelps prepared the way for their *Sabbath Hymn Book* (1858) with articles in Andover Theological Seminary's *Bibliotheca Sacra;* these pieces were later expanded as *Hymns and Choirs* (1860), a scholarly treatise that devotes considerable energy to justifying their hymnal (Benson, *English Hymn,* 475). In late 1855 Henry Ward Beecher devoted a series of columns in the *Independent* to defending his *Plymouth Collection* against criticisms printed in the *New York Evangelist.*

21. The hymns in the textual sample are listed here, alphabetized by beginning line: "Alas! And Did My Saviour Bleed," "Come, Thou Fount of Every Blessing," "How Firm a Foundation," "How Sweet the Name of Jesus Sounds," "I Love to Steal a While Away," "Jesus, Lover of My Soul," "Love Divine, All Loves Excelling," "Nearer, My God, to Thee," "Onward, Christian Soldiers," "Rock of Ages, Cleft for Me," "There is a Fountain Filled with Blood." These texts were published in seventeen hymnals, listed here chronologically: *Village Hymns for Social Worship* (New York: E. Sands, 1828); *Church Psalmody* (Boston: T. R. Marvin, 1831); *Psalms and Hymns, for the Use of the Reformed Church in the United States of America,* 62nd ed. (Philadelphia: Reformed Church Publication Board, ca. 1834); *Church Psalmist,* 52nd ed. (Philadelphia: Presbyterian Publication Committee, ca. 1843); *The Psalmist* (Philadelphia: American Baptist Publication and Sabbath School Society, 1844); *Hymns for the Use of the Methodist Episcopal Church,* rev. ed. (Cincinnati: R. P. Thompson, 1850); *Plymouth Collection of Hymns and Tunes* (New York: A. S. Barnes, 1860); *The Congregational Hymn and Tune Book* (New Haven: Durrie and Peck, 1856); *The Congregational Hymn Book* (Boston: John P. Jewett, 1857); *The Sabbath Hymn Book* (New York: Mason Brothers, 1858); *Church Book* (Philadelphia: Lutheran Book Store, 1882 [ca. 1868]); *The Church Hymnal with Canticles,* 73rd ed. (Medford, MA: Charles L. Hutchins, 1889 [ca. 1874]); *A Selection of Spiritual Songs* (New York: Century Co., 1881); *Hymnal of the Methodist Episcopal Church* (New York: Nelson and Phillips, 1878); *The Baptist Hymnal* (Philadelphia: American Baptist Publication Society, 1883); *The Seventh-Day Adventist Hymn and Tune Book* (Battle Creek, MI: Review and Herald Publishing House, 1899 [ca. 1886]); *The Hymnal* (Philadelphia: Presbyterian Board of Publication and Sabbath-School Work, 1909 [ca. 1895]).

22. G. W. Burnap, "Unitarian Christianity Expounded and Defended," in *The Old and the New* (Charleston, 1854), 124.

23. On Unitarian editing, see "Hymns and Hymn-Books," *Christian Examiner* 8

(1832): 163–81; James Warrington, "The Hymnal Revised and Enlarged," *Church Review* 54 (1889): 213, 230; Benson, *English Hymn*, 466–67.

24. "Another New Hymn Book," 53, 54; "The Sabbath Hymn Book," *Methodist Quarterly Review* 41 (1859): 151.

25. Biographical information from H[arold] W. Stephenson, *The Author of Nearer, My God, to Thee (Sarah Flower Adams)* (London: Lindsey Press, 1922), 12–15. John Julian, ed., *A Dictionary of Hymnology*, 2nd ed. (New York: Dover, 1957 [1907]), 1: 792–93.

26. *The Hymnal Revised and Enlarged* (New York: James Pott, 1889), no. 332. No. 344 in the same hymnal is the unaltered text of "Nearer, My God, to Thee." Episcopalians were given their choice.

27. Warrington, "The Hymnal Revised and Enlarged," 232.

28. James Strong, "Songs of the Church," *Methodist Review* (March 1893): 264.

29. William Henry Parker, *The Psalmody of the Church* (New York: Fleming H. Revell, 1889), 241.

30. *Hymns and Choirs*, 210.

31. Joseph Belcher, *Historical Sketches of Hymns, Their Writers, and Their Influence* (Albany, NY: Joel Munsell, 1873), 58.

32. Melvin Easterday Dieter, *The Holiness Revival of the Nineteenth Century* (Metuchen, NJ: Scarecrow Press, 1980); William Kostlevy, *Holiness Manuscripts: A Guide to Sources Documenting the Wesleyan Holiness Movement in the United States and Canada* (Metuchen, NJ: American Theological Library Association and Scarecrow Press, 1994).

33. Esther Rothenbusch, "'Is Not This the Land of Beulah?': The Search for the Holy Spirit in American Gospel Hymns," *Review and Expositor* 94 (1997): 58.

34. William Jensen Reynolds, *Hymns of Our Faith: A Handbook for the Baptist Hymnal* (Nashville: Broadman Press, 1964), 169–71.

35. *Hymns and Choirs*, 174–75, lists eighteen variants of fifteen passages.

36. Parker, *Psalmody of the Church*, 195; "Hymn Makers and Hymn Menders," 624–25.

37. C. H. Brigham, "Alteration of Hymns," *Christian Examiner* 72 (May 1862): 363.

38. Toplady's "Rock of Ages" quoted in *Hymns and Choirs*, 175.

39. Fernandez, "Persuasions and Performances: Of the Beast in Every Body, . . . And the Metaphors of Everyman," *Daedalus* 101 (1972): 42.

40. Ben Barker-Benfield, "Anne Hutchinson and the Puritan Attitude toward Women," *Feminist Studies* 1, no. 2 (1972): 72–73. Ivy Schweitzer argues in *The Work of Self-Representation: Lyric Poetry in Colonial New England* (Chapel Hill: University of North Carolina Press, 1991), that the Bridegroom tradition in Puritan culture was gendered.

41. Michael P. Winship, "Behold the Bridegroom Cometh! Marital Imagery in Massachusetts Preaching, 1630–1730," *Early American Literature* (1992): 171.

42. Susan Juster, "'In a Different Voice': Male and Female Narratives of Religious Conversion in Post-Revolutionary America," *American Quarterly* (1989): 41.

43. Stephen A. Marini, "Rehearsal for Revival: Sacred Singing and the Great Awakening in America," in *Sacred Sound: Music in Religious Thought and Practice,* ed. Joyce Irwin (Chico, CA: Scholars Press, 1983), 71–91, quotation from p. 81; Benson, *English Hymn,* 168, 362–64.

44. Wesley quoted in Parker, *Psalmody of the Church,* 169.

45. Hildebrandt et. al., *Works of John Wesley,* 7: 56.

46. Frederika Bremer, *The Homes of the New World,* trans. Mary Howitt (New York: Harper and Bros., 1853), 1: 307–9. Charles A. Johnson, *The Frontier Camp Meeting: Religion's Harvest Time* (Dallas: Southern Methodist University Press, 1985 [1955]), 192–207; John B. Boles, *The Great Revival, 1787–1805: The Origins of the Southern Evangelical Mind* (Lexington: University of Kentucky Press, 1972), 121–24.

47. B. St. James Fry, "The Early Camp Meeting Song Writers," *Methodist Quarterly Review* 41 (1859): 401–13.

48. Allen, *Psalms and Hymns,* xvi–xvii; Bird, "Sentimentalism in Hymns," 219–20, 227; "Literature and Fiction," *Methodist Quarterly Review* 57 (1875): 697.

49. John Fanning Watson, *Methodist Error,* quoted by Johnson, *The Frontier Camp Meeting,* 208, 294 n4.

50. *Church Psalmody,* v.

51. Quoted in Broyles, "*Music of the Highest Class,*" 79; the foregoing discussion is based on Broyles, "*Music of the Highest Class,*" 75–86.

52. Carol A. Pemberton, *Lowell Mason: His Life and Work* (Ann Arbor, MI: UMI Research Press, 1985); Broyles, "*Music of the Highest Class,*" 62–91.

53. Figures from Pemberton, *Lowell Mason,* 72. On the circulation numbers for *Church Psalmody* (Boston: Perkins and Marvin, 1831), see Benson, *English Hymn,* 383.

54. *Hymns and Choirs,* 151.

55. S. W. Christophers, *The New Methodist Hymn Book and its Writers* (London: Houder and Stoughton, 1877), 196–99; see also A. P. Hitchcock, "Hymns and Hymn-Tinkers," *Atlantic Monthly* 49 (1881): 344.

56. Brigham, "Alteration of Hymn," 360–61.

57. Fifty years after Mason and Greene defined the hymn as "public property" (*Church Psalmody,* viii), hymnologist Frederick M. Bird stated that "a hymn once printed belongs to all Christendom" ("Hymn Notes," *The Independent* 36 [June 5, 1884]: 711) and that "title to the best hymns and tunes is not to be obtained by copyright by any man" (Notice of *Ways of Life for the Sunday School, The Independent* 36

[August 7, 1884]: 1003). *Hymns and Choirs,* 141, discounted the importance of hymns' authorship: a hymnal "is not designed to perpetuate the renown of men." They maintained that textual alteration does not wrong poets, 143–51.

58. See, in particular, Fry, "Early Camp Meeting Song Writers," who reappears in this essay as the Ohio Methodist.

59. Mary De Jong, "'With my burden I begin': The (Im)Personal 'I' of Nineteenth-Century Hymnody," *Studies in Puritan American Spirituality* 4 (1993): 196–208.

60. Anglican bishop Christopher Wordsworth argued in *Holy Year* (London: Rivingtons, 1865), xxxviii–xli, that many hymns are "egotistical"; inappropriate self-consciousness is obvious in their reiteration of "I." He also remarked that indications that the singer is on familiar terms with God are "presumptuous" and probably "very offensive to Almighty God." According to eminent hymnologist Benson, *English Hymn,* 516, Wordsworth's views were influential.

61. According to De Jong "With My burden," 193, an editor remodeling Harriet Beecher Stowe's "Knocking, knocking" as a gospel hymn removed the explicitly female soul's address to the Lover.

62. "Hymn Makers and Hymn Menders," 620.

63. This point is supported by passages in the writings of Methodists Phoebe Palmer and Amanda Smith, both active in the Holiness movement; Harriet Beecher Stowe, reared as a Congregationalist but eventually an Episcopalian; and the Baptist and Congregationalist women's conversion narratives quoted in Juster, "'In a Different Voice,'" 41.

64. Dickson, "Hymn Book Making," 71, 73.

65. Fry, "Early Camp Meeting Song Writers," 405.

66. Dickson, "Hymn Book Making," 72–73.

67. "Hymn Makers and Hymn Menders," 622.

68. *An American Dictionary of the English Language,* rev. by Chauncey A. Goodrich (Springfield, MA: George and Charles Merriam, 1860), 141.

69. Dickson, "Hymn Book Making," 74.

70. "The Revised Methodist Hymnal," 523. *Hymns and Choirs,* 231–32, listed three "objectionable" passages in hymns; "bowels" had been cleared out of those lines in the *Sabbath Hymn Book.* J. O. M.'s notice of that hymnal specifically commended the editors for rewording Watts's reference to "the bowels of the poor" (*The Congregationalist* 10 [November 5, 1858]: 177).

71. Carroll Smith-Rosenberg, *Disorderly Conduct: Visions of Gender in Victorian America* (New York: Oxford University Press, 1985); Susan Curtis, "The Son of Man and God the Father: The Social Gospel and Victorian Masculinity," in *Meanings for Manhood: Constructions of Masculinity in Victorian America,* ed. Mark C. Carnes and Glyde Griffen (Chicago: University of Chicago Press, 1990), 67–78.

72. "Hymns from Compilers' Hands," 59.

73. Mary De Jong, "'I want to be like Jesus': The Self-Defining Power of Evangelical Hymnody," *Journal of the American Academy of Religion* 54 (1986): 476–78.

74. Robert S. MacArthur, "Rev. of *The Psalmody of the Church* by William H. Parker," *Baptist Quarterly Review* 11 (July 1889): 398.

5

Textual Changes in Popular Occasional Hymns Found in American Evangelical Hymnals

Samuel J. Rogal

IN HYMNODY, as in poetry in general, writers tend to respond to specific events that they believe deserving of hymnodic expression or praise by a congregation of worshipers. Those occasions may be of national or even international significance—war, exploration, peace, slavery, natural disaster; they may prove totally personal—birth, sickness, death, spiritual or physical recovery, spiritual or physical trauma; they may recognize a specific project, purpose, or organization. However, problems arise with those occasional pieces dating from the eighteenth and nineteenth centuries when (1) the specificity of the occasion becomes lost in history and fails to transcend the time in which it initially occurred; (2) the substance, language, or the tone of the hymn that one generation had embraced proves theologically, socially, or politically unacceptable or even repugnant to a later generation; (3) the single, personal experience proves too specific to apply to more general occasions or experiences. Thus hymnal editors, in much the same way as librarians, must periodically purge the collection to make room for new hymns. Unlike librarians, however, those hymnal editors do hold options that they may exercise: Has the text been—or can it be—revised to meet the spiritual needs and demands of contemporary worshipers while at the same time preserving certain of its original artistic and/or theological merits? The question stands, obviously, as a rhetorical one. The fascination for the scholar of hymnody, then, focuses upon those hymns that have been "saved" from the burial mounds of hymnodic oblivion and have remained, because of revision, standard hymnodic fare—the so-called classics of the genre. Further, can one infer from the textual changes the reasons for such revision: social? political? linguistic? denominational? Finally, in regard to those changes in the text, to what degree has an editor of one hymnal accepted the textual revision of another? How extensive has been the practice of revising revisions?

"Eternal Father, Strong to Save"

Since the preceding statements and questions do not raise a complexity of theoretical issues, problems, and concerns but simply require linguistic examination and discussion, there remains only the matter of selecting the appropriate hymn texts. To begin, the "Historical Edition" of *Hymns Ancient and Modern* (1909) contains a section of four hymns under the heading "On Behalf of Those at Sea"; the first of those (no. 561), "Eternal Father, Strong to Save," written in 1860 by the master of Winchester Choristers' School, William Whiting (1825–1878), certainly remains one of the most popular of occasional hymns, particularly within the last three-quarters of a century for funeral ceremonies of military and political dignitaries. Before turning to hymnals published in the United States, however, one needs to spend a textual moment in England in order to achieve a full examination and analysis of the revision process. Whiting's piece first appeared in the 1861 edition of *Hymns Ancient and Modern,* but not in its original form; Whiting's original text came forth seven years later in *The Anglican Hymn Book* (1868), with a third version—by Whiting himself—published in the 1869 *Psalms and Hymns* of the Society for the Propagation of Christian Knowledge. Placing the original text beside the 1861 revision (by the editors of *Hymns Ancient and Modern*) one sees (with the changes italicized):

> *Original (1860, 1868)*
> O Thou Who bidd'st the ocean deep,
> His own appointed limits keep,
> Thou, Who didst bind the restless wave,
> Eternal Father, strong to Save.
> O hear us when we cry to Thee
> For all in peril on the sea.
>
> O Saviour, Whose almighty word
> The wind and waves submissive heard.
> Who walkedst on the foaming deep,
> And calm amid the storm didst sleep;
> O hear us when we cry to Thee
> For all in peril on the sea.
>
> O Sacred Spirit, Who didst brood
> Upon the waters dark and rude,

Who bad'st their angry tumult cease,
And light diffused, and life, and peace.
O hear us when we cry to thee
For all in peril on the sea.

O Trinity of love and power
Our brethren shield in danger's hour;
From rock and tempest them defend;
To safety's harbour them attend;
And ever let there rise to Thee
Glad hymns of praise from land and sea.
Amen.

1861 Revision
Eternal Father, strong to save,
Whose arm hath bound the restless wave,
Who bidd'st the mighty ocean deep
Its own appointed limits keep;
O hear us when we cry to Thee
For *those* in peril on the sea.

O Christ, Whose *voice the waters heard*
And hushed their raging at Thy word,
Who walkedst on the foaming deep,
And calm amid the storm didst sleep;
O hear us when we cry to Thee
For *those* in peril on the sea.

O Holy Spirit, Who didst brood
Upon the waters dark and rude,
And bid their angry tumult cease,
And *give, for wild confusion* peace;
O hear us when we cry to Thee
For *those* in peril on the sea.

O Trinity of love and power,
Our brethren shield in danger's hour;
From rock and tempest, *fire and foe,*
Protect them wheresoe'er they go;
Thus evermore shall rise to Thee
Glad hymns of praise from land and sea. Amen.[1]

The revisions by the editors of *Hymns Ancient and Modern* appear, for the most part, syntactical and linguistic rather than substantive. For instance, beginning the piece with the appeal to the concrete "Eternal Father" rather than with the pronoun "Thou" definitely strengthens the immediate opening appeal of the hymn. The same holds true for the insertion of the clear Biblical image of the mighty "arm" of God. Indeed, the editors of *Hymns Ancient and Modern,* more than had Whiting, appeared strongly committed to the language of the source of the hymn, Psalms 89:9–10—"Thou rulest the raging of the sea: when the waves thereof arise, thou stillest them. / Thou has broken Rahab in pieces, as one that is slain; thou has scattered thine enemies with thy strong arm." In addition, the substitution in the refrain of the more specific "those" as opposed to the collective "all" preferred by Whiting sharpens the focus of those closing lines.

The attentiveness to sharp, active focus continues in the second stanza as the editors of *Hymns Ancient and Modern,* in their altering of Whiting's opening lines, present the image of Christ the peacemaker whose passivity alone can calm the brute forces of Nature: Whiting's "submissive" winds and waves *hear* the "almighty word"; in the revision, the "waters" both *hear* and *hush.* The editors of the 1861 book continue to intensify the tone of the piece, although the poetic quality of Whiting's original suffers from the change in stanza three, line four. Not until the end of the final stanza do the editors of *Hymns Ancient and Modern* tinker with the substance of Whiting's poem. The poet had essentially constricted his view of the danger from travel upon the sea to shipwrecks brought about by storms: "From rock and tempest them defend; / To safety's harbour them attend." The hymnal editors, perhaps being more modern and worldly than the poet, see fit to expand the dangers to fire and to natural and/or mortal enemies. The interesting point to be made from it all comes to light when one realizes that these changes occurred during Whiting's lifetime; he apparently raised no serious arguments against them and even proved willing to go forward with his own revisions. Nonetheless, the 1861 version in *Hymns Ancient and Modern* emerged from it all as the standard text of the piece.

One need not remain too alert for too long before realizing that Whiting's hymn, composed in an age of sail, steam, and rail, would not endure among the congregations—with or without the early revisions. Thus, once the hymn crosses the Atlantic and settles onto the pages of American hymnals, a number of textual changes slowly enter to affect both its sound and its sense. For example, the editors of the 1878 *Hymnal of the Methodist Episcopal Church* place "Eternal Father, Strong to Save" as the first of eight hymns headed "Miscellaneous—Mariners" and execute three changes in the text: (1) stanza two, line three, reading "And calm amidst the storm didst sleep" becomes "And calm amidst its *rage* didst sleep"[2]; (2) stanza three, line two, reading "Upon the waters dark and rude" has been revised to "Upon the *chaos* dark and rude"; and (3) stanza three, line three, reading "And bid their angry tumult cease" changes to "And bid *its* angry tumult cease" (an obvious necessity of grammar in light of the second change). The editors of the 1878 book have read their Scripture, since the language of Psalms 89:9 informs us that "Thou rulest the raging of the sea"; however, with the second change, they seek to broaden and intensify the image from the limited condition of the sea to the concept of a chaotic world about which Milton writes in Book I of *Paradise Lost*.[3] For their 1911 *Sunday School Hymnal*, the Methodists present four minor but interesting textual changes: (1) stanza two, line four shifts from "And calm amidst the storm did sleep" to "And calm amidst *its rage did* sleep"[4] (repeating essentially what had been found in the 1878 Methodist *Hymnal*); (2) the opening line of stanza three, "O Holy Spirit, Who didst brood," intensifies somewhat to "*Most* Holy Spirit! who didst brood"; (3) the original "Holy Spirit" of stanza three broods, in line two, "Upon the waters dark and rude," while in the Methodist Sunday school book the Spirit commits the same action "Upon the *chaos* dark and rude" (again a repetition of the 1878 Methodist revision); and (4) the necessary pronoun shift from "their" to "its" in stanza three, line three. Another interesting phenomenon occurs in 1917 on the page of the Lutheran *Common Service Book*, when, occasionally, the editors revert from the 1861 revision to Whiting's 1860 original. Before that, however, notice a minor tense change in stanza one, line two, wherein the 1861 text reads, "Whose arm hath bound the restless wave"; the Lutheran book intensifies the action by substituting "*doth bind*."[5] Then, in the opening lines of the second stanza, the editors of the 1917 hymnal present its worshipers with Whiting's 1860 version, "O Saviour, Whose almighty Word / The winds and waves submissive heard." They repeat their preference for the original language on two other instances: (1) stanza three, line three, "*Who bad'st* their angry tumult cease"; and (2) stanza four, line five, "*And ever let there rise* to Thee."

By the 1930s, at least for the Episcopalians and the Methodists, Whiting's "Eternal Father, Strong to Save" has moved from its previous category as a "mariner/maritime" hymn to one concerning the broader classification of "travel"—although neither organization appeared willing to recognize the possibility of travel by air. The 1933 *Hymnal* of the Protestant Episcopal Church confines its changes from the 1860 text to three—all in the third stanza and all of which we have previously noticed: "*Most* Holy Spirit! Who didst brood / Upon the *chaos* dark and rude, / And bid *its* angry tumult cease."[6] The 1935 Methodist *Hymnal* simply reprints the 1861 version—itself a nod in the direction of the hymnodic and social purity of the past.[7]

One recalls that in the original text of "Eternal Father, Strong to Save," Whiting had written, in stanza three, line four, "And light diffused, and life, and peace," which the editors of *Hymns Ancient and Modern* revised to "And give, for wild confusion, peace." Among their five revisions of the hymn (four of which we have already seen),[8] the 1958 Lutheran *Hymnal* offers one change that exists, really, as a composite of the original and revision. Looking at Whiting's original stanza three, line four—"And light diffused, and light, and peace"—and then at the 1861 revision—"And give, for wild confusion peace,"—they seek the best of both for their mid-twentieth-century congregations and produce "And gavest light and life and peace." Six years later, the editors of the 1964 Methodist *Hymnal,* surprisingly enough, do nothing with Whiting's hymn, reprinting the 1861 revision that appeared in the 1935 Methodist *Hymnal.*[9]

Interestingly, there had existed, since the publication of the 1936 Episcopal *Hymnal,* a fairly radical (at least to that point) revision of the second and third stanzas of the Whiting *Hymns Ancient and Modern* text undertaken by Robert Nelson Spencer (1877–1961), but his revision actually does not gain a significant hold upon hymnal editors until the 1960s and 1970s.[10] In 1964, the year in which the editors of the *Methodist Hymnal* took no steps to revise Whiting's hymn from its 1861 publication, the conservative Massachusetts preparatory schools founded by Dwight Lyman Moody at Northfield (for girls) and at Mount Hermon (for boys) published a *Hymnal* to serve both institutions. In terms of "Eternal Father, Strong to Save," the editors of that book included what we may label as the Whiting-Spencer version. The first stanza and all but the last line of the fourth remain fixed to the 1861 version; however, notice what happens to stanzas two and three as the result of Spencer's revisions (in italics):

Hymns Ancient and Modern (1861)
O Christ, Whose voice the waters heard
And hush'd their raging at Thy word,
Who walkest on the foaming deep,
And calm amid the storm didst sleep;
O hear us when we cry to Thee
For those who peril on the sea.

O Holy Spirit, Who didst brood
Upon the waters dark and rude,
And bid their angry tumult cease,
And give, for wild confusion, peace.
O hear us when we cry to Thee
For those in peril on the sea.

Northfield-Mount Hermon (1964)
O Christ, *The Lord of hill and plain,*
O'er which our traffic runs amain
By mountain pass or valley low;
Wherever, Lord, Thy brethren go,
Protect them by Thy guarding hand,
From every peril on the *Land.*

O Spirit, *Whom the Father sent*
To spread abroad the firmament;
O wind of heaven, by Thy might
Save all who dare the eagle's flight,
And keep them by Thy watchful care
From every peril *in the air.*

The editors of the Northfield–Mount Hermon book themselves attempt no further changes in the fourth stanza until the final line; Whiting had closed with "Thus evermore shall rise to Thee / Glad hymns of praise from land and sea"; the text for the 1964 version reads, "Thus ever-more shall rise to Thee, / Glad praise from *air and land and sea.*" With those changes, the sense of Whiting's hymn came out of the Victorian Age and into the twentieth century, embracing the major modes of transportation and thus being saved from extinction among the singers in the pews.

However, if Spencer had managed to bring "Eternal Father, Strong to Save" into the industrial age, it continued to bear the social restrictions of a single-gender language. Even with the inclusion of land and air transportation, there remained "Eternal Father," "Spirit whom the Father sent," and "Where ever, Lord, Thy brethren go." The editors of the 1970 Presbyterian *Worshipbook,* in addition to trading "thou" and "thee" for "you" and "yours," did manage a half-step forward in the second stanza by substituting "people" for Spencer's "brethren," but in the second line of the fourth stanza saw fit merely to substitute "brothers" for "brethren." Nonetheless, linguistic modernization becomes an empty exercise if it detracts from the sound and the imagery of the so-called antiquated original. Thus, one would be hard-pressed to argue the benefits to be gained by eliminating, in the final lines of the hymn, Whiting's "Thus evermore shall rise to Thee, / Glad hymns of praise from land and sea" and replacing them with the 1970 Presbyterian version, "Thus evermore with thanks shall we / Give praise from air and land and sea." Six years later, in the 1977 *Book of Praise*, although the editors cling fairly close to the 1861 revision, in stanza four, line two they substitute "our kindred shield in danger's hour" for "Our brethren shield in danger's hour," thus bowing ever so slightly in the direction of inclusive language.[11]

Three nondenominational hymnals from the 1990s inform us that, unless hymnal editors want to concern themselves with such recent technological modes of travel as space flight, the supersonic passenger planes, the England-France "channel," and the ultra-speed railway systems, Whiting's simple hymn of the sea has ingested all of the linguistic and substantive changes that it can bear. Thus the 1992 *Hymnal for Colleges and Schools* from Yale University, although updating the language, stands by the piece as a hymn of and for sea travel and does not stray too far from Whiting's original intent. A 1993 book, *Sing to the Lord,* generally follows the Whiting-Spencer text, but backs away from any attempts at linguistic inclusiveness, while the 1997 *Celebration Hymnal* follows the same trail.[12] After constructing a composite of the 140-year-old "before-and-after" look at Whiting's hymn, then, one sees:

Whiting (1860)
O Thou Who bidd'st the ocean deep,
Its own appointed limits keep,
Thou, Who didst bind the restless wave,
Eternal Father, strong to save.
O hear us when we cry to Thee
For all in peril on the sea.

O Saviour, Whose almighty word
The winds and waves submissive heard.
Who walkedst on the foaming deep,
And calm amid the storms didst sleep;
O hear us when we cry to Thee
For all in peril on the sea.

O Sacred Spirit, Who didst brood
Upon the waters dark and rude,
Who bad'st their angry tumult cease,

And light diffused, and life and peace.
O hear us when we cry to Thee,
For all in peril on the sea.

O Trinity of love and power,
Our brethren shield in danger's hour;
From rock and tempest them defend;
To safety's harbour them attend;
And ever let there rise to Thee
Glad hymns of praise from land and sea.

1970–1997[13]
Eternal Father, strong to save,
Whose arm has bound the restless wave,
Who bids the mighty ocean deep—
Its own appointed limits keep:
To you we pray most earnestly,
For those in peril on the sea.

O Christ the Lord of hill and plain
O'er which our traffic runs amain
By mountain pass or valley low;
Where-ever, Lord, your people go,
Protect them by your guarding hand
From every peril on the land.

O Spirit, whom the Father sent
To spread abroad the firmament;
O Wind of heaven, by your might
Save all who dare the eagle's flight;
And keep them by your watchful care
From every peril in the air.

O Trinity of love and pow'r,
Our kindred shield in danger's hour;
From rock and tempest, fire and foe,
Protect them where so e'er they go;
Thus evermore with thanks shall we
Give praise from air and land and sea.

The modernization of Whiting's hymn reflects clearly the seeming inability of late twentieth-century hymnal editors and worshipers to allow their imaginations to transcend language and to transfer their thoughts quickly and easily from one historical period to another. In other words, the typical worshiper of the present will not take the time to understand that a concept or image from one historical period can be transferred to another without having to change the language and thus upsetting the delicate artistic balance of sound and sense so necessary to poetry. Therefore, the nineteenth-century image of the sea, upon which relatively fragile sailing ships compete for survival against the seemingly uncontrollable tempests of a God-created and God-controlled Nature, cannot be imagined as synonymous with the hazards of jetliner travel without changing sea to *air*—as though one cannot understand the plays of Shakespeare or the operas of Handel unless characters appear in business suits and the language shifts from Elizabethan English or eighteenth-century Italian to Los Angeles rap.

"The Battle Hymn of the Republic"

There may arise some debate by certain purists as to whether "The Battle Hymn of the Republic" (1862) by Julia Ward Howe (1819–1910)—written in late 1861 or early 1862 and first published in the *Atlantic Monthly* for February 1862—constitutes a poem-song or a congregational hymn. However, because the piece appears in perhaps more hymnals than it does in anthologies of poetry, sustained argument on one side or the other proves unnecessary. The occasion of the hymn arose from the visit in December 1861 of Mrs. Howe and James Freeman Clarke (1810–1888)—the Massachusetts Unitarian, journalist, hymnal editor, and social liberal—to the Union troops commanded by General George Brinton McClellan (1826–1885). Clarke then suggested that Howe commemorate the occasion with a hymn that would underscore the theme of the sacredness of human liberty. Owing to the political context out of which "The Battle Hymn of the Republic" arose, the degree of its popularity depends, simply, upon the issue of geography.

Turning directly to the original text of "The Battle Hymn of the Republic," one sees a number of opportunities for those hands eager to wield the sharp pen of revision. In its pure state, the piece reads:

Mine eyes have seen the glory of the coming of the Lord:
He is trampling out the vintage where the grapes of wrath are stored;

He hath loosed the fateful lightning of his terrible swift sword;
His truth is marching on.

I have seen Him in the watch-fires of a hundred circling camps;
They have builded Him an altar in the evening dews and damps;
I can read his righteous sentence by the dim and flaring lamps.
His day is marching on.

I have read a fiery gospel, writ in burnished rows of steel:
"As ye deal with my condemners, so with you my grace shall deal;
Let the Hero, born of woman, crush the serpent with his heel,
Since God is marching on."

He has sounded forth the trumpet that shall never call retreat;
He is sifting out the hearts of men before his judgment-seat:
Oh! be swift, my soul, to answer Him! be jubilant, my feet!
Our God is marching on.

In the beauty of the lilies Christ was born across the sea,
With a glory in his bosom that transfigures you and me:
As he died to make men holy, let us die to make men free,
While God is marching on.

He is coming like the glory of the morning on the wave,
He is wisdom to the mighty, He is honor to the brave;
So the world shall be his footstool, and the soul of wrong His slave,
Our God is marching on.[14]

However, a careful reading of the hymn reveals that, given its heavily militaristic context, little can be done to neutralize its gender references without sacrificing its meaning (as indicated by the title) or its writer's intent. Perhaps the best that one could do would be to remove the third stanza, the "fiery gospel" being perhaps too suggestive of a kind of holy war, as well as to bring a number of verbs and pronouns into the twentieth century.

Nevertheless, as late as 1911 the editors of the Methodist *Sunday School Hymnal* include the initial five stanzas of "The Battle Hymn of the Republic," changing only (at the outset of the fourth stanza) "He has sounded" to "He hath sounded," perhaps for consistency with stanza one, line three. Also, those editors continue an earlier practice of substituting, in stanza three, line three, "I can read" for "I have read," emphasizing the present over the past.[15] Three years later, an edition of *Great Revival Hymns* reveals the elimination of the original third stanza, and one would reasonably conclude that, at least until the 1960s or 1970s, Howe's text would remain free from further editorial change.[16] Then in the 1933 Protestant Episcopal *Hymnal,* the original stanza three reappears unexpectedly, congregants apparently willing to deal, once more, with "a fiery gospel" and the Lord's "condemners."[17] However, another surprise remains. Upon examining a selection of eleven hymn books published in the United States between 1914 and 1958, one finds that eight of them have maintained the by-then traditional four-verse form of "The Battle Hymn of the Republic"—stanzas one, two, three, and five of the original— with the slight language changes noted heretofore.[18] Then, upon opening the 1964 Methodist *Hymnal,* what meets the eye? The editors of that book have added to the standard form a fifth stanza, that being stanza six of Howe's original poem and one that for a century hymnal editors essentially had ignored. Those lines, when one reads them carefully in relation to the preceding thought and context of the piece, transport Howe's hymn away from the battlefield and onto the broader areas of concern embodied within universal Christian mission: "So the world shall be His footstool and the soul of wrong His slave, / Our God is marching on."[19]

Within the last three decades of the twentieth century, one notes signs of editorial variety with regard to Howe's "Battle Hymn." The 1970 Presbyterian *Worshipbook* preferred the traditional four-stanza version, while the purely commercial *Illustrated Family Hymn Book,* perhaps in deference to its large illustrations, headnotes, and musical scores, allowed only for stanzas one, four, and five.[20] In 1992, the editors of the Yale *Hymnal* offered quite a different textual menu, beginning with stanza one (language changes in CAPS):

> Mine eyes have seen the glory of the coming of the Lord,
> WHO is trampling out the vintage where the grapes of
> wrath are stored,
> WHO HAS loosed the fateful lightning of his terrible swift sword;
> his truth is marching on.

Then follows stanza five, where the only language changes occur in the third line: "As he died to make ALL holy, let us LIVE to make ALL free"—which, of course, alter entirely Howe's thought and mood. The third stanza in the Yale text represents Howe's fourth stanza, again with the only (but expected) change in line two: "he is sifting out EACH HUMAN HEART before his judgment seat." Finally, for stanza four, the Yale editors resurrect the forgotten sixth stanza, with the language change occurring in line three: "so the world shall be his footstool, EVERY EVIL POWER his slave"—a more militant, strident, and less poetic note than that which Howe had originally sounded ("and the soul of wrong his slave").[21] The traditionalists might find refuge in the 1993 *Sing to the Lord,* whose editors appear content with the usual four-stanza version, and they may be equally content with the text offered by the editors of the 1997 *Celebration Hymnal*—until they come to stanza five, authored by another and later evangelical hand and having little or nothing to do with "Battle" or "Republic":

> We can almost hear the trumpet sound, the Lord's return is near;
> There are still so many people lost, His message they must hear,
> Father give us one more moment, one more day, just one more year—
> With God we're marching on.

Frankly, this addition, obviously an attempt to broaden the focus of the original, falls far outside the sound, the sense, and the occasion of Howe's 1862 hymn. The lines would be far better suited to an updating (should updating be necessary) of something along the lines of James M. Black's 1921 "When the Roll Is Called Up Yonder."[23] In the end, hymnal editors need to exercise their responsibilities to distinguish between meaningful—and even necessary—revision and ideological tampering with the text.

"Onward, Christian Soldiers"

The third and final hymn within the confines of this discussion has unnecessarily diminished in popularity within the last two decades, principally because a number of political and social guardians of linguistic morality have failed to consider both the occasion and context of its composition. The Reverend Sabine Baring-Gould (1834–1924), having been ordained a priest of the Church of England on Whit Sunday 1864, entered the day following his initial curacy at Horbury, three miles from Wakefield, in the West Riding of Yorkshire. In that same year, he wrote his hymn "Onward, Christian Soldiers" for the children's festival to occur in that parish, and the piece appeared in the *Church Times* for 1864 under the title "Hymn for Procession with Cross and Banners." What emerged from Baring-Gould's imagination and pen took the form of a children's hymn—admittedly a militant one—to which the children had to march, with banners flying, from one village to another.[24] Further, one must consider the world events of that moment, the larger background against which Baring-Gould wrote his hymn: civil wars in Afghanistan and the United States; the French capture of Mexico City; Polish uprising against Russia; war between Austria-Prussia and Denmark over Schleswig; military actions to achieve the unification of Italy; war between the Boers of the Orange Free State and the Basutos; war between Paraguay and Argentina; and war between Brazil and Uruguay. Once Sir Arthur Seymour Sullivan (1842–1900) united his hymn tune, "Gertrude," to Baring-Gould's "Onward, Christian Soldiers," the piece enjoyed unrivaled popularity as a processional hymn in churches and at public functions throughout Britain and the United States for a century, until such time as the word *war* in a congregational hymn fell almost to the level of vulgarity. Rather than engaging in the usual exercises involving textual changes, hymnal editors, particularly those representing the "mainline" Protestant denominations in the United States, simply dropped the piece from their tables of contents.

One should not forget that in the general context of language changes the observation that a given hymn has undergone only infrequent and insignificant alteration does not necessarily detract from the discussion. Notice how that statement applies to Baring-Gould's "Onward, Christian Soldiers." As written, the hymn contains six eight-line stanzas, each followed by the well-remembered refrain:

> Onward, Christian soldiers,
> Marching as to war,
> With the Cross of Jesus
> Going on before.

However, the fourth stanza never really gained acceptance by hymnal editors, and one becomes hard-pressed to find it—most likely because of the sudden shift in tone and substance from the collective to the personal:

> What the saints established,
> That I hold for true,
> What the saints believed
> That believe I too.
> Long as earth endureth
> Men that faith will hold,—
> Kingdoms, nations, empires,
> In destruction ruled. (lls.25–32)[25]

In addition, the editors of the 1868 edition of *Hymns Ancient and Modern* altered stanza three (changes in italics) to read:

1864
Like a mighty army
Moves the Church of God;
Brothers, we are treading
Where the Saints have trod;
We are not divided.
All one body we,
One in hope, in doctrine,
One in charity.

1868
Like a mighty army
Moves the Church of God;
Brothers we are treading
Where the saints have trod;
Though divisions harass,
All one body we,
One in hope *and* doctrine,
One in charity.

However, in the United States, the revision of line five never became a fixture; in a survey of eighteen American hymnals published between 1878 and 1997, all of the editors chose to revert to Baring-Gould's original "We are not divided," while the majority offer to their congregations between three and four stanzas from the complete original text.[26]

Although changes in the text of "Onward Christian Soldiers" from the version offered in *Hymns Ancient and Modern* by editors of American hymnals tend to be isolated, they ought to be noted. The 1917 Lutheran *Common Service Book* (as well as its 1958 offspring) begins stanza six ("Onward, then, ye people") with "Onward, then, ye FAITHFUL," a nod in the direction of the truly committed as opposed to the "people" who merely occupy the pews. The Unitarian *Services of Religion* (1937) undertakes a further revision of the third stanza:

1864
Like a mighty army
Moves the Church of God;

Brothers, we are treading
Where the saints have trod;
We are not divided.
All one body we.
One in hope, in doctrine,
One in charity.

1937
Like a mighty army
Moves the church of God;
Brothers, we are treading
Where the saints have trod;
May we not divided,
But one body *be,*
One in hope and *duty,*
One in charity.

The revisions in lines five and six appear to change the tone of the stanza from the outward positivism expressed by Baring-Gould to a mood of doubt—or at least to the need for reassurance, while *duty* may well manifest the broader notion of doctrine. A stroke against antiquated pronoun forms appears in the 1970 *Worshipbook,* wherein the editors strike down the "ye" in the first line of the sixth stanza and offer, in its place, "Onward, then, YOU people," which neither contributes to nor detracts from the original. Interestingly enough, the editors of the *Illustrated Family Hymnal* (1980) in stanza three, line seven, revert to Baring-Gould's original text ("One in hope, IN doctrine"), while the compilers of *Sing to the Lord* (1993) and the *Celebration Hymnal* strive for gender equity by removing "brothers" from stanzas two ("CHRISTIANS, lift your voices") and three ("CHRISTIANS, we are treading"). That same purpose appears to have been accomplished in the 1997 *Book of Praise,* where the editors simply do not include stanzas two and three and in stanza six, line eight, substitute "WE WITH Angels sing" for the original "Men and Angels sing." Nonetheless, hymnal editors have, for almost a century and a half, exercised relatively few revisions within Baring-Gould's text—one reason being that the hymnodist continued to live on some sixty years after the publication of his hymn. In any event, and to reemphasize a previous point, those who hold strong political or social objections to the piece, realizing that revision really means practically a complete rewriting, have simply chosen to ignore it. What may well keep "Onward, Christian Soldiers" afloat in certain congregations perhaps has more to do with Sullivan's hymn tune than with linguistic "correctness," but that raises a totally separate issue.

Reasons for and Legitimacy of Hymn Textual Change

It requires little effort, other than searching through a myriad of hymnals, to uncover language changes in scores of popular occasional hymns that continue to be sung by American congregations. The more important point focuses not so much upon those actual changes in the texts, but the reasons for doing so. That problem, in turn, raises another question, one concerning the propriety of one person or group altering the poetic composition of another under the guise of congregational hymns, once produced, becoming the public property of the worshipers. In other words, copyright considerations aside, do textual changes constitute a necessary and legitimate exercise?

Three-quarters of a century ago, the prominent American hymnologist Louis Fitzgerald Benson (1855–1930), while explaining the relationship between of the congregational hymn and *belles-lettres,* stated clearly that, "There is no reason why hymn writing should not be recognized as a legitimate type of lyrical art. There is no reason why the poet's imagination and the poet's craftsmanship should not bring fresh offerings of strength and beauty into the sanctuary of God through the medium of the modern hymn as well as through the ancient Psalm."[27] Benson noted and then placed his stamp of approval upon the notion that, even as early as 1927, the vast caverns of hymnody in English contained ample room to accommodate sources originating from both the language of Scriptures and the creative minds of twentieth-century hymnodists. At present, there appears no need to challenge or to alter Benson's statement; indeed, the number of *original* congregational hymns produced within the last two decades, a fair proportion of them arising from specific occasions, has proven more than sufficient to meet the spiritual needs of all generations of contemporary worshipers. Again, one may be tempted to inquire as to why clergy, church musicians, and hymnal editors continue to seek changes in the texts of the "older" congregational hymns. Why have individuals and committees attempted to force into their own timeframes hymns that have emerged from far different thematic and chronological contexts? Does "ownership" by the congregation come with a license to alter the text? Does the acceptance of Benson's conviction that a true relationship exists between hymnody and legitimate lyrical poetry mean, really, a responsibility to preserve the truth—the purity, if you will—of the literary text?

Practically hidden within the preface of the 1972 Presbyterian *Worshipbook* lies this announcement (and one can uncover similar statements within the prefaces of at least a dozen other hymnals of the last half of the twentieth century): "There is contemporaneity in the hymns. New hymns have been written. Old hymns have been altered, where copyright and literary structure permit, so that archaic language is eliminated, and excessive introspective use of the first person singular pronoun is diminished."[28] The third sentence of that statement arouses considerable interest, particularly since ownership and the ability to alter tend to be determined by date of copyright. Thus, one dare not lay a pencil upon any poem or "hymn" by William Butler Yeats (1865–1939), for instance, because that writer's work remains under copyright by both his heirs and his publishers. Therefore, the nontraditionalists will have to endure (or simply not read) certain of that poet's lines because they appear anchored too steadfastly to masculine and first-person references. Notice these lines from Yeats's "Meditations in Time of Civil War" (my italics):

> Two *men* have founded here. A *man*-at-arms
> Gathered a score of horse and spent *his* days
> In this tumultuous spot,
> Where through long wars and sudden night alarms
> *His* dwindling score and *he* seemed castaways
> Forgetting and forgot;
> And *I*, that after *me*
> *My* bodily heirs may find,
> To exalt a lonely mind,
> Befitting emblems of adversity. (lls.21–30)[29]

Should an editor or scholar choose to alter Yeats's language (and thus probably his poetic meter), then, of course, the weight of legal and scholarly liability would assuredly come bearing down upon his or her moral and intellectual shoulders. All effort would indeed be lost.

However, what would result should a literary editor or scholar decide to include the *substance* of a poetic piece—a piece conveniently beyond the liabilities of copyright restrictions—but found the poet's language too "limited"? Consider, for example, the refrain of a well-known verse from the 1696 *New Version of the Psalms of David* by Nahum Tate (1652–1715) and Nicholas Brady (1659–1726). Their paraphrase of Psalm 34:1–9, "Through all the changing scenes of life, in trouble and in joy," emphasizes the *individual's* need for permanent, all-encompassing commitment to God, no matter how positive or negative the events of the moment may appear. The refrain reads,

O magnify the Lord with me,
With me exalt His name;
When, in distress to Him I called,
He to my rescue came. (lls.5–18)[30]

Understanding the present sociolinguistic campaign to purge the American English of gender bias and excessive introspection (actual, implied, or totally innocent), one might be tempted to revise the lines from Tate and Brady to read,

O magnify the Lord with us,
With us exalt God's name;
When in distress to God we called,
God to our rescue came.

The result, of course, yields a sanitized, collective, and gender-free version of the original text; one can certainly argue that the revision takes absolutely nothing from the sound or the sense of the original—which leaves one with no other choice than to rewrite Psalm 34! However, a larger issue hovers above both the original and the revised versions. Essentially, do those who practice language revision on behalf of social and/or linguistic equality fail to respect the sanctity—the right, if you will—of the original poet's sound, sense, and purpose? Does language change prostitute and sacrifice those qualities? Further, for poets of the sixteenth through the nineteenth centuries for whom the word *copyright* meant little, how do they rise from their graves to protect the purity of that which they have created?

Consider once more Benson's notion that hymnody and poetry should indeed share the same bed. From the minds and the hearts of artists and creators endowed with lyrical invention, as well as from scholars possessed of linguistic imagination, the works of the "traditional" hymnodists of the Christian Church—from Isaac Watts of the early eighteenth century to F. Bland Tucker of the 1940s—hardly require editorial renovation from those editors of the present moment who have determined that the spirit of contemporary worship must douse every spark from the past. That point of view to the contrary, hymnal editors and denominational governing boards continue their assaults upon the original texts: "We have sought," claim the editors of the Yale *New Hymnal,* "to be particularly sensitive to the need for more inclusive language of praise. In this regard we have been greatly helped by the work of editors of other recent hymnals, and we have made our own contribution to this process. The Psalter in this book depends heavily upon inclusive language versions prepared by the United Methodist Church and the National Council of Churches. In the hymns, taken as a whole, masculine references have been significantly reduced, and some hymns which use feminine imagery in speaking to or about God have been included."[31] Despite such practice, as we have seen through the majority of examples offered throughout this discussion, the textual revamping has bequeathed little positive improvement to the original versions. If anything, changes in the text prove only that to revise the work of another hand exists as a far less demanding exercise than that of original composition.

To those persons for whom hymnody represents merely an exercise in singing words—any words—to a popular tune, linguistic and/or substantive revisions of hymn texts hold little or no cause for question. After all, in the instances of "Mine eyes have seen the glory of the coming of the Lord," "Eternal Father, Strong to Save," and "Onward, Christian Soldiers," the music of each rises (rightly or wrongly) as the single, most important element to stir the hearts and the spirits of the congregations. Indeed, hardly an American Thanksgiving-day service passes without voices raising to "St. George's Windsor" by George Job Elvey (1816–1893) or to the arrangement from *Nederlanditsch Gedenckelanck* (1626) by Edward Kremser (1838–1914); hardly an American dignitary goes to his or her grave without a military band offering forth the somber strains of "Melita" by John Bacchus Dykes (1823–1876). Who, among the majority of American congregations or ceremonial attendants, really cares if *bidd'st* becomes *bids, brethren* shifts to *brothers* or *sisters, ourselves* transposes to the entire *world,* or if HMS *Cutty Sark* or Herman Melville's *Pequod* sprouts aluminum wings, propellers, or jet engines? As long as the music of hymnody remains of primary importance for those who rise weekly from their pews, as long as those persons pay little or no attention to the texts of the hymns that they sing, then hymnal editors and denominational organizations will see little or no need to demonstrate allegiance to the sound and the sense of the original—particularly, as has already been admitted—if the copyright has expired!

However, there exists another group to come forward and to declare the validity of changing the language of the hymnodic text. Its members do so because revision looms large as a sociological necessity. Consider the instance late in the 1970s or early 1980s of one member of a hymnal committee—himself a poet, hymn writer, and the holder of a PhD in English literature. He and his colleagues on the text committee for an American Episcopalian hymnal came upon the occasional hymn, "God of the Prophets! Bless the

Prophets' Sons," written in 1884 for the centennial of the New Brunswick (New Jersey) Theological Seminary, by Denis Wortman (1835–1922)—a former president of the General Synod of the Reformed Church—and usually sung, thereafter, on Ember Days and at ordination of clergy. Concerning Wortman's hymn, the poet, hymnodist, and literary scholar explains:

> There were some problems with the text, first with regard to language, which used to read, "God of the prophets bless the prophets' sons." Since we were already ordaining women . . . this made it less than useful for an ordination hymn. There had been some earlier attempts to revise the text, and everyone had agreed that they just weren't good enough. So I was given that text as an assignment to take care of the language. Also there were some difficulties in the middle stanzas, with enjambment in some of the middle lines. Then in the third stanza that began "Anoint them priests" had a doctrine of ordination that was very hierarchical and completely out of line with what we understood priesthood to be about. . . . Eventually, I decided that stanza was so contrary to what we really believe that it just couldn't be salvaged; it had to be rewritten. That's how I got into this hymn writing business; through the back door.[32]

One may look at early versions of Wortman's hymn and observe and appreciate fully the problems that American Episcopal priests, men and women, of the 1980s and 1990s would have with it and certainly agree with the criticism of its key phrases: "Anoint them prophets"; "Anoint them priests"; "Anoint them kings! Aye, kingly kings, O Lord!"; "Make them apostles! Heralds of Thy cross. . . ."[33] However, the question arises: would not Episcopal congregations be best served with a fresh hymn to celebrate the ordination of its priests rather than with a patchwork of revisions applied to a century-old hymn that has long outgrown its effectiveness as part of the worship service?

Indeed, if revision and rewriting of others' hymnodic verse assume precedence over original composition, if revision and rewriting continue to serve as the "back door" entrance to "this hymn writing business," then original hymn texts have little hope for survival for and among future generations. Today's hymnodic composition will almost assuredly become tomorrow's revised text, with that revision due, within two or three decades, for further linguistic, substantive, or contextual refinement. In the end, congregational hymnody—by its very existence a by-product of occasional verse—instead of standing as a form of legitimate creative literature set to serious music and serving the spiritual needs of those in attendance at public worship, will face the danger of being reduced to the level of so many popular songs manufactured to complement the social and denominational fads of the all too temporary moment.

Notes

1. *Hymns Ancient and Modern for Use in the Services of the Church. With Accompanying Tunes.* Historical Edition (London: William Close and Sons, 1909), 704; all references to the 1860 and 1861 versions of "Eternal Father, Strong to Save" are to this edition.

2. *Hymnal of the Methodist Episcopal Church: With Tunes* (New York: Phillips and Hunt; Cincinnati: Cranston and Stowe), 419.

3. See *Paradise Lost*, 1: 9–10, 44–83, in John Milton, *Complete Poems and Major Prose,* ed. Merritt Y. Hughes (New York: Odyssey Press, 1957), 211, 212–13.

4. *The Methodist Sunday School Hymnal,* ed. John R. Van Pelt and Peter C. Lutkin (New York: Methodist Book Concern, 1911), 267.

5. *Common Service Book of the Lutheran Church* (Philadelphia: Board of Publication of the United Lutheran Church in America, 1917), 507.

6. *The Hymnal as Authorized and Approved for Use by the General Convention of the Protestant Episcopal Church* (New York: Church Pension Fund, 1933), 515.

7. *The Methodist Hymnal* (New York: Methodist Book Concern, 1935), 553.

8. *Service Book and Hymnal. Authorized by the Lutheran Churches* (Minneapolis: Augsburg Publishing House, 1958), 338; the first four changes: (1) "O Saviour, whose almighty word / The winds and waves submissive heard" (2:1–2); (2) "O SACRED Spirit, who didst brood" (3:1); (3) "Upon the CHAOS dark and rude" (3:2); (4) "WHO BAD'ST ITS angry tumult cease" (3:3).

9. *The Methodist Hymnal* (Nashville: Methodist Publishing House, 1964), 538.

10. See *The Northfield and Mount Hermon Hymnal* (n.p: Published by Northfield and Mount Hermon Schools, 1964), 221; *The Worshipbook* (Philadelphia: Westminster Press, 1970), 356.

11. *The Book of Praise* (Quebec: Presbyterian Church in Canada, 1997), 420–21.

12. See *A New Hymnal for Colleges and Schools,* ed. Jeffery Rowthorn and Russell Schulz-Widmar (New Haven: Yale University Press and The Yale Institute of Sacred Music, 1992), 508; *Sing to the Lord* (Kansas City, MO: Lillenas Publishing, 1993), 764; *The Celebration Hymnal: Songs and Hymns for Worship* ([United States]: Word Music/Integrity Music, 1997), 808.

13. I have constructed this composite form from the 1970 *Worshipbook* (see note 10) and the three books cited in note 12.

14. *American Poetry: The Nineteenth Century. Volume One, Philip Freneau to Walt Whitman* (New York: Literary Classics of the United States/Library of America, 1993), 709–10.

15. *Methodist Sunday School Hymnal*, 272–73.

16. *Great Revival Hymns No. 2*, ed. Homer A. Rodeheaver, B. D. Ackley, and Charles H. Gabriel (Chicago: Rodeheaver, 1914), 247.

17. *The Hymnal of the Protestant Episcopal Church* (1933), 540–41.

18. *Great Revival Hymns No. 2*, 247; *Elmhurst Hymnal and Orders of Worship for the Sunday School, Young People's Meetings, and Church Services* (St. Louis, MO: Eden Publishing House, 1921), 254–55; *Hymns of Praise for the Church and Sunday School*, ed. F. G. Kingsbury (Chicago: Hope Publishing, 1922), 283; *The Excell Hymnal for the Church and Sunday School*, ed. Hamp Sewell, Edwin O. Excell, and W. E. M. Hackman (Chicago: E. O. Excell, 1925), 276; *Songs of Faith and Triumph, Numbers One, Two, and Three Combined*, ed. J. Lincoln Hall, Adam Geibel, C. Austin Miles, and B. D. Ackley (Philadelphia: Hall-Mack Company, 1919), 146; *The Hymnal for Young People*, ed. Milton S. Littlefield and Margaret Slattery (New York: A. S. Barnes, 1930), 212–13; *Hymns of Praise, Numbers One and Two Combined, for the Church and Sunday School*, ed. F. G. Kingsbury (Chicago: Hope Publishing, 1934), 283; *The Hymnal . . . of the Protestant Episcopal Church* (1933), 540–41—five stanzas; *Services of Religion for Use in Churches of the Free Spirit* (Boston: Beacon Press, 1937), 567—three stanzas; *A.M.E. Hymnal, with Responsive Scripture Readings Adapted in Conformity with the Doctrines and Usages of the African Methodist Episcopal Church* (Philadelphia: A.M.E. Sunday School Union, 1959), 376; *Service Book and Hymnal* (1958), 356—three stanzas.

19. *Methodist Hymnal* (1964), 545.

20. *The Worshipbook* (1970), 474–475; *The Illustrated Family Hymn Book*, ed. Tony Jasper (New York: G. S. Schirmer, 1980), 94–95.

21. *New Hymnal for Colleges and Schools* (1992), 573.

22. *Sing to the Lord* (1993), 756; *Celebration Hymnal* (1997), 804.

23. For an early version see *The Excell Hymnal* (1925), 182, beginning:

> When the trumpet of the Lord shall sound, and time shall be no more,
> And the morning breaks eternal, bright and fair;
> When the saved of earth shall gather safely on the other shore,
> And the roll is called up yonder, I'll be there.

24. *Handbook to the Church Hymnary*, ed. John M. Barkley, 3rd ed. (Oxford: Oxford University Press, 1979), 174.

25. *Hymns Ancient and Modern* (1903), 775; *A Dictionary of Hymnology*, ed. John Julian, 2nd ed. (London: John Murray, 1907; New York: Dover, 1957), 1: 870.

26. Figures after page or hymn number in () refer to the stanzas: *Hymnal of the Methodist Episcopal Church* (1878), 206 (1, 2, 3, 5, 6); *Hymnal of the Methodist Episcopal Church, with Tunes* (New York: Hunt and Eaton; Cincinnati: Cranston and Stowe, 1889), 206 (1, 2, 3, 5, 6); *Common Service Book* (1917), 388–89 (1, 3, 5, 6); *Elmhurst Hymnal* (1921), 186 (1, 3, 5, 6); *University Hymns, with Tunes Arranged for Men's Voices,* ed. Harry B. Jepson and Charles R. Brown (New Haven: Yale University Press, 1924), 346–47 (1, 3, 5, 6); *Excell Hymnal* (1925), 167 (1, 2, 3, 6); *Hymnal for Young People* (1930), 179 (1, 3, 5, 6); *Hymnal . . . of the Protestant Episcopal Church* (1933), 670–71 (1, 2, 3, 5, 6); *Services of Religion* (1937), 331 (1, 3, 6); *The Hymnal. Containing Complete Orders of Worship. Authorized by the General Synod of the Evangelical and Reformed Church* (St. Louis, MO: Eden Publishing House, 1941), 292 (1, 3, 5, 6); *A.M.E. Hymnal* (1958), 191 (1, 5, 6); *Service Book and Hymnal* (1958), 560 (1, 2, 3, 5, 6); *Methodist Hymnal* (1964), 305 (1, 3, 5, 6); *Worshipbook* (1970), 542–43 (1, 3, 5, 6); *Illustrated Family Hymn Book* (1980), 116–17 (1, 2, 3, 5, 6); *Sing to the Lord* (1993), 644 (1, 2, 3, 5, 6); *Book of Praise* (1997), 636–37 (1, 5, 6); *Celebration Hymnal* (1997), 731 (1, 2, 3, 6).

27. Louis Fitzgerald Benson, *The Hymnody of the Christian Church* (New York: George H. Doran, 1927), 138.

28. *Worshipbook* (1972), 6.

29. *The Variorum Edition of the Poems of W. B. Yeats,* ed. Peter Allt and Russell K. Alspach (New York: Macmillan, 1968), 420.

30. *New Hymnal* (1992), 200.

31. Ibid., i.

32. Harry Eskew, "An Interview with Carl Daw," *The Hymn* 40 (1989): 26.

33. *Hymnal* (1933), 563.

6
Indices

More Than Meets the I

Mary Louise VanDyke

NAMES, ACTING AS "pointers"—to people, to ideas, and to things—have power. Words of hymns—nouns, adjectives, adverbs—are important; but names chosen for titles and indices can superimpose on hymn texts new and different insights. Editors of hymnals organize not only texts but also thoughts in deliberate ways to direct their use and dictate their meaning. In American hymnody new standards of word usage progressively replace old ones, sometimes by popular consensus and other times by individuals and committees delegated to ensure a hymnal's theological or political correctness. The character and uses of a hymnal may also be affected by the editorial choices of stanzas included, added, or omitted. And the organization of a hymnal can affect attitude toward worship. Editors and editorial committees who choose the contents of a hymnal and design its indices make word choices for their denominations or for their congregations in many ways. For example, Table 6.1 is a progressive listing of some subject names that appear under the letter I from hymnals selected for this study.

Sometimes indices use the hymnal as a teaching resource, extracting ideas hidden deep in inner stanzas. Sometimes they show the use of the hymnal as a preaching tool, or as a way of defining the church year or reinforcing a creed, and at still other times as a list of resources for use in the worship service. At some times, hymnal indices may have been used to advance an agenda or a style of evangelism. And still others may have been designed by individual clergymen to empower their sermons directly or indirectly.

Scholars have described the power of congregational song, whereby a thought introduced in the sermon may be reinforced by a hymn, or a resolution to act may be encouraged by a stirring refrain. But this study proposes that some nineteenth-century evangelical hymnals were indexed in a way that encouraged a minister to consult topical or subject headings before he began to write his sermon. A proper Subject Index, if compiled by a renowned evangelical preacher, could supply not only a topic but also the correct vocabulary

Table 6.1 Names for headings beginning with the letter "I" in my database, arranged chronologically

---

INVOCATION of the Holy Spirit (1827), __and General Praise (1845);

INVITATION and warning (1845), __to the Mercy Seat (1845), __of the Savior (1851), __of the gospel (1851), __to the Gospel Feast (1851), __to return to God (1856), __to repentance (1856), __to receive the gospel (1856), __of disconsolate to God (1864), __to Jesus of wanderer (1864), __and acceptance (1926);

INVITATIONS of Christ to Sinners (1851); __of the Savior (1851);

INVITED TO CHRIST, the prodigal (1851);

INSUFFICIENCY of worldly happiness (1851), __of self righteousness (1851);

INDWELLING OF CHRIST implored (1864);

INFIDELITY deplored (1864);

INGRATITUDE deplored (1864);

INTERCESSION of Christ (1864), __ Glory to Christ for (1864);

INTERCESSOR, Christ the (1864);

INSTALLATION, hymns for (1864);

INSPIRATION of Bible (1864);

INCARNATION (1864);

IMMINENT, death is (1864);

INTRODUCTORY to Worship (1867);

INSTITUTIONS OF THE GOSPEL: Baptism, __Ministry, __Sabbath, __The church (1867);

IMMORTALITY (1878);

INTERFAITH (1958).

---

of words and phrases to go with it. A fledgling or insecure preacher could expound with confidence and authority if he knew he was preaching ideas and issues endorsed by recognized evangelical leaders. This may help explain the burgeoning of topics in subsequent editions of the same hymnal.

Two studies below enable a closer look at this phenomenon; the first compares two editions of *Psalms and Hymns* published by the Connecticut Association in 1845 and 1851, and the second compares editions of Methodist Episcopal hymnals 1857–67 and 1878. The names chosen for subjects and topics in the indices of seventeen evangelically oriented hymnals between 1827 and 1958 were the focus of my research. Other fields in my database include number of stanzas printed, occasional scriptural references, and authors cited. For a description of the seventeen hymnals published between 1827 and 1958 in the study see Table 6.2.

Table 6.2
Hymnals analyzed

ID#11 *New Baptist Hymnal*, Nashville, TN: Broadman Press, 1926. 407 hymns + doxologies

ID#19 *The Broadman Hymnal*, Nashville, TN: Broadman Press, 1940. 480 hymns + aids to worship

ID#33 *Pilgrim Hymnal*, Boston, MA: Pilgrim Press, 1958. 584 hymns + amens

ID#58 *New Christian Hymn and Tune Book*, Cincinnati, OH: Fillmore Bros., 1882. 710 hymns + doxologies

ID#69 *The Methodist Hymnal*, 1905, Nutter and Tillett, NY and Cincinnati, Jennings and Graham, ca. 1907 pp. 169–77.

ID#77a–c *Hymnal of the Methodist Episcopal Church*, 1867 (1,148 hymns) and 1878 (1,117 hymns) editions.

ID#114 *Songs for Service*, Chicago: Rodeheaver Gospel Music Co., 1918. 333 hymns

ID#121 *Christian Service Songs*, Chicago: Rodeheaver, 1939, ca. 1934. 312 hymns

ID#122 *Tabernacle Hymns Number 3*, Chicago: Tabernacle Publishing Co., 1931. 352 hymns

ID#132 *Plymouth Collection*, H. W. Beecher, NY: A. S. Barnes, 1856 edition and 1864 edition. 1,374 hymns

ID#181 *Village Hymns,* Asahel Nettleton, NY: E. Sands, 7th ed., 1827. 600 hymns + doxologies

ID#S1 *Psalms and Hymns for Christian Use and Worship*, CT Assn. 1845. 1845, 1851 printings. 1,202 hymns

ID#S2 *Church Service Hymns*, Chicago: Rodeheaver, 1948. 448 hymns

ID#S3 *Triumphant Service Songs*, Chicago: Rodeheaver, Hall-Mack Co., 1934. 447 hymns

ID#S4 *The Social and Sabbath School Hymn Book,* G. N. Allen, Oberlin, OH: Fitch, 1846, 5th ed., 1854. 218 hymns + doxologies. Supplement of 69 hymns

ID#S5 *Hymns for Social Worship*, 1844, Oberlin, OH: 6th ed. rev. and remodeled, 1863, and 7th ed., 1868. 299 hymns

ID#S6 *Gospel Hymns Nos.1–6 Complete*, I. Sankey, J. McGranahan, G. Stebbins, Chicago/New York: John Church Co./Biglow and Main, 1894. 739 hymns

Table 6.3
Identification letters used in this paper for hymnals analyzed in this study

Code: Year/Den./Total/Organization/Title/PD/ID#

a: 1827/II/600 + doxs/Titles, Sections, 289 subj./*Village Hymns*/181

b: 1845/II/1202/Titles or scripture, Psalms and Hymns, 19 major topics (see APPA)/*Psalms and Hymns for Christian Use*/S1

c: 1846/II/218/Titles, Sections only/*Social and Sabbath School Hymn Book*/S4

d: 1851/II/1202/Identical contents as 1845, expanded index to 844 topics/*Psalms and Hymns for Christian Use*/S1

e: 1854/II/287 (218+69)/Titles, Sections, Index of Headings, Supplement (see App. C)/*Social and Sabbath School Hymn Book*/S4

f: 1856/II/1374 + doxs/Sections, 73 topics, 243 subheadings/*Plymouth Collection*/132

g: 1857–67/V/1129 + doxs/No sections, duplicate titles and indices, meters in 1867 ed./*Hymnal of the Methodist Episcopal Church*/77a, c

h: 1863/II/299/Table of contents only /*Hymns for Social Worship*/S5

i: 1864/II/1384 (1374 + supp)/No titles, sections, 908 topics, 2192 subheadings/*Plymouth Collection*/132

j: 1878/V/1117/No titles, organized by meters, scriptural index, major topics/*Hymnal of the Methodist Episcopal Church*/77b

k: 1882/IV/711/No titles, no sections, 33 major headings/*New Christian Hymn and Tune Book*/58

l: 1894/IX/739/Titles, no sections, scripture references nos. 1–547, 46 topics/*Gospel Hymns 1–6 Complete*/S6

m: 1905/V/748/No titles, sections, 181 major topics/*The Methodist Hymnal*/69

n: 1918/IX/333/Index intermixes titles, refrains, first lines/*Songs for Service*/114

o: 1926/I/407/Titles, sections, titles indexed with first lines, 399 topics (33 in God, 50 in Jesus, 13 in Holy Spirit)/*New Baptist Hymnal*/11

p: 1931/IX/352/Titles, no sections, 38 topics, no subheadings/*Tabernacle Hymns No. 3*/122

q: 1934/IX/295/Titles, no sections, 57 topics, subheadings only for Christ (10)/*Triumphant Service Songs*/S3

r: 1939/IX/312/Titles, no sections, 67 topics, subheads only for Jesus Christ (8)/*Christian Service Songs*/121

s: 1940/I/480/Titles, no sections, 60 topics, no subheads/*Broadman Hymnal*/19

t: 1948/IX/448/Titles, no sections, titles and choruses indexed, 81 topics/*Church Service Hymns*/S2

u: 1958/II/543+/No titles, sections, 168 major topics, 61 subtopics/*Pilgrim Hymnal*/33

Table 6.4
Hymns from PD indexed as Atonement

Hymn	Hymnal	Subject/Topic
Alas, and did my	m, n, s, q	ATONEMENT
Savior bleed	f, i	ATONEMENT, Gratitude for
Arise, my soul, arise	m	ATONEMENT
Blow ye the trumpet,	j	ATONEMENT, Fullness of
blow	j	ATONEMENT, Universality of
	i	ATONEMENT For all
Christ the Lord is risen today	j	ATONEMENT Completed
Hail, thou once	j	ATONEMENT, Fullness of
despised Jesus	t	ATONEMENT
Hark, the voice of love and mercy	j	ATONEMENT, Completed
Jesus, keep me near the cross	q	ATONEMENT
Jesus, lover of my soul	m	ATONEMENT
My hope is built on nothing less	s	ATONEMENT
Not all the blood of	a	ATONEMENT
Beasts	i	ATONEMENT, Sufficiency of
	k	CHRIST, Atonement
On a hill far away	r, t	ATONEMENT
Rock of ages	m, s, t	ATONEMENT
	i	ATONEMENT OF CHRIST, Sufficiency of
Sweet the moments rich in blessing	a	ATONEMENT
There is a fountain filled with blood	m, n, p, s	ATONEMENT
When I survey the wondrous cross	a, m, s	ATONEMENT

The analyses of the subject/topical indices direct attention to their changing vocabulary and content through 150 years of American religious history.
It is assumed that the hymnal editors have customized their collections to the
needs of particular groups; or, as we will see, some can bear the personal
stamp of individual compilers. Topical indices reflect social, political, and religious changes as well as liturgical or denominational issues. Table 6.4 shows
a variety of hymns indexed as ATONEMENT.

In the second section twenty hymns extracted from the database are ar-

ranged in tables that show subject references for each text. The format of subject and/or topical indices is not standardized. Some, like *b* and *d*, *f* and *i*, and
m list headings alphabetically but refer to texts by page numbers only, making
the subject index complicated to use. Neither *s* nor *l* use any subheadings.
With the exception of *m*, subject indices are bound into the back of each
book. Although for *m* a subject index with 287 headings appears in Oliver
Baketel's concordance to the hymnal,[1] the subject index published in *The
Hymns and Hymn Writers of the Church*[2] was used for this study because it
was designed to unify the Methodist Episcopal Church. In it 748 texts are indexed using 175 major headings with numerous subheadings (forty-two under CHRIST and ten under GOD, for example).

The physical evidence alone validates the study of the subject/topic indices.
Some terms in nineteenth-century subject indices (now archaic by our standards) would have been selected either to add weight to sermons or to give
power to the hymns. They grew in importance as educational tools, designed
to generate sermon material for pastors and service ideas for worship leaders.
Indices are indicators of trends; as new topics are introduced and others are
deleted, one can track how ideas progressively have gained or lost their effectiveness. Some of the topics we now take for granted were introduced at interesting times in American history. For example, PATRIOTIC and MIS-
SIONS did not appear until 1856; EASTER was first used as a topic in 1878;
PROCESSIONAL and BROTHERHOOD did not appear before 1934. The
subheadings for the major heading CHURCH in 1851 included *going to, stability of, Gentile,* and *abiding.* In 1864 CHURCH, *love for* was added. Later, in
1878, CHURCH subtopics included *security of, beloved by God, immovable,
militant, triumph of,* and *foundation of.* The topic TEMPERANCE appeared
in 1894, but not again until 1939 in hymnals researched. Table 6.5 shows the
introduction of some other topics into hymnals.

The information given in first-line indices varies from hymnal to hymnal.
Only the first lines in alphabetical order with corresponding hymn numbers
appear in *a.* Hymnals *b* and *d* list first line, author, and the number for the
page but not for the hymn. Editors of *g* improved on this by citing the number
of each hymn as well as its first line, author, and page number. In *j* and *k* the
unnecessary references to page numbers are dropped. With *l* the style changes
to add familiar titles to the first-line index, inserting them in alphabetical order. Titles are printed in small capitals and first lines in Roman, using upper
and lower case. The index in *n* is confusing because refrains, titles, and first
lines are all printed in the same type. Were the editor/publishers setting a new
trend or following common practice of naming hymns? Now titles such as

Table 6.5
Some noteworthy terms found in research of subject indices

---

a. (1827) DOCTRINES OF THE GOSPEL/GRACES OF THE SPIRIT/
CHARACTERS OF CHRIST

b. (1845) THE SPREAD OF THE GOSPEL/SPECIAL OCCASIONS, Sacramental, Ecclesiastical, Civil

d. (1851) BALM, grace the noblest/REVELATION, Scriptures a divine/
PROTECTION, divine continued

e. (1854) CONSOLATION/FREEDOM/IMMORTALITY/PILGRIM
FATHERS/REFORMS

f. (1856) BIBLE, Influences of/CHRIST, Joy in/GOD discerned in nature/
SABBATH, spiritual influence of

g. (1857–67) BREVITY, UNCERTAINTY OF LIFE/REJOICING: Prospect
of heaven/SUNDAY SCHOOL

h. (1863) EXPERIMENTAL: Faith, Courage, Zeal/HEAVEN/HORTATORY:
Encouragement

i. (1864) ABASEMENT OF SELF/ARMOR of Gospel/PRAYER, description
of/SLEEP, refreshed by

j. (1878) COVENANT/CROWNS OF GLORY/HALLELUJAHS/MARRIAGE
HYMNS/SATAN/STORMS

k. (1882) RECLAIMED/TIMES AND SEASONS

l. (1894) ADOPTION/FEAR NOT/INVITATION/MISSIONARY/REFUGE/
TEMPERANCE

m. (1905) APOSTASY/BACKSLIDER/BROTHERLY LOVE AND SERVICE/
BUSINESS/POOR

n. (1918) CHRISTMAS/CHORUSES/CONFESSION/DECISION/
PERSONAL WORK

o. (1926) BETHEL/CHASTENING/DOUBT/THE FALL/SOCIAL
BETTERMENT

p. (1931) CHILDREN'S/CALVARY/NAME OF JESUS/SECOND COMING/
SOLOS

q. (1934) AGGRESSIVENESS/CHOIR SELECTIONS/CHRISTIAN
EDUCATION/SOUL WINNING

r. (1939) ALLEGIANCE/EASTER/JUNIOR CHOIR/MOTHER/
PATRIOTIC/TEMPERANCE

s. (1940) MOTHERS DAY/QUARTETS/SOCIAL SERVICE/
STEWARDSHIP/YOUTH HYMNS

t. (1948) CLEANSING/GOOD FRIDAY/SOUL WINNING/SPECIAL DAYS:
Rally Day/WITNESSING

u. (1958) ALL SAINTS' DAY/BEAUTY/HOSPITALS/MEMORIAL DAY/
REFORMATION DAY

Table 6.6
CHARACTERS OF CHRIST (hymns 125–40) in *a*

Advocate, Friend, Fountain, Hiding Place, Lamb of God, Light, Pearl of
Great Price, Physician of Souls, Priest, Savior, Star of Bethlehem, and Way to
Canaan

Table 6.7
DOCTRINES OF THE GOSPEL (hymns 141–70) in *a*

Adoption, Atonement, Communion with God, Decrees of God, Depravity,
Sin and misery connected, Election, The Lord's Call, Grace Reigning,
Salvation by Grace, Pardon, The Converted Thief, Perseverance, Precious
Promises, Christ: The Believer's Ark, Redemption, Efficacious Grace, and
Sanctification and Pardon.

"He Lifted Me," "His Grace Is Satisfying Me," and "The Haven of Rest" are
intermixed with refrains and first lines. Other gospel hymnals—*p, q, r,* and *t*—
improved this greatly by going back to using *l*'s system of spelling titles with
capital letters, making it easier to distinguish between titles and first lines.
For example, in the General Index of *q*, the title of 240 (WE'RE MARCHING
TO ZION) follows "We Praise Thee, O Lord"; and the first line of 240 ("Come
We That Love the Lord") follows COME TO THE SAVIOR. Only *u* includes
the name of the tune with each first line and its hymn number.

The way the contents of a hymnal are organized can be interpreted as the
hymnal's mission statement. The "Arrangement" of *a* tells us much about its
intended use; the sections appear in this order: Universal Praise, Scripture,
Alarming, Inviting, Penitential, Christ (seven subheadings), Characters of
Christ in alphabetical order (Table 6.6), Doctrines of the Gospel in alphabetical order (Table 6.7), The Christian, Worship, The Sinner Awakened, Conviction, Conversion, The Convert, Rejoicing in a Revival, Baptism, Monthly
Concert, Missionary Meetings, Collections, Times and Seasons (eleven subheadings), Funeral Hymns, Time and Eternity, Resurrection, Day of Judgment, and Death and Heaven.

One of the unique features of the index in *a* is the list of characteristics
defining GRACES OF THE [HOLY] SPIRIT. The characteristics also appear
in italics as titles above each hymn in that section (see Table 6.8).

There are no sections as such in either the 1857 or 1867 edition of the Methodist hymnal (g). Philip Phillips's 1867 edition does not print the texts in numerical order; no. 1 is followed immediately by no. 75, making it difficult to navigate this collection. A commendable feature of this hymnal, however, is that each text is complete on one page and no hymns require an awkward page turn. The Methodist hymnal of 1878 (j), like g, is not divided into sections; but its Table of Contents provides major headings of Worship, God, Christ, The Holy Spirit, The Scriptures, The Sinner (four subheadings), The Christian (seven), The Church (five), Time and Eternity (five), Miscellaneous (four), Doxologies, Occasional pieces and chants. In the later Methodist Hymnal m, the classifications appear at the top of the corresponding pages as well. Hymnals f and i arrange the contents into many subheadings in the following order: Sabbath and Sanctuary; The Bible; God (five subheadings); Christ (three); Warning and Invitation; Christian Experience (four); The Church (two); Time, Eternity, Life and Death; Heaven; Times and Seasons; Children's Hymns; and Doxologies. The Contents in u (pp. ix, x) are in this order: Worship (four subheadings); God the Father (three); Our Lord Jesus Christ (eight); The Holy Spirit; The Trinity; The Bible; The Church of Christ (five); The Christian Life (six); The Kingdom of God on Earth (four); Seasons (three); Special Services and Occasions (four); Children; Youth; The National Anthem; Service music. Hymnals k, l, p, q, r, and t do not offer any plan of organization.

Beyond a choice of stanzas and their order, an editor could ascribe each text a title. Titles, when used, gave the editor more latitude to interpret the texts. Often the title placed at the head of the hymn is the reader/singer's first encounter with the text; a well-chosen title focuses the singers' thoughts. For instance, G. N. Allen, who compiled the hymnbooks used during Charles Finney's tenure at Oberlin, surely must have felt it necessary to reflect Finney's preaching. One can sense Finney's influence in such titles as "Vigilance Enjoined," "Entire Consecration," or "Christ our Salvation." It is in l that we encounter the greatest use of titles different from first lines; in most cases these titles are the first lines of the refrains, such as "Seeking to Save," "Have Courage, My Boy, to Say No," or "Scatter Seeds of Kindness."

Items other than titles often appear as headings of hymn texts. In a, hymn number, meter, author, title, and/or scriptural reference is provided for each hymn. As mentioned above, an alphabetical arrangement of the forty "graces" comprises a section in a; they also appear as italicized headings for hymns 183 to 230 (see Table 6.8).

Also in a, reference to a passage of scripture may take the place of the title.

Table 6.8
Graces of the Spirit as listed in *a*

Bearing the Cross	Happy Poverty	Christian Love
Charity	Hatred of Sin	Peace of Conscience
Comforts—true and false	The Christian's Hope	Rejoicing
Confidence in the Mediator	Hope encouraged	Resignation
Delight in God	Hoping, yet trembling	Self-denial
Contrite heart	Humility	Sincerity and truth
Faith conquering	Joy in the Holy Ghost	Submission
Faith connected with salvation	Heavenly joy on earth	Submission to Christ
A living and a dead Faith	Justice and equity	Trust and love God
The power of Faith	Love to God	I will trust
Holy Fortitude	Love to Christ	True wisdom
Humble gratitude	Love to Christ, present or absent	Zeal—true and false
Gravity and Decency	Lovest thou me?	

As a matter of style, perhaps, chapters of scripture as headings are written in Roman numerals but in the index of scriptural references in the back of the book they are not. As one would expect, the largest number of biblical references is to Psalms with thirty-five citations. References to Isaiah total thirty; to Jeremiah eleven; to Job seven; to Genesis and Proverbs six each; to Numbers, 1 Samuel, and Ezekiel three each; to Deuteronomy, Ecclesiastes, Canticles, Daniel, Hosea, Habakkuk, and Zechariah two each; and to Joshua, Judges, Ruth, 1 Kings, 1 Chronicles, Nehemiah, Esther, Joel, Amos, Jonah, Micah, Haggai, and Malachi one each.

Scripture passages are given with each title in *l* for hymns 1 through 547 only; numbers 548 through 739 have titles without accompanying scripture references.

Although a few earlier individual collections had placed tunes and texts on the same page, it was *The Plymouth Collection (f)* that Henry Ward Beecher published for his Brooklyn congregation in 1855 that was the first hymnal designed for use in formal worship to place a tune at the top of the page with a group of appropriately metered texts immediately below it. This arrangement became more or less the standard format for hymnals to follow for many years.

In the Methodist Episcopal hymnals analyzed, the 1857 edition indicates at the head of each text a page number in the tune collection, *The New Lute of Zion,* to which it can be sung. This is replaced in the 1867 edition with the metrical initials that designate the meter of the text. This 1867 edition also shows the hand of Phillips in the addition of headings giving instructions about ways to sing or interpret the hymn. Some suggestions are *spirited* for "Come Ye That Love the Lord" and "Grace, 'Tis a Charming Sound"; *mournful* for "He Dies, the Friend of Sinners Dies"; and *with gentleness* for "By Cool Siloam's Shady Rill." Some of the other interpretive directions include *with fervor, affettuoso, with ardor,* or *not too bold.* Tempo indications appear such as *poco adagio* and *not too fast.* Duplicate texts, titles, and indices are in 1857 and 1867.

A Comparison: *Psalms and Hymns for Christian Worship,* Prepared and Set Forth by the General Association of Connecticut, 1845 and 1851

Metrical psalmody began to loosen its stranglehold on Presbyterian collections after the revivals of George Whitefield swept through New England during the 1740s. The hallowed literal versifications gradually gave way to more and more of Isaac Watts's "Christianized" freer style. The same standards of correctness had to be upheld for hymns as well, and hymnal committees were invested with heavy responsibilities for selecting politically correct texts and rejecting others. By 1845, some felt it necessary to refresh the supply of congregational songs.

A close look at these two editions of *Psalms and Hymns for Christian Worship*, published within six years of each other, reveals some interesting facts. The contents of the two are exactly the same; the title page of the 1851 edition merely adds Seymour and Co. to the name of the Rochester publisher Wm. E. Alling. The two Prefaces, both dated 1845, are the same. There are no changes in the pages headed "Directions for the Use of This Book." The page numbering and the contents of the pages are exactly the same throughout, including titles, biblical references, and number of stanzas. Hymn numbers are identical through #680 where a printing error occurs and persists to the end of the 1845 edition, which modifies the sequential numbering of its final twenty-six hymns; this error has been corrected in the 1851 printing. The same thirteen doxologies appear on the same pages, 657 and 658. Fifty-two selections of "Selected Psalms and Hymns in Parallelisms for Chanting" begin in both books on page 659 and are ordered the same way with identical contents; the only change is the addition of pointing in the 1851 publication.

A survey of this section suggests various foci of mid-nineteenth-century worship; in addition to the general subjects of worship and praise, there are categories for Confession and Penitence, The Lord's Supper, Gathering of a Church, Dedication of a House of Worship, Fast Day, Thanksgiving Day, Ordination, Missionary Meetings, Funereal [*sic*], and a concluding doxology citing verses from Luke and Isaiah. The eight chants in four-part chordal harmony are identical. The same one-page table suggesting which of the chant tunes should be used with which text is placed after the "Index of Topics and Uses" in 1845, but for convenience, no doubt, it is inserted between the selections and the tunes in 1851. In both hymnals the "Index of First Lines" is identical, citing first line of text, author, and page number.

In the subject/topical indices, however, the two editions differ. A marked increase in the number of subjects and subheadings can only reflect more widespread use; hymns grew in importance as a means not only to shape the service but also to lend power to the sermons. Even the headings of the indices differ; in 1845 one page of General Index is followed by four pages titled Index of Topics and Uses organized into three major headings of ORDINARY PUBLIC WORSHIP, SPECIAL OCCASIONS, and PRIVATE AND FAMILY WORSHIP. The ORDINARY PUBLIC WORSHIP comprises 1. *Introductory*

(Invocation and General Praise with three sections); 2. *Various Topics* (sixteen listed below); and 3. *Close of Worship*. Within SPECIAL OCCASIONS are Sacramental, Ecclesiastical, Sabbath School, Missionary, Charitable and Benevolent, Civil, Funereal, and Miscellaneous. PRIVATE AND FAMILY WORSHIP lists twenty-four subheadings. Material listed under the heading "Various Topics" is organized into sixteen subheadings: Scriptures, God, Jesus Christ, Holy Spirit, Trinity, Man, The Way of Salvation, Invitation and Warnings, The Christian, The Church, The Spread of the Gospel, Time, Death, The Resurrection, The Judgment, and Heaven. None of the page references appear in two places; in fact, double listing seems to be carefully avoided. For instance, those numbers given to "Invocation and General Praise" do not appear under any other topics. This makes a total of twenty-seven major headings if one counts "Private and Family Worship" as a heading.

The 1851 edition, in contrast, changes the title of the index from "topics" to "subjects" and organizes the material under 834 headings with hundreds of subheadings. The subjects that carry the longest lists of subheadings are CHRIST (124), GOD (122), PRAYER (seventy-two), GOSPEL (forty-one), CHRISTIAN (thirty-eight), HEAVEN (thirty-six), SIN (thirty-five), GRACE (thirty-five), SAINTS (thirty-four), SINNERS (thirty-two), MAN (thirty-two), HOLY SPIRIT (twenty-eight), CHURCH (twenty-six), and LOVE (twenty-six). A total of 705 psalms and hymns are ordered consecutively through 655 pages. Because the page numbers are the same in both editions, one can track how a given text was indexed more fully as its usefulness grew. For instance, #409 "How sad our state by nature is" (four) appears in no less than sixteen different places in the expanded index, including ATONE, *The blood of Christ only can;* CORRUPTION *of nature;* DEPRAVITY *by nature;* GOSPEL, *grace of;* GOSPEL, *sufficiency of;* JESUS, *salvation through him alone;* JUSTIFICATION *not by works;* JUSTIFICATION *through the blood of Christ alone;* MAN *depraved by nature;* MAN *justified by grace, not by works;* MERCY, *man's only hope;* SIN, *deep the stains of;* SALVATION *by grace;* SLAVERY OF SIN, *Christ saves his people from the;* SUFFICIENCY *of the gospel;* VOWS *cannot expiate human guilt.* "Give me the wings of faith to rise" on p. 563 is indexed in *d* in fifteen different ways, including EXAMPLE *of ancient worthies;* EXAMPLES OF FAITH; FAITH, *ancient examples of;* FAITH, *prayer for;* HEAVEN, *followers of those who have gone before to;* HEAVEN, *glories of;* HEAVEN, *joys of;* HEAVEN, *rest in;* LAMB OF GOD, *Victory ascribed to;* REST *in heaven;* REST, *saints above possess the promised;* SAINTS, *joys of in heaven;* SCRIPTURE CHARACTERS, *for our imitation;* WORTHIES, *the ancient, examples to us;* and WRESTLING WITH SIN.

A Comparison: Several Editions of Methodist Episcopal Hymnals

According to Hymnologist Donald Hustad, "With the advent of the 'gospel singer' about 1840, it became possible for many people to devote themselves full-time to a ministry of music in evangelism. The first may have been Philip Phillips (1834–1895), the 'Singing Pilgrim.'"[3] It was Phillips who totally rearranged the textual material within g. With many of its texts set to new tunes, it was published under his editorship in 1867 as *New Hymn and Tune Book: An Offering of Praise.* Texts maintained their numbering from the earlier volume but were scrambled. The same numbers for the same texts appear in the subject/topic indices of both publications.

Scarcely nine years later, the Methodist General Conference of May 1876 decided that "a thorough revision of the Hymn Book now in use is imperatively demanded," and a committee was formed. The instructions, reported in the Preface, were that "no hymn now in use shall be excluded without a vote of two-thirds of the committee . . . no hymn not now in the collection shall be admitted without a vote of two-thirds of the committee in its favor." This hymnal appeared with an "Address to the Members and Friends of the Methodist Episcopal Church" dated January 12, 1878, in which the committee wrote of rejecting, adding, or "changing the phraseology" of the hymns in the collection and commending it "as one of the choicest selections of evangelical hymns ever published." It was their hope that it would "increase the interest of public worship, give a higher inspiration to social and family services, and aid in private meditation and devotion." By comparing the contents of the two hymnals and the various ways in which hymns were titled and indexed to be "used," we see what materials the committee thought necessary to accomplish its purpose.

Within the hymnal, the forty-three texts "new" to the 1878 edition, shown in Table 6.9, were spread over nineteen categories. The highest number, nine, appear in the section *THE CHRISTIAN—*PRAYER AND PRAISE. Six are placed within *THE CHRISTIAN—*TRIAL, SUFFERING AND SUBMISSION; four in *THE CHRISTIAN—*ACTIVITY; three in WORSHIP; three in *GOD—*BEING AND ATTRIBUTES; two each in *CHRIST—*LIFE AND CHARACTER, HOLY SPIRIT, *THE SINNER—*REPENTANCE, and *THE CHRISTIAN—*JUSTIFICATION AND ADORATION; and one each in *CHRIST—*INCARNATION AND BIRTH, *CHRIST—*RESURRECTION, PRIESTHOOD AND REIGN, THE SCRIPTURES, *THE SINNER—*PROVISIONS OF THE GOSPEL, *THE CHRISTIAN—*CONSECRATION, *THE CHURCH—*GENERAL HYMNS, *THE CHURCH—CHURCH WORK:*

Table 6.9
Texts in *j* that are not in *g*

Amazing grace [16]	Majestic sweetness sits enthroned [42]
Come, Holy Spirit, come [??]	More love to thee [67]
Come, thou fount of every blessing [72]	Must Jesus bear the cross alone [45]
Come, thou long-expected Jesus [72]	My country 'tis of thee [23]
Faith of our fathers [66]	Nearer, my God, to thee [23]
God is love [68]	O worship the King [57]
He leadeth me [50]	On the mountain's top appearing [60]
Holy Ghost with light divine [64]	Onward, Christian soldiers [49]
Holy, holy, holy [29]	Safely through another week [49]
How firm a foundation [4]	Stand up, stand up for Jesus [42]
I heard the voice of Jesus say [63]	Sun of my soul [51]
I love to tell the story [52]	Sweet hour of prayer [45]
I need thee every hour [56]	The day is past and gone [69]
In the cross of Christ [48]	The heavens declare thy glory [69]
Jerusalem the golden [72]	The morning light is breaking [52]
Jesus, I my cross have taken[35]	'Tis midnight and on Olive's brow [54]
Jesus, the very thought of thee [65]	What shall I render to my God [75]
Joy to the world [11]	What a friend we have in Jesus [53]
Just as I am [17]	When Thou, my righteous judge [71]
Lead, kindly light [57]	Work, for the night is coming [54]
Lord, I hear of showers of blessing [75]	

MISSIONS, *TIME AND ETERNITY*—JUDGMENT AND RETRIBUTION, *TIME AND ETERNITY*—HEAVEN, and NATIONAL OCCASIONS.

The Methodists were particularly thorough in extracting topics from inner stanzas of hymn texts. "Glorious things of thee are spoken" customarily is found under ZION, CITY OF GOD, or ROCK OF AGES. But for Methodists in 1878 it was indexed under HOSANNAS; RIVER OF LIFE; CHURCH, *Security of the;* CHURCH, *Beloved by God;* CHRISTIANS, *Joy of;* CHURCH, *Foundations of.* None of the other editors of the seventeen hymnals in this study pointed to "Jesus, lover of my soul" in the Methodist terminology of THE SINNER, *Penitential,* SINNERS, *Confessing,* or CHRIST, *Love of, for Man.* For other editors or editorial committees the term HEAVEN was sufficient as a topical reference for "On Jordan's stormy bank I stand"; but for the Methodists in 1867 it was "Rejoicing in the Prospect of Heaven," and in 1878 there were "longings" for it and "bliss" of it. Closer study of the Subject Index of the 1878 hymnal shows it to be quite abstract, raising the possibility that it was compiled as a tool for academics and professors more learned than the man or woman in the pew. Most people in a congregation take the hymnal at its face value—a collection of hymns and tunes; who, then, but a clergyman would have had any reason to scan it for topics such as PANOPLY, *Wrestling Jacob;* or LEPROSY, *Spiritual?* How many were studious enough to delve beyond the first line and/or title for treasures of hidden references in Tables 6.10 and 6.11?

Hymnals as Individual Statements

Of the seventeen hymnals analyzed in this study, four bear a personal stamp and reflect differing evangelistic stances. They show the influence of well-known personalities of their day—Asahel Nettleton (1783–1844), Charles G. Finney (1792–1875), Henry Ward Beecher (1813–1887), and Dwight Moody (1837–1899). History has put these ministers of the gospel into separate corners. Yale historian Sydney E. Ahlstrom described Asahel Nettleton as a representative figure of the Second Awakening, in demand as a revivalist in Connecticut, New York, and elsewhere in New England: "Yet his invariable success in calling sinners to repentance undermined the idea that a revival was the work of God."[4] In addition to his powerful pulpit appeal, Nettleton used systematic home visitations, personal conferences, inquiry meetings, and follow-up instruction. Nettleton first regarded Charles Finney as a threat in New England and publicly denounced him during a conference in July 1827 in New Lebanon, New York. It was not so much Finney's doctrine of "entire sanctification" nor his belief that holiness was a human possibility that inflamed Nettleton: rather, he objected to Finney's methods.[5]

"Following the camp meeting movement of 1800 and the eastern seaboard ministry of Charles G. Finney in the 1820s, revivalism became an important influence in American church life."[6] In Oberlin and other schools founded in the mid-nineteenth century to train young ministers "men of piety and scholarship purged American revivals of their fanaticism, grounded them on liberalized Calvinist or Arminian doctrines, and set their course in a socially responsible direction."[7] Finney was appointed to teach theology at the Oberlin Collegiate Institute in 1834, so the earliest hymnbooks compiled for use in Oberlin College and village would have been dependent on Finney's approval for content and organization.

The social orientation of another evangelist's theology as well as his individual style is shown in the content, arrangement, and indices of the hymnal Henry Ward Beecher compiled for use by his own Plymouth Church congre-

Table 6.10

Hidden references within hymns to topics in *j*, the 1878 Methodist Hymn Book

First line	Subject Heading	Hidden Reference
1. "My soul, be on thy guard"	PANOPLY	4a "Thine armor is divine"
2. "Great God while Zion sings"	GOD: Light of saints	3a "God is our sun; he makes our day"
3. "With joy we meditate the grace"	CHRIST: High Priest CHRIST: Sympathy of CHRIST: Grace of	1b "Of our High Priest above" 2a "Touched with a sympathy within" 5c "We shall obtain delivering grace"
4. "Return, O wanderer, return"	GOD: Father	1b "And seek thy Father's face, 4c "Thy Father calls-no longer mourn"
5. "O for a closer walk with God"	HOLY SPIRIT, *invoked* RENOUNCING ALL FOR CHRIST BACKSLIDING *Lamented* BACKSLIDING, *Return from* DOVE, heavenly	4a 'Return, O Holy Dove, return'
6. "Come, ye disconsolate"	HOLY SPIRIT: invitations of CHRIST: Bread of heaven LOVE-FEAST HYMNS	3a "Here see the bread of life, see waters flowing" 3c "Come to the feast of love, come ever knowing"
7. "Come, my soul, thy suit prepare"	CHRIST, *Guide*	3c "As my guide, my guard, my friend"

8. "The morning light is breaking"	RIVER OF LIFE	3a "Blest river of salvation"
9. "Give me the wings of"	CHRISTIANS: Conquerors through Christ SAINTS in heaven	3c "Ascribe their conquest to the Lamb" 1c "The saints above, how great their joys "
10. "When thou, my righteous Judge"	HEAVEN, Society of ARCHANGELS: *Trumpet* CHRIST: hiding place HEAVEN: Praise of LOVE: For the church SAINTS: humility of	4a " Among thy saints let me be found" 4b "Whene'er the archangel's trump shall sound" 3b "Be thou my only hiding place" 4e "While heaven's resounding mansions ring" 2a and b "I love to meet thy people now, Before thy feet with them to bow" 1d "Shall such a worthless worm as I"

Table 6.11

Topics within *j* (the 1878 Methodist Hymn Book) referring to inner
stanzas of hymns

CHRIST, *Physician*/"Hark the glad sound" (4c)
CHRIST, *Prince of grace*/"Plunged in a gulf of dark despair" (2a)
CHRIST, *Bread of heaven* and LOVE-FEAST/"Come, ye disconsolate" (3a
   and 3c)
COURAGE/"My Savior, my almighty Friend" (3c)
DEATH, *Fear of, overcome*/"My God, the spring of all my joys" (5a)
DEATH, *Second* and VANITY *of earth*/"O where shall rest be found" (4d and
   1c, d)
DEVILS and FAITH, *work of*/"My soul, be on thy guard" (1c and 3c)
GOD, *Light of the saint*/"Great God, attend, while Zion sings" (3a)
GOD, *Father* and PARDON *Offered*/"Return, O wanderer" (1b, 4c and 3d,
   5c, d)
GRACE, *Miracle of*/"Sweet the moments, rich in blessing" (3d)
HELL, *Place of Punishment*/"That awful day will surely come" (4c, d)
HOLINESS, *Highway of* and SINNERS, *Slavery of*/"Jesus, my all, to heaven is
   gone" (2c and 3c, d)
IMMORTALITY/"I'll praise my Maker while I've breath" (1e, f, g and 4e, f, g)
RIVER OF LIFE/"The morning light is breaking" (3a)
SINNERS, *Slavery of* and TRUST *in God*/"How sad our state by nature is"
   (1d, 2d)

---

gation, *The Plymouth Collection.* Both Finney and Beecher were able to move
sinners to repentance, but their styles were opposite. Of Beecher, it was said
by Reverend J. H. Chadwick, a Unitarian preacher of Brooklyn, "He spoke
oftener from his emotions than from his beliefs."[8] Meanwhile, Finney wrote:
"I insisted that our reason was given us for the very purpose of enabling us
to justify the ways of God."[9]

Not many years later, another powerful evangelist, Dwight Moody, with
his own musician Ira Sankey (1840–1908), changed the course of conventional
evangelical hymnody. Working as co-laborers in evangelistic crusades in Britain and America wherever they went they reached people "eager for the rich
and soul-subduing melodies which he [Sankey] poured out upon them in
floods." In Britain they found "a multitude who were weary of the stupid,
drawling hymns and tunes so common before the evangelists appeared on
British soil."[10] Edgar Goodspeed, whose book chronicles in detail Moody's
evangelistic campaigns, refers to hymns sung in great revival gatherings in

England and Scotland from "Sacred Songs"; I have found Goodspeed's num-
bers correlate with the numbers for the hymns in *Gospel Hymns and Sacred
Songs* by P. P. Bliss and Ira Sankey published in America by John Church and
Company and Biglow and Main in 1875. Many from that book are included in
I in this study.

Asahel Nettleton and HARMONY

Nettleton wrote in his preface that he compiled *Village Hymns* as "A Supplement to the Psalms and Hymns of Dr. Watts" in response to the proposal
made by the General Association of Connecticut in 1820 for a new Selection
of Hymns. It was published "in this forty-eighth year of the independence of
the United States of America." He, like conscientious editors before and after
him, struggled over the indexing. "With respect to the arrangement, it has
cost me much labor. I am aware that many of the hymns placed under different heads, might have been arranged under the same; and yet all these heads
seem indispensable. . . . But there are so many things peculiar to the *commencement* of the Christian life, that it was deemed highly proper to collect
a number suited to his case, and place them under the eye of the young convert." [11] Accordingly, this subject so important in his ministry merits fifty-one
hymns; CONVERT lists hymns 372–423 with three subheadings *in darkness,
humbled,* and *true.* Seven additional hymns appear under DARKNESS, *new
convert in,* and CONVERT, *true* lists two. The Subjects in *a* reflect Nettleton's
predisposition to identify and qualify experiences. "Spiritual pride leads to a
certain unsuitable and self-confident boldness before God and man. Humility
leads to the opposite," he argued. [12] Opposite terms abound in his Subject Index; COMFORT is true or false, FAITH is living or dead, the WAY is broad
or narrow, and ZEAL is true or false. In a letter attacking Finney, Nettleton
complained that no attention was being given to the "danger of a spuri-
ous conversion": "It is an important part of a preacher's duty in a season of
powerful revival, to discriminate between true and false conversion." [13] Ac-
cordingly, two hymns appear under a heading CONVERT, *True.*

A contemporary account describes Nettleton's characteristic quietness:
"The stillness, at times, seemed to be have something like a mystery about it;
it was sublime, it was awful; you almost seemed to be in eternity." [14] Subjects
such as WATCH, *Pray* and WATCH *and Knock* as well as HOLY SPIRIT, *His
influences* and PRAYER *to the Spirit* reflect this. Nettleton describes the graces
of the Spirit as the distinguishing marks of true religion. "Their absence cannot be compensated by flaming zeal." [15] He warns against the hypocrisy of ex-

hibiting Christian graces "in theory alone"; they must show in one's actions. And it is the preacher's mandate to "expose every counterfeit" (a volley aimed directly at Finney). Forty-seven total texts (183–230) are devoted to the Christian graces. Only CHRIST (with forty-three subtitles) and SINNER (with thirty-four subheadings) merit this much space in his hymnal. HYPOCRITE earns its own heading.

After two unsatisfying meetings with Finney in the winter of 1826–27, Nettleton agonized that Finney was destroying harmony within the associations of ministers, creating a "civil war in Zion, a domestic broil in the household of faith."[16] Reflecting his deep regard for the Church as an institution, most of the seventeen hymns under his Subject heading CHURCH are devoted to *glory of*; the others are distributed among *love to, prayer for, children of, prayed for, wheat and tares in,* and *meetings*.

Nettleton, deploring Finney's "new measures," upheld Jonathan Edwards's Calvinistic doctrinal system. Material in *a* parallels these views; we find thirty texts under DOCTRINES distributed among DECREES OF GOD, DEPRAVITY, ELECTION, FALL OF MAN, PERSEVERANCE, and REGENERATION, with additional texts indexed under CONVERSION GIVES JOY TO SAINTS, DAY OF JUDGMENT, and JUDGMENT DAY. SCRIPTURES includes the subheadings *excellence of, a lamp, glory of, attended with the Spirit,* and *reveal Christ*.

Charles Grandison Finney and Early Oberlin Hymnals (COUNTERPOINT)

George Nelson Allen published his *Social and Sabbath School Hymn Book* in Oberlin in 1846. It included 218 hymns; there was no index. In 1847 the same 218 hymns were published with an "Index of Subjects" on the back page. The Index duplicated the organization of the book. The major headings were, in this order: Scriptures, Exhortatory, Devotional and Experimental (with sixteen subheadings), Sabbath, Family Worship, Missionary (three subheadings), Special Occasions (six subheadings), and Doxologies. Allen's use of "Experimental" is curious, but in 1855 Philip Schaff observed that all the German churches in America had adopted the system of revivals with the emphasis upon "subjective, experimental religion."[17] In 1854 a fifth edition of *The Social and Sabbath Hymn Book* appeared with a Supplement of sixty-nine texts grouped together on pages 182–238 between the doxologies and the "Index of First Lines." The supplementary texts were inserted alphabetically into the "Index of First Lines," but there are no references to them in the "Subject

Index." The material included in this supplement is noteworthy. Although they are not categorized by subject, some of the hymns bear titles such as *Loving-kindness, The Christian Race, God a Sovereign, Pilgrim's Song, Christ the Judge, Christian Watchfulness.* Table 6.12 shows parallels between Finney's personal expressions and texts or titles found in the Oberlin books.

The last example in Table 6.12 cites another hymnbook used in early Oberlin, *Hymns for Social Worship,* first published in 1844, revised and "remodeled" through seven editions, the last appearing in 1868. The sixth and seventh editions, five years apart, are duplicates save for the deletion in the final edition of the section labeled Bondmen and the substitution of two jubilee hymns for two earlier hymns that had decried "fetters, chains, stripes" and asked heaven to comfort the mourning slave. We can assume that this hymnal, also edited by Allen, reflects Finney's theology. Its order is substantially different. Terms seem interchangeable; in the section titled EXPERIMENTAL the earlier (1854) terms Petition, Repentance, and Confession do not appear, but Humiliation, Submission, Penitence, Rest, Communion, Gratitude, and complete subheadings titled "Faith, Courage, Zeal" and "Compassion for others" are added. SPECIAL OCCASIONS is expanded considerably, adding to hymns for sickness, death, and funeral suggestions for hymns for Our Country, New Year's Day, Christmas Day, Thanksgiving Day, Fast Day, and Communion Day. In many ways, the organization of this hymn appears Finney's "stamp." EXPERIMENTAL/*Self-examination* nos. 60–63 includes "A Charge to Keep I Have"; EXPERIMENTAL/*Penitence and Confession* nos. 64–74, includes "Alas, and Did My Savior Bleed" (five) and "Not all the Blood of Beasts"; and EXPERIMENTAL/*Consecration and Sanctification* nos. 137–146 include "O for a Heart to Praise My God" (four); "Jesus I My Cross Have Taken" (two) and "Love Divine, all Loves Excelling" (two).

The most noticeable shift between the two Oberlin hymnals occurs in the treatment of judgment. In the earlier 1854 (*e*) hymnbook Judgment and Heaven are subtopics assigned three pages at the end of SPECIAL OCCA-SIONS. In *Hymns for Social Worship,* 1863 (*h*) the major topic JUDGMENT AND ETERNITY covers pages 279–86 and HEAVEN covers pages 287–99.

H. W. Beecher and *The Plymouth Collection* (LYRICISM)

In the preceding comparisons of editions of *Psalms and Hymns* and hymnals of the Methodist Episcopal Church, skillful indexers ferreted out hidden references within the texts in the hymnals. In both cases, the collection came first and the "meat" was extracted later. Given Henry Ward Beecher's style in

Table 6.12
Parallels between Finney's sermons and Oberlin hymnals

A. "Let us look into some of the promises. . . .I might occupy many pages in the examination of the promises, for they are exceedingly numerous, and full, and in point." (Charles G. Finney, *Lectures on Systematic Theology*, ed. J. H. Fairchild, 1878, republished 1987. Lecture 37, "Sanctification," 409).

Social and Sabbath-School Hymn Book, no. 60 "Approach, my soul, the mercy-seat" Title: Pleading The Promises

B. "The sovereignty of God consists in the independence of his will, in consulting his own intelligence and discretion in the selection of his end, and the means of accomplishing it."
"The sovereignty of God is an infinitely amiable, sweet, holy and desirable sovereignty . . .the perfection of all that is reasonable, kind and good." (Charles G. Finny, *Lectures on Systematic Theology*, ed. J. H. Fairchild, 1878, republished 1987. Lecture 45, "Divine Sovereignty," 516, 522).

Social and Sabbath-School Hymn Book: Supplement no. 289, "God moves in a mysterious way"
Title: *God a Sovereign*
5. His purposes will ripen fast
Unfolding every hour;
The bud may have a bitter taste
But sweet will be the flower.
6. Blind unbelief is sure to err
And scan his work in vain;
God is his own interpreter,
And He will make it Plain.

C. Jer. 31:31–34, "Upon this passage I remark: This is undeniably a promise of entire sanctification. It is a promise that the 'law shall be written in the heart.'" (Charles G. Finney, *Lectures on Systematic Theology*, ed. J. H. Fairchild, 1878, republished 1987. Lecture 45, "Divine Sovereignty," 411).

"Weakness of heart does not mean a divided heart. . . A weak heart is not a wicked heart. . . In order to strengthen our hearts, we need to know and thoroughly consider those truths which are calculated to wean us from sin and strengthen our will and purpose in the spiritual life. It also involves an increase of faith. Strengthening the heart must necessarily depend upon an increase of faith." (Charles G. Finney, *Principles of Christian Obedience*, comp. and ed. Louis Parkhurst, Jr., Minneapolis, MN: Bethany House Publishers, 1990. Lecture 12, "Weakness of Heart," 166).

Table 6.12. *Continued*

"While a man's heart is wrong, he cannot heartily approve of what is right without contradiction. It appears that the manner of preaching which calls forth the greatest enmity of heart is best. . . *we insist that holy things are offensive to unholy hearts.* While hearts remain unholy, they are pleased with that which is unholy." (Charles G. Finney, *Principles of Revival,* comp. and ed. Louis Parkhurst, Jr., Minneapolis, MN: Bethany House Publishers, 1987. Principle 45, 197).

Social and Sabbath-School Hymn Book, no. 58, "O for a heart to praise my God"
Section: Consecration and Sanctification
Title: *Jesus' Heart A Copy*

D. "Repentance is the turning from an attitude of rebellion against God, to a state of universal submission to his will, and approbation of it as wise and good." (Charles G. Finney, *Lectures on Systemic Theology,* ed. J. H. Fairchild, 1878, republished by Colporter Kemp. Lecture 34, "Repentance and Impenitence," 371).

Hymns for Social Worship
EXPERIMENTAL: *Submission and Trust,* nos. 75–86 included in this section: "Guide me, O thou great Jehovah" and "Father, whate'er of earthly bliss."

---

other aspects of his work and life, it is highly possible that the contents of his hymnals were chosen for their specific use in his evangelical ministry—a classic "chicken or the egg" situation. A look at the subject indices of *The Plymouth Collection* discloses much about the man himself—his philosophy, his stance on issues. Chauncey Burr once said: "Of the cleverness of H. W. Beecher both as a writer and speaker there can be no question. . . . His sermons are always exceedingly clever—not as sermons, but . . . as specimens of word-weaving . . . of words with little original thought, they are almost marvellous."[18] Perhaps "word-expanding" better defines the burgeoning of topics in editions of Beecher's hymnal. In the 1856 edition, seventy-two categories or major headings and 243 subheadings appear, whereas in the 1864 edition the "Subject Index" covers seventeen pages, comprising 908 major headings and 2,192 subtopics. Over the course of eight years Beecher had learned how to "use" the material in the back of the hymnal as a way to reinforce his ideas.

Changes in the format itself show that Beecher had given much thought to hymn classification. The "Subject Index" in the later edition was much easier to use. In both editions, the subheadings were italicized, but where the 1856 edition printed them in random nonalphabetized paragraph format, the 1864 edition printed them in a neat system of indentations, alphabetically arranged. The range of topics reveals Beecher's broad interests. John Howard wrote of him: "Few minds since Shakespeare's have laid hold on such a wondrous number and diversity of matters for treatment."[19] Another contemporary observed that in Beecher's forty years at Plymouth Church, "his sermons and lectures abounded in thoughts and expressions such as have fallen from the lips of no man since the days of Shakespeare."[20]

Beecher planned to break new ground with his hymnal. "Should it prepare the way for another work," he wrote in the Introduction to the 1856 edition (dated August 10, 1855), "we shall rejoice to have wrought as a pioneer." And indeed he had changed forever the look of American hymnals by putting music and text together and by interlining first stanzas. But through his indices he also changed the way people looked at hymns. He defined a hymn as "a lyrical discourse to the feelings." And in spite of the disclaimer "we have carefully avoided a narrow adherence to our own personal taste in the selection of hymns," the indices undeniably expound his individual style.[21] The vocabulary is often flamboyant and sensual. Glory and glories are two of his favorite expressions; only Beecher's hymnal uses the words "glory" and "glorying" in references to "All Hail the Power" or "When I Survey the Wondrous Cross." He is the only editor to extract from "All Hail the Power" the term SUPREMACY or from "When I Survey the Wondrous Cross" the terms AGONY and IMMENSITY, or to describe the Love of Christ as BOUNDLESS. He finds Music in Christ's Name, the glory of Christ's Face, and refuge in The Bosom and/or The Breast of Jesus.

In his selection of topics, Beecher is not so much a preacher as an interpreter. "From all that dwell below the skies" is indexed in most hymnals under PRAISE or WORSHIP; but in *i* we find it under GLORY TO GOD, *All Invoked to Join.* His tendency to interpret is nowhere more evident than in his indexing of "On Jordan's Rugged Banks I Stand" under nine different subjects including CANAAN, *Fair Fields of;* PESTILENCE, *None in Heaven;* HEAVEN *Separated by Jordan of Death.* Even the names designated for topics in *i* bear the individual personal stamp of Beecher. Common generic terms such as Praise, Worship, or Devotional are not for him; no committee would create NAME OF CHRIST, *Music of,* and other such colorful commentary. For the Methodists, Hell was a place of punishment, but for Beecher it is *deserved by the sinner* and *dreaded.* The Sinner by other indexers/editors is *burdened, con-*

victed, or *addressed;* but according to Beecher he/she *walks the broad way, is wept over by Christ,* or *overcome by Christ's love.* In most other collections the hymn "How Tedious and Tasteless the Hours" appears under topics Christ, Praise, or Loving-Kindness. But Beecher sermonizes with *Banishment from Christ unendurable, Blessings naught without Christ, Estrangement from Christ unendurable,* and *Winter of separation from Christ.*

Beecher also used *The Plymouth Collection* to reinforce his individual thoughts about sleep, evolution, symbols of God, angels, heaven, ordinances, Sabbath, and so forth. On sleep, Beecher said, "The order of nature is that a man should rise from his bed in the morning as birds rise, singing and in perfect health . . . a man rises buoyant and has his best hours in the early day . . . [though] the fancy may not be so brilliant in the early day, the judgment is better."[22] Of the several hymnals researched for this study, only *The Plymouth Collection* and the copiously indexed Methodist Hymnal of 1878 include a major heading SLEEP; and *The Plymouth Collection* alone includes SLEEP, *refreshed by.* "Glory to Thee, My God, This Night" and "Awake, My Soul, and with the Sun" are included in that category.

Beecher's also emphasized the all-encompassing glory of God in Christ: "There is no food for soul or body which God has not symbolized. He is light for the eye, sound for the ear, bread for food, wine for weariness, peace for trouble."[23] It is no surprise to see "Now to the Lord a Noble Song" (indexed in other hymnals under Praise to God or Anticipations of Heaven) under GLORY OF CHRIST'S FACE and "O Thou in Whose Presence" (indexed in other hymnals under Worship or Adoration), under LOOKS OF CHRIST, *Glorious;* CHRIST, *Voice of, charming;* and VOICE OF CHRIST, *Charm of.* "Guide Me, O Thou Great Jehovah" is found under BREAD OF HEAVEN, *Christ is* and MANNA, *Christ the.*

"Just as I Am" in *i* appears under CEREMONIES, OUTWARD, *Vain;* but in other hymnals it was indexed under such subjects as Blood of Christ, Decision, Repentance, Seeking pardon, and Abasement of self.

Beecher's topic index goes at great length to stress ALL, based on his belief that, "The unity of Christians does not depend upon similarity of ordinance and methods of worship. . . . I do not believe the millennium will see one sect, one denomination. . . . The unity of the church is to be the unity in the love of Christ and in the love of each other."[24] ALL, *invited to praise Christ* includes "Mortals, Awake, and Join," "Joy to the World," and "Glory to God on High." ALL, *atonement for* points to "Blow Ye the Trumpet, Blow."

The topics of Separation, Banishment, and Estrangement loom large.

Again, this is based on Beecher's ideas: "I do not care about one system or another; . . . any system that lets down the curtain between God and men . . . anything that blurs the presence of God, that makes the heavens black and the heart hopeless—I will fight it to the death."[25] "How Tedious and Tasteless the Hours," found in other hymnals under Christ, *loveliness of,* or under Christ, *provisions of,* is indexed in *i* as WINTER *of Separation from Christ,* BANISHMENT FROM CHRIST *Unendurable,* and ESTRANGEMENT FROM CHRIST *Unendurable.* The topic ESTRANGEMENT FROM CHRIST *Deplored* includes "How Oft, Alas, This Wretched Heart."

Dwight Moody and Ira Sankey's Gospel Hymns (MINIMALISM)

One Moody contemporary quoted him addressing a congregation: "If you can't sing as well as the person next to you, don't mind that. If you can't sing at all, just talk the words out. It will do you good."[26] Hustad writes that nineteenth-century evangelical musicians established a pattern of compiling and publishing gospel songbooks, used first in their evangelistic crusades and then released to the public. "The pattern," writes Hustad, "was set by the time Dwight L. Moody (1837–1899) came on the scene. His own musician was Ira David Sankey (1840–1908) who may be considered the archetype of his profession."[27] Goodspeed cites eighty-three or more hymns in Moody/Sankey services in the United States and Great Britain. Of those eighty-three, eighteen were not published in *l.* The Moody revival texts most frequently cited in Goodspeed are #1. "Hold the Fort" (9x); #2. "There Were Ninety and Nine" (9x); #3. "Rock of Ages" (5x); #4. "Jesus of Nazareth Passeth By" or "Too Late" (5x); #5. "Nothing but Leaves" (4x); #6. "Safe in the Arms of Jesus" (4x); #7. "Jesus, Lover of My Soul" (4x); and #8. "I Need Thee Every Hour" (4x). These appear in the Topical Index of *l* in the following categories: #1 appears only in WORK; #2 in CHRIST SEEKING/CHRIST THE SHEPHERD; #3 in BLOOD OF CHRIST/PRAYER/REFUGE/WORSHIP; #4 in WARNING/RESURRECTION; #5 in WARNING/WORK; #6 in ASSURANCE/FELLOWSHIP WITH CHRIST/FUNERAL/HEAVEN/LOVE; #7 in FUNERAL/REFUGE/WORSHIP; and #8 in CONFESSION/FAITH/FELLOWSHIP WITH CHRIST/PRAYER/TEMPTATION/TEMPERANCE/WORSHIP. Yet "I Need Thee Every Hour" and "Just as I Am," each indexed under six or seven headings in *l,* are scarcely mentioned in Goodspeed's biography. Goodspeed says of Moody, "He preaches the gospel, clearly, broadly, pointedly; but there is no Moody type of doctrine, except in so far as the attentive and loving study of the Bible is a Moodyism."[28] There is no subject heading in *l* labeled BIBLE.

Indices: More Than Meets the I   149

Instead there are fifteen hymns about words or the Word under PRECIOUS PROMISES.

Goodspeed quotes Moody as saying, "The churches need awakening; it is too easy now to be a church member," and "In the summer season never mind the church, leave it to the owls and bats; . . . go out on the first street corner you come to and preach. . . . We must have plainer churches."[29] So it is no surprise to find that the topic CHURCH is missing. In Goodspeed we hear Moody complaining, "There is too much preaching. It's preach, preach, preach, all the time." In one sermon he advised: "You, young men, have heard sermons enough here in Brooklyn to convert every one of you. What you need is to work among yourselves. . . . Then you'll see results," and in another: "The quickest way to train young converts is to put them to work."[30] It is not surprising to find sixty-one hymns in the category of WORK.

Goodspeed also recorded that a common complaint about Moody's sermons concerned their lack of direct application to the relations and duties of everyday life—that they did not aim to make men less selfish and cold-hearted or more charitable, generous, and kind. Remember, he warned the critics that, "the great preacher is a firm believer in the immediate second coming of Christ. . . . Why trouble himself about the affairs of the household, the street, and the mart, when he expects every moment to see the world rolled up like a scroll?"[31] In *l*, then, as one would expect, THE COMING OF CHRIST is in large print and thirty-one hymns are listed under it. "We ought to be limited in our range of selection of hymns," Moody once declared. "I have a profound conviction that the great size of our congregational hymn-books is killing congregational singing."[32] Not the body of *l* but its topical index reflects this conviction by its sparseness. Arranged in order of the number of hymns cited, CHRIST and CHRIST-related hymns head the list with 169 hymns distributed among FELLOWSHIP WITH CHRIST (thirty-seven hymns); THE BLOOD OF CHRIST (thirty-one); THE COMING OF CHRIST (thirty); THE CROSS OF CHRIST (twenty); CHRIST SOUGHT BY THE SINNER (fifteen); SUFFERINGS OF CHRIST (fourteen); CHRIST A FRIEND (nine); CHRIST SEEKING (nine); and CHRIST THE SHEPHERD (four). The next thirteen topics, in descending order are HEAVEN (eighty-four hymns); SALVATION (eighty-three); INVITATION (seventy-three); WORSHIP (sixty-eight); PRAISE (sixty-five); PRAYER (sixty-four); WORK (sixty-one); CONSECRATION (forty-three); LOVE (forty-three); CONFESSION (thirty-six); WARNING (thirty-four); REFUGE (thirty-four); and JOY (thirty-three).

Moody advocated limiting not only the selection of hymns, but also their length: "Two or three verses well sung and bearing upon the key-note or sub-ject of the meeting will do more good than a dozen verses poorly sung."[33] He admitted to preaching the same sermon over and over again.

Coda

Noting Moody's pungent, direct manner and use of apposite illustrations, Goodspeed compared Moody to Nettleton.[34] And there the study of four evangelists, four styles, four ways of looking at hymns comes full round. Moody is the minimalist, the master of the simple statement [theme] and variations. If we extend the musical analogy, Nettleton enjoyed the harmony implicit in chordal structure; Beecher gloried in the soaring melodies of the most lyrical passages; and Finney delighted in the reasoned logic of the coun-terpoint.

Through these four individuals, then, one glimpses how the indexing of hymnals advanced particular agendas or styles of evangelism. This becomes especially evident when these evangelists' hymnals are compared with others whose indexers had less overt personal agendas.

Notes

1. *The Methodist Hymnal* (New York: Eaton and Mains, 1907), 169–77.

2. Charles Nutter and Wilbur Tillett, *The Hymns and Hymn Writers of the Church* (New York: Eaton and Mains, 1911), 471–81.

3. Donald Hustad, *Jubilate! Church Music in the Evangelical Tradition* (Carol Stream, IL: Hope Publishing, 1981), 207.

4. Sydney E. Ahlstrom, *A Religious History of the American People* (New Haven: Yale University Press, 1972), 421.

5. Ahlstrom, *Religious History,* 60.

6. Hustad, *Jubilate!,* 207.

7. Timothy L. Smith, *Revivalism and Social Reform* (Baltimore: Johns Hopkins University Press, 1980), 60.

8. Thomas Know, *Life and Work of Henry Ward Beecher* (Hartford, CT: Hartford Publishing, 1887), 537.

9. Charles Grandison Finney, *Memoirs of Rev. Charles G. Finney Written by Him-self* (New York: Fleming H. Revell, 1876), 63.

10. Edgar J. Goodspeed, *A Full History of the Wonderful Career of Moody and Sankey in Great Britain and America* (Mt. Union, OH: L. U. Snead, 1870), iv.

11. Asahel Nettleton, *Village Hymns,* 7th ed. (New York: E. Sands, 1827) Preface, 5–6.

12. Bennet Tyler, *Memoir of the Life and Character of Rev. Asahel Nettleton, D.D.* (Boston: Doctrinal Tract and Book Society, 1850), 263.

13. Tyler, *Memoir of Asahel Nettleton,* 259.

14. R. Smith, *Recollections of Nettleton and the Great Revival of 1820* (Albany, NY: E. H. Pease, 1848), 73.

15. Tyler, *Memoir of Asahel Nettleton,* 261.

16. Ibid., 239.

17. Smith, *Revivalism,* 31.

18. John R. Howard, *Henry Ward Beecher, A Study of His Personality, Career, and Influence in Public Affairs* (New York: Fords, Howard and Hulbert, 1891).

19. Howard, *Henry Ward Beecher,* 13.

20. Know, *Life and Work of Henry Ward Beecher,* 320.

21. Henry Ward Beecher, *Plymouth Collection,* 1856, viii, iv.

22. N. A. Shenstone, *Anecdotes of Henry Ward Beecher,* (Chicago: R. R. Donnelly, 1887), 407.

23. Shenstone, *Anecdotes,* 418.

24. Howard, *Henry Ward Beecher,* 601.

25. Ibid., 592.

26. Goodspeed, *Moody and Sankey.*

27. Hustad, *Jubilate!,* 208.

28. Goodspeed, *Moody and Sankey,* 38.

29. Ibid., 238, 398.

30. Ibid., 238, 398, 239.

31. Ibid., 274.

32. Ibid., 584.

33. Ibid., 381.

34. Ibid., 202–3.

7

Fanny Crosby, William Doane, and the Making of Gospel Hymns in the Late Nineteenth Century

Edith L. Blumhofer

ONE SPRING DAY IN 1867, Fanny Crosby, a blind poet of growing repute, sat in a small upstairs apartment in lower Manhattan thinking through a new poem on the subject of Christlikeness. She dictated her lines to the first available amanuensis and summoned a messenger to carry her words to William Doane, a man she knew only by reputation. Doane, a church musician, inventor, and millionaire Cincinnati business executive, was visiting Manhattan, and Crosby's messenger found him in conversation with the Reverend W. C. Van Meter, superintendent of the Howard Mission, or Home for Little Wanderers, in the city's notorious Five Points neighborhood. The two were discussing Van Meter's wish for a new hymn for the Howard Mission's upcoming anniversary. Doane's objection that he had neither text nor tune was interrupted by the messenger's arrival with Crosby's "More Like Jesus Would I Be," and a note that read, "Mr. Doane: I feel impressed to send you this hymn; may God bless it! Fanny Crosby." To Van Meter's delight, Doane promptly composed a tune, and the hymn debuted at the mission's May anniversary:

> More like Jesus would I be,
> Let my Savior dwell in me;
> Fill my soul with peace and love,
> Make me gentle as a dove.
> More like Jesus while I go,
> Pilgrim in this world below
> Poor in spirit would I be;
> Let my Savior dwell in me.
>
> If he hears the raven's cry,
> If his ever watchful eye
> Marks the sparrows when they fall,

Surely he will hear my call;
He will teach me how to live,
All my sinful thoughts forgive;
Pure in heart I still would be;
Let my Savior dwell in me.

So began a Doane-Crosby collaboration, a partnership that left an enduring imprint on global evangelical song. The association accelerated Crosby's rise in the emerging business of Victorian hymnody. Crosby's lyrics set to Doane's tunes enjoyed enormous success, and during the late nineteenth-century heyday of D. L. Moody's revivals, they expressed and defined Victorian popular evangelicalism. Crosby's work with Doane perhaps best exemplifies the varieties, limitations, and possibilities that the world of late nineteenth-century American gospel song offered women.

First, the Howard Mission was a fitting endeavor to facilitate a Doane-Crosby connection. Both Crosby and Doane had a history of involvement through Protestant voluntary associations with the masses of humanity crowding the old downtowns of America's cities. Decades earlier, Protestants had begun taking in hand the problems associated with urban growth by supporting an ambitious array of schools, homes, industrial training, and feeding programs. In the late 1860s, faith-based outreaches played a central role in the gradual transformation of Manhattan slums even as they plied away at ameliorating other urban ills. Crosby in Manhattan, like Doane in Cincinnati, understood involvement in rescue missions and related endeavors as part of their Protestant social obligation. Since the 1840s, annual anniversary celebrations of their organized work for the common good had been a spring ritual for the greater New York area's Protestants. And new hymns for those celebrations offered powerful imaginative reminders of the core of piety at the heart of these strivings for a Christian America. Crosby had a circuit of rescue missions at which she occasionally spoke and more often sat among the wayward offering prayers and encouragement. Their anniversaries elicited from her pen hymns of celebration of the testimonies she heard of transformed lives.

Upon receiving Crosby's lyrics, "More Like Jesus," Doane located Crosby's rooms, paid her generously for the text, and stayed long enough to cement a friendship. By the time of this meeting in 1867, both Crosby and Doane had established reputations in the expanding world of gospel hymn production, Crosby's more recent than Doane's. Neither believed Doane's visit to Crosby a coincidence. Over decades the story of their meeting became part of the myth that nurtured convictions about providence, gospel hymnody, and Protestant evangelism. For their part, publishers quickly recognized a profitable opportunity. From 1867, the Doane-Crosby partnership proved lucrative for religious publishers, especially Biglow and Main, yielding some lasting "gospel favorites" that quickly made their way around the world. Among these molders and mirrors of contemporary evangelical priorities were "Jesus, Keep Me Near the Cross"; "Rescue the Perishing"; "Safe in the Arms of Jesus"; "Pass Me Not, O Gentle Saviour"; and "I Am Thine, O Lord."[1]

When Crosby and Doane met in 1867, the market for new forms of religious music was expanding exponentially. Their style of text and tune had clear antecedents in revival and camp meeting songs as well as in the Sunday school music that flourished after the 1840s. But the genre stood poised to tighten its hold on popular Protestantism in the 1870s, in large part through the unanticipated popularity across Britain and the United States of evangelist Dwight L. Moody and his songster, Ira Sankey.[2] Before Moody and Sankey, gospel hymns, with their choruses and simple message, had often been relegated to Sunday schools, conventions and the "social meetings" of the churches. They seldom intruded on the decorum of Sunday morning services, where church musicians complained that congregational singing languished. Moody and Sankey set American and British Protestants to singing catchy melodies that carried testimonies, stories, doctrine, and hope. In short, the evangelists collected and published resources to promote in song their "take" on evangelicalism, and their devoted public embraced the genre with enormous enthusiasm. Sankey found Crosby's texts, often set to Doane's tunes, among the most useful for his purposes. Under her own name and scores of pseudonyms, with Doane, Sankey, and others providing tunes, she crafted a substantial percentage of the text in Sankey's multiple *Gospel Hymns*, regarded in its day as "the most valuable musical property in the world."

When Crosby and Doane began to partner in 1867, questions about musical propriety had long agitated in America's Protestant churches. On the one hand, urbanization, industrialization, immigration, and other social and class tensions brought relentless and constant pressure for cultural relevance and accessible hymnody. On the other, church musicians voiced strong opinions about reverence and style. Amid the varied pressures that the larger patterns of social change exerted on religious life, Moody and Sankey came to represent a popular adaptation of the "old-time religion" that expressed itself in part in new eminently singable music and invigorated congregational song.[3] Independently and together, Crosby and Doane held a prominent place in Moody's and Sankey's efforts, and these indefatigable evangelists played an enormous role in popularizing their texts and tunes around the world.

In their personal lives, Doane and Crosby had striking similarities, yet profound differences. Both came of hardy English stock, and both spent their formative years in the northeast. From youth, Doane enjoyed expanding business success and traveled widely. Crosby's adult life focused almost entirely on the streets of Manhattan and Brooklyn. Doane enjoyed financial prosperity. Crosby, generous to a fault with her meager earnings, owned little. Doane was prominently associated with the Northern Baptist Convention. Crosby had far less direct denominational involvement until after the age of sixty when she joined Manhattan's Cornell Methodist Episcopal Church. Doane's business choices determined how some of Crosby's most popular lyrics were disseminated and remembered. It is impossible to do justice to either without the other, and together they offer a unique glimpse into the ethos of an emerging economic powerhouse of gospel song.

Fanny J. Crosby

Fanny Crosby took enormous pride in her lineage. The first Crosby's had arrived in Boston in 1635. Some of the clan married into Mayflower families, and Crosby cherished family lore that assigned family members places of influence in the Revolutionary War.

Intermarriage among the extended clan was common, and both of Fanny Crosby's parents were Crosbys.[4] John Crosby and his second wife, Mercy Crosby, welcomed Fanny into their modest home in Southeast, New York, on March 24, 1820. A few weeks later, ill-advised treatment of an eye irritation left the infant blind. The family determined to make the child's life as normal as possible, and so they refused to allow her blindness to keep her from performing daily chores or romping with playmates. She early displayed a decided ability to express herself in rhyme. Her first published poem appeared before 1835 in one of P. T. Barnum's earliest entrepreneurial ventures—a weekly paper published in Bethel, Connecticut, and called *Herald of Freedom*.

In 1835, Mercy Crosby enrolled Fanny in the New York Institution for the Blind, a new residential school in Manhattan.[5] Crosby thrived in her new surroundings. Her music and English teachers honed her skills and challenged her to excel. She learned to play the harp, organ, and piano as well as to compose texts and tunes. Her vocal music instructor, George Root, opened the world of popular music to her. She provided lyrics for his cantata, "The Flower Queen," a piece that enjoyed enormous success (from its debut in 1851) in schools as well as in the grassroots normal institutes of music that offered adult music education and teacher training around the country.[6] Root (who wrote tunes for religious songs as well as popular music) collaborated with Crosby on a second cantata and other popular songs that gained enormous vogue.[7] Root, not Crosby, reaped the financial gain.

In Manhattan, this daughter of the Puritans discovered her spiritual home in Methodism. At a fall revival in November 1850, during the singing of Isaac Watts's "Alas, and Did My Saviour Bleed," Crosby felt her heart warmed and responded to an evangelist's invitation at Manhattan's 30th Street Methodist Church. From 1850, Crosby's activated faith drove her to the streets and tenements of New York where she conversed with the lonely or assisted workers at the city's rescue missions. She tended the ill, worked for the temperance movement, and did what she could after the Civil War to support the YMCA, Christian Endeavor, and other nondenominational youth and camp meeting efforts. Her later songs would have wide appeal in part because her piety and values were shaped in a variety of Christian contexts and honed in the endeavors with which many ordinary Protestants identified. They welled from a Methodist's warmed heart, but they drew also from a Puritan heritage and the Episcopal liturgy, and they addressed topics of immediate concern to revivalist Protestants of the day.

Without any break, Crosby moved from student to teacher of English and history at the Institute, leaving the school only in 1858 when she married Alexander Van Alstine, a sight-impaired musician whom she had come to know at the school. For the next forty years, the couple lived, sometimes together, sometimes apart, in either Manhattan or Brooklyn. At her husband's request, Crosby continued to use her maiden name.

In 1864, Crosby made the acquaintance of William Bradbury, proprietor of Bradbury Publishing and the Bradbury Piano Company. A prosperous Manhattan publisher, composer, organist, choral director, and music instructor as well as a fixture among the city's middle-class Protestants, Bradbury first introduced Crosby to the circle of people who supplied texts and tunes for the rapidly expanding market in religious song.[8] Bradbury played a central role in the evolution of new Protestant music, contributing tunes still paired with perennial favorites like "Jesus Loves Me" and "Just as I am." He had vision and aptitude and a business through which to realize his ambitions.

Crosby had written many song lyrics, and some had achieved a degree of popular acclaim, but she had never tried her hand at a hymn. From 1864, her output exceeded Bradbury's expectations, and until she died in 1915, Crosby's name was inextricably linked to the new music that poured from his press. Most of Crosby's enduring hymns were written early in her hymn-writing career. They brought her to the attention of the era's evangelists—Moody,

Sankey, Philip Bliss, Daniel Whittle, Philip Phillips—whose popularization of her lyrics and regard for their author helped make her name a household word among Protestants. She had known success before, but the response to her hymns far exceeded any acclaim accorded her earlier achievements.

William Howard Doane

Hymns are born of the marriage of text and tune, and for these tunes, Crosby often depended on William Doane. Like her, Doane traced his American ancestry to Boston in the 1630s. He was born in Connecticut in 1832 and showed an early aptitude for both music and business. In 1851, he became financial director for J. A. Fay and Co., manufacturers of woodworking machinery. He performed so well that in 1856 the company sent him to Chicago to superintend its western interests. In 1861, Doane, not yet thirty years old, took over the company, moving to Cincinnati where the firm's main offices had been expanding since 1852.

Doane displayed a genius for improving and inventing woodworking machinery. Over the course of his career, he registered over seventy patents and was widely acknowledged for his mechanical as well as his business acumen. His business achievements brought him wealth, but his musical religious work gave him enduring satisfaction.

Doane devoted himself to religious music after an experience in 1862 that bore the familiar hallmarks of classic conversion narratives. Plagued by heart problems and desperate for healing, he vowed that if God restored him to health, he would dedicate his musical interests to evangelism and write texts and tunes for the masses. His gradual recovery followed, and he promptly pursued his new purpose. "This vow I have sacredly kept," he testified in his declining years, "and every dollar received from this source has been given back to the Lord."[9] Those dollars were much more than an average salary: Doane's daughter later estimated that her father earned between $20,000 and $25,000 per year from his music.

Doane wrote gospel songs and did religious work as a hobby—a hobby that consumed him. He preached Sunday mornings at Cincinnati's Bethesda Mission (which he also largely supported) and superintended Sunday school Sunday afternoons at Mt. Auburn Baptist Church near his hilltop Cincinnati home. He used both settings as musical laboratories and wrote many of his tunes for these congregations, always with a larger public in mind. Active in his Baptist denomination, he filled a term as president of the American Baptist Publication Society and editor of its official hymnal.

Collaborators

Doane's many interests necessitated frequent travel, and so a blind woman at home in Manhattan tenements and a denizen of a Cincinnati mansion found collaboration possible. Doane first wrote Sunday school and evangelistic songs in response to a sense of calling and found immediate venues for his compositions in his own Sunday school and religious work. Observing that children sang "mournful lays" and that few religious songs were addressed to the unconverted, he attempted to supply a perceived need. Crosby, meanwhile, wrote her first hymn texts under contract with Biglow and Main. She might be given a subject or a tune; she then supplied text—"hymns on demand," one reporter called it. As her songs were published in the inexpensively bound songbooks that served Sunday schools and social meetings, she gained repute that expanded her opportunities. Music publishers both created and responded to a constant demand for new materials and so Crosby's many texts, good or bad, generally appeared in print, at least briefly. Beyond her contract with Biglow and Main, Crosby collaborated and published wherever she chose. Doane expanded her world and carried her texts into new venues, including the hymnal he edited for his denomination.

Biglow and Main counted Doane among its authors, too; also prominent in the company was the era's most important single gospel song figure, Ira Sankey. Doane's first book, *Sabbath School Gems,* appeared in 1862, followed by *Little Sunbeams* in 1864. 1867 saw the publication of *Silver Spray,* a collection that sold 300,000 copies in two months. He released these first efforts through the John Church Company, a Cincinnati firm in which he had an interest. Like other hymnal editors, Doane brought such books out as quickly as possible. They were cheaply assembled and not intended to last. New editions or entire new collections were constantly forthcoming. Publishers seemed to adopt the policy of publishing as much as possible and allowing popular taste and demand to determine what survived. Songs that failed to "catch on" or that were appropriate only to specific occasions simply disappeared after a few months or years. Crosby wrote thousands of such texts, many under contract for specific books or publishers, but fewer than twenty remain in general use, and some were never published. She owned the rights to none of them.

Crosby and Doane collaborated in different settings, and Crosby's versatility enabled her to respond to any request Doane made. Her visits to the Doane family yielded some of the duo's best-known collaborations. During Crosby's stay at Sunny Side in 1875, for example, Doane played a melody for Crosby. In the evening, as the family sat outside watching the sunset, they conversed about the nearness of God. Before retiring that night, Crosby composed words for Doane's new tune—words that arose from her musings on the family's evening conversation. Doane published them as the hymn, "I Am Thine, O Lord," a song Sankey and Moody soon popularized:

> I am thine, O Lord; I have heard thy voice,
> And it told thy love to me;
> But I long to rise in the arms of faith
> And be closer drawn to thee.
>
> Refrain:
> Draw me nearer, nearer blessed Lord
> To the cross where thou hast died;
> Draw me nearer, nearer, nearer blessed Lord
> To thy precious bleeding side.

When they did not have the luxury of prolonged periods together, Crosby adapted to Doane's schedule. He wrote to request songs on particular topics, and Crosby responded with text to suit. For example, he once asked Crosby for a hymn on the cross, and she framed the poem, "Jesus, Keep Me Near the Cross":

> Jesus, keep me near the cross,
> There a precious fountain
> Free to all, a healing stream,
> Flows from Calvary's mountain.
>
> Refrain:
> In the cross, in the cross
> Be my glory ever,
> 'Til my raptured soul shall find
> Rest beyond the river.

In the next stanzas, Crosby moved from prayer to testimony and resolve:

> Near the cross, a trembling soul,
> Love and mercy found me;
> There the Bright and Morning Star
> Shed its beams around me.

Near the cross I'll watch and wait,
Hoping, trusting ever,
'Til I reach the golden strand
Just beyond the river.

Like many Crosby texts, these words echoed familiar passages of the King James Version of the Bible. Crosby sent them to Doane who, at a meeting in Baltimore used them with a tune he had recently composed, and a widely loved hymn was born. Doane's tune was simple and singable, suited to congregational use in four-part harmony.

This hymn reveals reasons for the wide contemporary popularity of Crosby-Doane hymns. Crosby's use of the first person seemed to make Crosby transparent and vulnerable—to bare her soul while also providing language to assist congregations to form and articulate corporate desire (and holding up for any who did not yet have the desire a description of spiritual hunger to which to aspire). Such personal language had the dual task of showing the errant what they lacked and helping the convinced to define a common goal and then measure experience by it. These interwoven prayers and testimonies, then, expressed ideals for evangelical piety. As songs of the pilgrimage that *was* the Christian life, they were highly personal, with exhortation implied indirectly (in prayers and testimonies) as well as directly. Texts described emotions and sentiments appropriate to the evangelical experience; sung corporately, they enabled singers to participate in a community shaped by evangelical sentiment.

"Jesus, Keep Me Near the Cross" quickly came into its own. Moody and Sankey returned to the United States in 1875 from a two-year evangelistic blitz that took Britain by storm and made their American debut in November 1875 in Brooklyn. The city's five hundred churches scrambled to find nearly 1,000 volunteer musicians, ushers, and counselors. When Moody strode to the platform of DeWitt Talmage's cavernous Brooklyn Tabernacle on November 19, 1875, Sankey was seated at his pump organ opening the service with this new Crosby-Doane hymn—"Jesus, Keep Me Near the Cross."[10]

In February 1876, Moody and Sankey returned to New York for a more ambitious effort at the New York Hippodrome. There Sankey introduced another new Crosby-Doane hymn to his 1,250-voice choir—"Rescue the Perishing," another text Crosby provided in response to Doane's written request for lyrics on the subject:

Rescue the perishing, care for the dying,
Snatch them in pity from sin and the grave;

Weep o'er the erring one, lift up the fallen,
Tell them of Jesus, the mighty to save.

The choir easily mastered the simple text, and the *New York Times* recognized immediately that it had what it took to become a Protestant favorite. Doane's stirring marchlike tune summoned Christian soldiers to duty in a musical style recently made familiar by the Salvation Army. Crosby's text expressed her sense that the "lost" were not beyond help. Like Moody's sermons, Crosby's hymns did not dwell on damnation and judgment; rather, they addressed wandering errant individuals who could respond to loving concern. Broken lives, Crosby insisted, could best be reached by Christians whose hearts brimmed with compassion:

Down in the human heart, crushed by the tempter,
Feelings lie buried that grace can restore.
Touched by a loving heart, wakened by kindness,
Chords that are broken will vibrate once more.

Not all Crosby-Doane hymns found immediate enduring popularity, and some that did proved to lack staying power. The hymn for which the two have been best known since World War II, "To God Be the Glory," seemed unremarkable when it appeared in 1875, and Ira Sankey—who could presumably have given it visibility—overlooked it when he compiled his definitive hymnal, *Gospel Hymns 1–6*. Although it appeared occasionally in hymnals, it was not widely known until 1954 when Billy Graham's song leader, Cliff Barrows, discovered it during Graham's London Crusade and taught it to the crusade choir. Their enthusiasm proved contagious, and the hymn has since appeared in a wide array of Protestant hymnals, evangelical and other, often in the opening section among hymns of adoration:

To God be the glory, great things he hath done!
So loved he the world that he gave us his son
Who yielded his life an atonement for sin,
And opened the life-gate that all may go in.

Refrain:
Praise the Lord! Praise the Lord!
Let the earth hear his voice!
Praise the Lord! Praise the Lord!
Let the people rejoice!

O, come to the Father through Jesus, the Son,
And give him the glory, great things he hath done.

O perfect redemption, the purchase of blood—
To every believer the promise of God.
The vilest offender who truly believes
That moment from Jesus a pardon receives!

Refrain

Great things he hath taught us; great things he hath done!
And great our rejoicing through Jesus, the Son;
But purer, and higher, and greater will be
Our wonder, our transport, when Jesus we see.

The process of preparation of another popular Crosby-Doane hymn (perhaps the most popular of all in their lifetimes), "Safe in the Arms of Jesus,"
illustrates how adept the two became at working together. The story is deeply
embedded in Crosby lore. It varies slightly, depending on the narrator, but
the different renderings have enough in common to suggest the facts. Doane
was changing trains in New York, en route from Cincinnati to Philadelphia,
when on impulse he called on Crosby, whistled a tune he had composed on
the train, and requested fresh text in twenty minutes. She complied effort-
lessly, dictating text on a topic she had been mulling over, and Doane made
his train connection. He sang "Safe in the Arms of Jesus" that night in the
St. Denis Hotel in Philadelphia. This hastily prepared number became perhaps the era's most popular American hymn. Its use in the 1880s in the public mourning for Presidents Garfield and Grant testified to its place in the
Protestant imagination.[11] Its themes of safety and repose and its focus on the
loving Christ appealed widely in an era of cultural uncertainty and high mortality. Crosby and Doane saw the text as descriptive of the believer's relationship to Christ in this life, but the public seized on the text to comfort the
grieving:

Safe in the arms of Jesus, safe on his gentle breast,
There by his love o'ershaded sweetly my soul shall rest.
Hark! 'tis the voice of angels borne in a song to me,
Over the fields of glory, over the jasper sea.

Refrain:
Safe in the arms of Jesus, safe on his gentle breast,
There by his love o'ershaded, sweetly my soul shall rest.

Safe in the arms of Jesus, safe from corroding care,
Safe from the world's temptations, sin cannot harm me there.
Free from the blight of sorrow, free from my doubts and fears;
Only a few more trials, only a few more tears!

Refrain

Jesus, my heart's dear refuge, Jesus has died for me;
Firm on the Rock of Ages ever my trust shall be.
Here let me wait with patience, wait till the night is o'er;
Wait till I see the morning break on the golden shore.

Doane promptly filed for copyright for both text and tune. He thereafter routinely refused permission to use the text without the tune, thus assuring that the two, if remembered at all, would be remembered together. This became Doane's ploy. However text or tune evolved—whichever came first, whoever suggested the topic—Doane copyrighted both as a single unit.[12] In addition to composing the tunes that sang Crosby's words into millions of hearts, then, Doane wielded enormous influence on the public use of Crosby texts through his initiative in copyrighting them. The copyright laws evolved in the late nineteenth century, and confusion about changing regulations as well as blatant violations plagued the era. Doane followed legislative and legal developments closely and exploited his connections to push for fairness.

In the highly competitive world of gospel song publishing, Doane kept close watch on the use of his and Crosby's collaborations. If he favored a project or valued a colleague, he might agree to the use of a song like "Rescue the Perishing" for $10. To discourage use, he simply raised the price to $50 or more. He always rejected requests to publish text only. He often gave permission to use hymns free of charge, or he might opt to charge a single modest fee for the use of several songs.[13] Sometimes he traded with friends, giving permission for the use of a song for which he held the copyright in exchange for the use of another. In the 1890s, Doane and Baptist songwriter Robert Lowry drew up a formal agreement to share their songs without compensation for publication in hymnals either edited.[14] They also agreed with Biglow and Main on a fixed percentage for their songs published in Biglow and Main hymnals.

Some requests for permissions came from sources that reveal the extent of the popular appeal of certain gospel hymns. In 1890, Doane granted the Watchtower Bible and Tract Society (Jehovah's Witnesses) permission to use "Near the Cross," "Safe in the Arms of Jesus," and several other hymns for $80 in their *Poems and Hymns of Millennial Dawn.* Certain Doane-Crosby songs could not be obtained for any price: Biglow and Main identified a few "stock pieces" they insisted should be theirs alone, among them the blind Crosby's widely popular anticipation of seeing Christ, text for which Doane composed a tune:[15]

> Some day the silver chord will break
> And I no more as now shall sing,
> But, oh, the joy when I awake
> Within the palace of the king.
>
> Refrain:
> And I shall see him face to face,
> And tell the story, "saved by grace."

Doane knew the pitfalls of the business side of hymn production. He sat on the board of directors of the financially troubled Newhall and Evans Music Company, a Cincinnati-based firm that failed in the 1880s. He knew well the affairs of another Cincinnati-based publisher, John Church and Company. On close terms with the owners of Biglow and Main, he worried about change when Lucius Biglow retired and Sankey's son, Ira Allen Sankey, took the helm of the business. Doane and his cohorts dreaded generational change and considered that the stalwarts of the gospel hymn movement were being displaced by unknown new voices. In the end, he found the young Sankey a friend rather than a foe, but not everyone agreed. Musical Evangelist Charles Alexander and Moody Bible Institute's D. B. Towner failed to get along with Allen Sankey. The two sought permissions from Biglow and Main without manifesting any inclination to cooperate. Sankey accused Alexander of attempting to use Biglow and Main material to build up a rival publishing business and responded by allowing his requests for permissions to languish.[16] Doane couched the permissions he gave Towner (always reluctantly granted) in the language of ministry and regretted Charles Alexander's disinterest in cooperation. On his part, though, Ira D. Sankey exercised his prerogative as the best-known gospel song promoter of the period to insist that Biglow and Main publish no other collection of gospel hymns during the first year of the

American publication of his own *Gospel Hymns*. Issues surrounding copyrights and sales always haunted collaborative endeavors.

Handling permissions was one way in which copyright owners wielded limited control over the burgeoning industry. Some blatantly flaunted copyright laws. Doane sometimes protested. When he noticed Crosby's "Rescue the Perishing" published with another tune without permission, for example, he promptly dictated a stern letter demanding an explanation. He often received inquiries about copyrighted songs from small independent publishers eager to advance their own interests but wary of breaking copyright laws. Some who flaunted the law ran short-lived operations and simply disappeared from the scene. Others flirted with the letter of the law, making slight adaptations to the work of others. And still others simply violated the rules, paid off small complainants, and dared others to sue.

Composers and text writers whose work gained international renown faced added copyright woes. During the 1880s, American literary figures as well as hymn writers agitated for an international copyright law. The February 1886 issue of the *Century* devoted space to opinions from forty-five prominent American authors demanding an international copyright law as part of "an honorable public policy." The magazine then polled musicians and discovered similar sentiment fueled by impatience with legislators indifferent to the need. The overwhelming argument that the point was moral, not economic, seemed lost on a Congress more concerned with preserving special interests than with crusading for change. Crosby's former teacher and collaborator, George Root, made the effort to review the musical catalogue of the British Museum searching for English reprints of American music. He found over twenty-three pages listing his own music, published in England, for which he received no compensation. This situation, repeated many times over, troubled especially writers of tunes whose music could easily be "pillaged by the whole world."[17]

The enormous popularity of gospel songs assured their rapid translation and use wherever Protestant missionaries traveled. Their direct appeals and catchy tunes made them attractive evangelistic tools. Some of the translation work occurred in the United States and proceeded under American copyright conventions. Walter Rauschenbusch, the German Baptist social gospeler, for example, undertook to translate numerous Crosby texts and other gospel hymns himself; for others, he commissioned translations. Rauschenbusch and Sankey together edited several German hymnals based on Sankey's bestselling *Gospel Hymns*. Biglow and Main copyrighted the translations, and the German texts were set to their common American tunes.[18] Further, the collaboration of Rauschenbusch and Sankey indicates how music pushed at theological boundaries that often otherwise seemed impermeable. Rauschenbusch moved on to endorse a radically different style of hymnody, but his work with Sankey left an enduring imprint on German evangelicalism in the United States and abroad.

Individuals who held copyrights to texts or tunes did not necessarily make much money.[19] Sometimes publishers held copyrights, as Biglow and Main did on many Crosby texts. Under early copyright laws, publishers learned through difficult experiences how to proceed more efficiently.[20] For example, Biglow and Main once copyrighted a hymnal only to learn later that since the hymns were not copyrighted individually the copyright was good only under the title and in the collection in which the songs first appeared. When the book went out of print, copyright on the hymns effectively lapsed. The sheer cost of copyrighting influenced such decision-making. The charge to copyright a single item—book or hymn—was 50 cents. Whoever held copyright had to complete a separate form for each item, and a return certificate cost an additional 50 cents. A book with three hundred songs could cost $300 or $1 to copyright, and thrifty publishers opted at first for the obvious choice. They also had to pay permission fees for songs copyrighted by individuals. Smaller publishers often found the costs of complying with copyright regulations could be daunting. The law further provided that no copyright was valid unless notice was given by inserting in every copy published notice of copyright. It imposed a fine of $100 for inserting copyright notice without actually holding copyright. Original copyrights ran for twenty-eight years. The holder or their heirs could renew for an additional fourteen years. At the end of that period, others might obtain copyright. For example, Crosby and Doane collaborated on "Hide Me," a song first copyrighted by Biglow and Main. At the expiration of the original copyright in 1913, Doane renewed it in his name, gaining the rights for an additional fourteen years. Editors sometimes seized such opportunities to copyright individual hymns, thus assuring personal benefit from the work of others. For better or worse, the hymn publishing business exposed the competitive greed as well as the business genius of a cohort of people who wielded expanding power in American evangelicalism.

The editorial cost for compiling hymnals could be considerable. For example, Doane bought the right to use "No Not One" for $5 for his book, *Precious Jewels*.[21] Higher fees for other permissions offset that low cost. It was obviously cheaper to solicit new material than to compile books of other people's work. Sometimes instead of charging for use, Doane allowed a hymn to be used for a percentage of sales. So, in 1908 he received $7.50 from Biglow and Main from the sale of hymnals that included his and Crosby's "Rescue the Perishing." Such royalties were typically paid quarterly and were generally 1 cent per copy of a book. Doane and Robert Lowry had a formal agreement with Lucius Biglow and Sylvester Main for royalties that ranged from 1 to 10 cents on their Biglow and Main books.

Fanny Crosby did not benefit directly from the copyrights Doane held for her texts and his tunes. Indirectly, though, she realized more from her association with Doane than a fee or a set percentage on her hymn texts might have yielded. A generous and principled man, Doane showered Crosby with kindness and thoughtfulness. Occasional trips to his Cincinnati mansion became the highlights of her life. Enveloped in the warmth of a loving family and surrounded by all that money could provide, Crosby found renewal and inspiration. Doane's wife and daughters doted on her, and when she could not attend family occasions, she sent poems filled with fond expressions to this, her second family. Occasional gifts of money, furnishings or warm apparel from the Doanes added lavish comforts to Crosby's sparse life. And Doane looked out for her interests when he felt people manipulated her for their own advantage. His frequent travels and, later, his prolonged stays at his summer home in Rhode Island, brought Doane and Crosby into regular contact, and their common circle of close friends—most of them other gospel hymn writers—helped Doane look out for Crosby even from a distance.

Neither Doane nor Crosby admitted feeling limited or taxed by contracts or requests. Doane always carried a small notebook in which he made notations when subjects or tunes came to mind. He whiled away long hours of railroad travel by devoting himself to gospel music. He liked to say that he never used gospel music that did not "move" him. And apparently his music "moved" others, too. In 1892, at the closing meeting of a huge Christian Endeavor Convention in Manhattan's Madison Square Garden, four of the five hymns "which burst from the hearts of the different delegations to express their desire" were William Doane's, and some of the texts were Crosby's.[22]

Although blind, Crosby liked to compose while holding a book. She worked on her poetry in her highly disciplined mind, retaining, reviewing, and editing it until someone called to whom she could dictate. Stories abound of hymns that poured spontaneously from her at the suggestion of a subject or the playing of a tune, but she said she composed best in the quiet of the night and when moved by particular circumstances.[23] Crosby hymns often followed a pattern. Like much of the Protestant piety of the period, conservative and liberal, they tended to focus on Christ—the Savior, Friend, Protector. They often exulted in the prospect of sight—"And I shall see Him face to face and tell the story, Saved by Grace"; "When with the ransomed in glory His face I at last shall see"; "But purer, and higher, and greater will be our wonder, our transport, when Jesus we see." And they typically moved from the realities of life to the certainties of the hereafter: "All the way my Savior leads me; O the fullness of his love! / Perfect rest to me is promised in my father's house above." Like many evangelicals, Crosby also found compelling the twin notions of safe shelter from the worldly unrest and personal submission to divine sovereignty.

After serious illness in the winter of 1900, Crosby moved to Bridgeport, Connecticut, where her sisters and nieces provided care until her death in February 1915. (Her husband died in Brooklyn in 1902 and was buried in an unmarked grave in an out-of-the-way corner of a Queens cemetery.) As she grew older, her irrepressible cheerfulness and encouraging spirit made her a popular participant in youth conventions under the auspices of the YMCA or Christian Endeavor. A member of the King's Daughters, Crosby appeared occasionally on the platform of the Northfield Conferences, at Chautauqua assemblies, and at the Methodist campground at Round Lake, New York, where, in 1901, she was crowned poet laureate. In her later years, Protestant churches chose to honor her by setting aside Fanny Crosby Sundays near her March 24 birthdate.[24] On these Sundays, congregations of many denominations acknowledged her influence on their religious practice by singing her hymns, interspersing them with a narrative of her life and incidents of the songs, thus reinforcing the sense among Protestants that they knew this woman whose turns of phrase helped mold their identity.

Doane received similar adulation. His friends insisted that Doane "made" Crosby while hers thought she "made" him. The truth was somewhere in between. Crosby and Doane mirrored as well as molded one popular venue of American Protestant piety. Crosby's lyrics and Doane's tunes arose out of their lived experience of American Protestant Christianity as it played itself out in the Sunday schools, revival meetings, youth conventions, and rescue missions they frequented. Legends in their day, the two made an enduring contribution to the corpus of American Protestant song. Over the years, critics have debunked her poetry and his tunes, but millions of Protestants nonetheless enthusiastically embraced both, using her words to focus their spiritual yearnings and finding his tunes accessible and catchy.[25] Some critics have been as uneasy about the larger spiritual and cultural tradition Crosby and Doane represented as about their specific creations.[26]

The hymns Crosby and Doane created offered their singers common voice, with text and tune shaping a community of believers around the texts printed in the hymnal. Both text and tune played roles in popularizing metaphors and perceptions of meaning that nurtured evangelical spirituality across Protestant denominations and movements. Crosby and Doane seemed to illustrate a contemporary's observation: "There is no surer road to popularity than to become the author of a popular tune that can be sung in church, Sunday school and home."[27]

Crosby remained active until a few weeks before her death in Bridgeport, Connecticut, on February 12, 1915. She dictated her last hymn the evening before she died. By then, Doane was gravely ill. He died at his Watch Hill, Rhode Island, home December 23, 1915.

Despite the inevitable sifting that set aside many of their hymns, Crosby and Doane crafted enduring gospel hymns that molded and mirrored American evangelical Protestantism and took their place in its expressions worldwide.

Notes

1. For a contemporary assessment of Doane, see special issue of *Christian Endeavor World,* January 25, 1912, in honor of his eightieth birthday; Woodman Bradbury, "William Howard Doane," *The Standard,* January 29, 1916, 681–82; John Emerson Montague, "William Howard Doane," *Watchman-Examiner,* September 24, 1931, 1228–29.

2. Wilbur F. Crafts, *Song Victories of "the Bliss and Sankey Hymns"* (Boston: D. Lothrop, 1877); Ira Sankey, *My Life and the Story of the Gospel Hymns* (New York: Harper, 1907); Ian Bradley, *Abide with Me: The Social World of Victorian Hymnody* (Chicago: GIA Publications, 1997); Bruce Evensen, *God's Man for the Gilded Age* (New York: Oxford University Press, 2003).

3. Sandra Sizer analyzed aspects of the social implications of gospel hymnody in her *Gospel Hymns and Social Religion: The Rhetoric of Nineteenth-Century Revivalism* (Philadelphia: Temple University Press, 1978).

4. The principal sources for Crosby's life are her several autobiographies: *Memories of Eighty Years* (Boston: J. H. Earle, 1906); Samuel Trevena Jackson, ed., *Fanny Crosby's Story of Ninety-Four Years* (New York: Fleming H. Revell, 1915); Fanny Crosby and Robert Lowry, *Bells at Evening* (New York: Biglow and Main, 1897). As Crosby's fame grew, many periodicals carried sketches of her life. See, for example, G. H. Sandison, "Fannie Crosby: Writer of Hymns," *National Magazine* 9 (1898–99): 548–50; J. L. Harbour, "A Blind Singer," *Union Signal* June 5, 1902, 7; "A Life of Service," *Union Signal,* March 23, 1905, 5; Henry L. Shumway, "New England's Hymn-Writer, *New*

England Magazine 32 (1905): 313-15. A standard biography is Bernard Ruffin, *Fanny Crosby* (Philadelphia: United Church Press, 1976). See also Edith L. Blumhofer, *"Her Heart Can See": The Life and Hymns of Fanny J. Crosby* (Grand Rapids, MI: William B. Eerdmans, 2005).

5. A history is posted at www.nyise.org/history.

6. The best source for the extent, growth, and content of the normal institute movement in the 1850s is the *New York Musical World,* successor to the *Message Bird* (1849-52) and predecessor of the *Musical Review and Musical World,* each of which document the activities and opinions of the major advocates of public music education.

7. Lydia Avery Coonley, "George F. Root and His Songs," *New England Magazine* 19 (January 1896): 555-70.

8. Ellen Jane Porter, "William Bradbury, the Camp Meeting Spiritual, and the Gospel Song," *The Hymn* 34 (1983): 34-40.

9. William Howard Doane, "How I Came to Write Sacred Music," Doane Collection, American Baptist Historical Society (ABHS), Colgate-Rochester Seminary, Rochester, N.Y.

10. "Moody and Sankey," *New York Times,* November 20, 1875, 2.

11. See, for example, "Northern Ohio Doing Reverence to Garfield," *New York Times,* September 26, 1881; "Playing on Muffled Bells," *New York Times,* August 10, 1885.

12. All of Crosby's collaborators did not proceed in similar fashion. The words for "Blessed Assurance," written as Crosby's response to her first hearing of a tune by her friend, Brooklyn socialite Phoebe Palmer Knapp, were copyrighted separately from the tune. Knapp's millionaire husband, Joseph Fairchild Knapp, copyrighted his wife's music, a custom he followed with all of her compositions. He copyrighted only what she created. Nonetheless, Knapp's tune is never sung to other words, and Crosby's words are seldom sung to another tune.

13. William J. Kirkpatrick to William H. Doane, March 10, 1909, Doane Collection, ABHS.

14. Lowry to Doane, October 21, 1895, Doane Collection, ABHS.

15. Hubert P. Main to Doane, March 9, 1904, Box 9, Doane Collection, ABHS.

16. Ira Allen Sankey to Doane, January 28, 1909, Doane Collection, Box 4, ABHS.

17. "Open Letters," *The Century* 33 (1887): 969-73.

18. *Evangeliums-Lieder 1 und 2 mit deutschen Kernliedern, ausgewählt und herausgegeben von Walter Rauschenbusch und Ira D. Sankey* (New York: Biglow and Main, 1890).

19. The best account of the business side of nineteenth-century American music

is Russell Sanjek, *American Popular Music and Its Business,* 3 vols. (New York: Oxford University Press, 1988).

20. On copyright, see Aubert J. Clark, *The Movement for International Copyright in Nineteenth-Century America* (Washington, DC: Catholic University of America Press, 1960; Ronald V. Bettig, "Critical Perspectives on the History and Philosophy of Copyright," *Critical Studies in Mass Communication* 9 (June 1992): 131–55.

21. George C. Hugg to Doane, n.d., Doane Collection, ABHS.

22. Mary Carr Merritt, "A Maker of Sweet Melodies," *Christian Endeavor World,* January 25, 1912, 323.

23. Ira Sankey included numerous "incidents" of Crosby hymns in his autobiography, *My Life and the Story of the Gospel Hymns.* Crosby includes a chapter of hymn stories in her *Memories of Eighty Years.*

24. For example, "Fanny Crosby Day," *New York Times,* March 27, 1905, 3.

25. Mrs. A. B. Blake, "Church Music in America," *Harpers Monthly Magazine* 58 (April 1879): 734.

26. Keith Watkins, "A Few Kind Words for Fanny Crosby," *Worship* 51, no. 3 (May 1977): 248–59

27. Matthew Hale Smith, *Sunshine and Shadow in New York* (Hartford, CT: J. B. Burr, 1869), 219.

III
Understanding the Classical Era of American Protestantism through Hymns

8
Heritage and Hymnody

Richard Allen and the Making of African Methodism

Dennis C. Dickerson

WESLEYAN EVANGELISM IN the Delmarva Peninsula during the mid-eighteenth century resulted in numerous conversions among poor and middling whites and free and slave blacks. Francis Asbury, "the builder of American Methodism," arrived in Philadelphia on October 27, 1771, and thereafter preached throughout the Middle Atlantic. In 1775 he landed in Virginia and added the Upper South to his itinerary. Neither Asbury nor other Methodist ministers neglected Delaware, where in 1772 he preached at Newcastle "where the Lord favoured me," and then filled his mind with "Divine peace." These efforts in Delaware proved crucial to the future of Methodism. There in 1777 the conversion of Richard Allen unleashed forces that neither Asbury nor the Delaware slave could have envisioned.[1]

Richard Allen, the founder of the African Methodist Episcopal Church (AME), established the denomination to reclaim the spiritual fervor and the religious zeal that American Methodism had gradually lost. He strictly adhered to the Methodist Discipline, he eschewed growing Wesleyan formalism, and he vigorously encouraged the singing of hymns. In fact, Allen's total embrace of hymnody became the principal means through which he developed the African Methodist Episcopal Church into a thoroughly Protestant and a conspicuously Wesleyan denomination.

Richard Allen, born a slave on February 14, 1760, in Philadelphia, Pennsylvania, was sold as a boy with his family in around 1768 to Stokeley Sturgis of Kent County, Delaware. Benjamin Chew, the family's Pennsylvania owner, had a 1,000-acre plantation that was near the Sturgis farm.[2] Although Allen remembered Sturgis as "a very tender, humane man," he was an impecunious owner. Economic difficulties compelled Sturgis to sell Allen's mother and three of his siblings. Allen observed: "I had it often impressed upon my mind that I should one day enjoy my freedom; for slavery is a bitter pill, notwithstanding we had a good master." Because Sturgis was constantly in debt,

Allen feared that after his owner's death "we were liable to be sold to the highest bidder." Hence, Allen and his brother convinced Sturgis to allow them to purchase their freedom. Allen achieved this objective in 1783 after he earned money by cutting wood, working in a brickyard, and performing other arduous chores.[3]

Allen was a quintessential Wesleyan. He was among the first generation of Americans both black and white whom Methodist circuit riders converted to Christianity. He imbibed their zeal for the gospel, their burden to save the lost, and their ubiquitous presence in various venues where they preached in churches, in camp meetings, and in the countryside to rich and poor, black and white, free and slave. Methodist evangelicalism and egalitarianism depended upon deep religiosity and spirituality. These Methodist characteristics became a standard by which Allen would judge future Wesleyan practices and assess their adherence to the Christian faith as he understood it.

Allen conspicuously bore the marks of Methodism. Wesleyan evangelists initially came to New York City in 1766. In that year, Betty, a New York slave, was reputed to be the first Methodist convert in the British North American colonies. A decade later a Methodist minister converted Allen to Christianity. Allen's conversion experience, which he recounted years after the event, conformed to testimonies typical to the late eighteenth and early nineteenth centuries. "I was awakened and brought to see myself, poor, wretched and undone," he declared, "and without the mercy of God must be lost." Thereafter, he "obtained mercy through the blood of Christ." Subsequently, after conversations with "many, old, experienced Christians," Allen doubted the authenticity of his conversion. He then sought "the Lord afresh." Allen recollected that, "I went with my head bowed down for many days. My sins were a heavy burden. I was tempted to believe there was no mercy for me. I cried unto the Lord both day and night. One night I thought hell would be my portion. I cried unto Him who delighteth to hear prayers of a poor sinner, and all of a sudden my dungeon shook, my chains flew off, and, glory to God, I cried. My soul was filled. I cried, enough for me—the Saviour died. Now my confidence was strengthened that the Lord, for Christ's sake, had heard my prayers and pardoned all my sins."[4] In the narrative account of his conversion, Allen relied on language that Methodists often used to describe their encounter with the Holy Spirit. At the point of his conversion Allen fervently exclaimed in 1777 that, "my dungeon shook, my chains flew off." Another Methodist convert, an English soldier in 1743, similarly, declared that, "my chains fell off, my heart was free."[5] Allen clearly had learned the lexicon of conversion and had mastered the rituals of spiritual discovery that characterized Methodist people.

After his conversion, Allen, still a slave of Stokeley Sturgis, joined a Methodist Society, belonged to John Gray's class, and met "his class for several years." His evangelical fervor soon affected his mother, a brother, a sister, and Sturgis himself. Allen convinced Sturgis to allow visiting Methodist preachers, including the prominent Freeborn Garrettson, to hold services at his house. Garrettson showed Sturgis the sinfulness of slave owning. As a result, Sturgis was converted and allowed Allen and his brother to purchase their freedom. After his manumission, Allen traveled throughout the Middle Atlantic colonies as a Methodist preacher and was invited to accompany Francis Asbury and later Richard Whatcoat of the Baltimore Circuit. During the early 1780s, Allen developed attributes that his Wesleyan affiliations probably nurtured. Hence honesty, integrity, and piety became characteristics automatically associated with him. When Allen accumulated sufficient funds to pay Sturgis for his freedom, he also offered to his debt-ridden owner "a gift of eighteen bushels of salt, worth a guinea per bushel at the time, in consideration of the uncommon kind Treatment of his Master during his servitude." Historian Gary Nash concluded that, "such a gift, representing at least half a year's wages for a common laborer, testified to Allen's regard for his master and to his adoption of the Methodist disdain for the things that money could buy." Concerning Allen as a "dyed in the wool" Methodist, Nash pointed to comments in 1787 by Thomas Attmore, a white Philadelphian. "I have been acquainted with Richard Allen (for) some considerable Time," he said, "and have found him to be of a Christian temper, given to Hospitality, often visiting the Sick and Afflicted, and Administering according to his Ability, and when he hath it not in his power to help them, he hath place in the Minds of People of Affluence, and Frequently is intrusted by them with Cash for the help of the Necessities of the . . . Neady."[6]

Attmore's assessment of Allen's reputation, however, failed to uncover deeper concerns that motivated the manumitted minister. As he lingered in sadness in 1776 over the sale of his family to another slave owner, Allen in 1777 heard the preaching of a Methodist circuit rider. That was when his "dungeon shook" and his "chains flew off" and he experienced conversion. One result of Allen's deepening religiosity was an unquenchable desire to be free. He attributed this to the Methodists.[7]

Allen possessed a particular understanding and appreciation for Methodism. These Wesleyan evangelists preached to poor whites and slave blacks.

African Americans were so receptive to them that Allen testified that "in their first rise and progress in Delaware state, and elsewhere, the colored people were their greatest support; for there were but few of us free; but the slaves would toil in their little patches many a night until midnight to raise their little truck (gardens) and sell to get something to support them more than what their masters gave them, but we used often to divide our little support among the white preachers of the gospel." And why did blacks respond with such generosity? Allen declared that, "the Methodists were the first people that brought glad tidings to the colored people." Speaking for himself, Allen asserted, "I feel thankful that ever I heard a Methodist preach. We are beholden to the Methodists, under God for the light of the Gospel we enjoy; for all other denominations preached so high-flown that we were not able to comprehend their doctrine." Methodism through extemporaneous preaching, Allen added, "has proved beneficial to thousands" of people.[8]

During the 1780s, however, Methodism changed. The Wesleyan movement that initially drew Allen's loyalty became an increasingly unfamiliar religious body. The fervor with which the gospel was advanced, openness to the poor and to blacks, and staunch abolitionism all started to wane. In Allen's mind, two unfortunate developments were responsible. The formation of an American Methodist denomination at the 1784 Christmas Conference in Baltimore, Maryland, conferred an ecclesiastical elitism and formality upon the Wesleyan movement that Allen eschewed. Moreover, as it became a respected religious body, the new denomination manifested less zeal against slavery. Concerning the Christmas Conference Allen recalled, "this was the beginning of the Episcopal Church amongst the Methodists. Many of the ministers were set apart in holy orders at this conference, and were said to be entitled to the gown; and I have thought religion has been declining in the church ever since. There was a pamphlet published by some person, which stated, that when the Methodists were no people, then they were a people; and now they have become a people they were no people." He added that these developments "had often serious weight upon my mind."[9]

The racial incident that precipitated Allen's establishment of Bethel African Methodist Episcopal Church and the denomination that developed out of it should be understood within this context. Allen, disappointed with American Methodism, founded African Methodism to recapture authentic Wesleyanism in America. Allen, a member of Old St. George, had earlier raised the idea of starting a separate black church. His rebuff by church officials, however, convinced Allen to respond to their offer to hold special services for blacks in the St. George facility. Allen's stirring sermons seemed to draw increased numbers of blacks into the Methodist congregation. But these successes drew negative reactions from white Wesleyans. Allen observed that "when the colored people began to get numerous in attending the church, they moved us from the seats we usually sat on, and placed us around the wall, and on Sabbath morning we went to church and the sexton stood at the door, and told us to go in the gallery. He told us to go, and we would see where to sit. We expected to take the seats over the ones we formerly occupied below, not knowing any better. We took those seats. Meeting had begun, and they were nearly done singing, and just as we got to the seats, the elder said, 'Let us pray.' We had not been long upon our knees before I heard considerable scuffling and low talking." Allen then saw a trustee pull Absalom Jones from his knees. The altercation continued with another trustee trying to do the same thing with someone else in Allen's party. The prayer period ended, however, before any further disruption occurred. Allen said, "we all went out of the church in a body, and they were no more plagued with us in the church."[10]

When Allen and his followers left Old St. George, they turned to the Free African Society (FAS), a mutual aid organization with quasi-religious functions that they established in 1787. The FAS provided the framework for a separate black church. The majority within the FAS decided to affiliate with the Episcopal Church and invited Allen to become their minister. Allen declined and retained his Wesleyan commitment. St. Thomas Protestant Episcopal Church and Bethel African Methodist Episcopal Church, both dedicated in 1794, were the two congregations that emerged out of the Free African Society. Absalom Jones became rector of St. Thomas while Richard Allen served as pastor of Bethel.

What happened in November 1787 at Old St. George was on one level an ugly racial incident. Allen's founding of an African Methodist Episcopal congregation was the direct and unambiguous response to white Methodist racism. But for Allen the matter was more than a reaction to racism. The mistreatment of blacks in a Wesleyan setting was simply a symptom of a larger sickness that afflicted Methodism. When Allen was converted, Methodists would disrespect neither a parishioner nor a potential convert on account of race. Allen viewed the racial egalitarianism of white Wesleyans as a byproduct of authentic Christianity and genuine religiosity. Things had changed by 1784 and again by 1787 at the time of the Old St. George incident. Racism could flourish because Methodists had become respected as a denomination and pretentious as a people. For Allen, the founding of African Methodism represented an opportunity to rescue the authentic Wesleyanism that American Methodism had despoiled. Years later he regretted that "it is awfully feared that the simplicity of the Gospel that was among them (American Methodists) fifty years ago, and that they conform more to the world and the fashions thereof, they would fare very little better than the people of the world. The discipline is altered considerably from what it was. We would ask for the good old way, and desire to walk therein."[11] While he nurtured African Methodism, Allen considered himself a Methodist. When several FAS members joined the Episcopalians, Allen recalled that, "in 1793 a committee was appointed from the African (St. Thomas) Church to solicit me to be their minister, for there was no colored preacher in Philadelphia but myself. I told them I could not accept of their offer, as I was a Methodist. I was indebted to the Methodists, under God, for what little religion I had; being convinced that they were a people of God, I informed them that I could not be anything else but a Methodist, as I was born and awakened under them." But it seemed that Allen, in developing his institutional commitments in an autonomous African Methodist congregation, viewed himself as one of the few true practitioners of "the good old way."[12]

Although Allen severed all of Bethel's ties with the Methodist Philadelphia Annual Conference in 1801 and established in 1816 an independent African Methodist Episcopal denomination, he consistently called himself a Methodist, nurtured a reputation as a Methodist, and adhered strictly to Wesleyan doctrines and practices. His self-identification as a Methodist while he developed an autonomous African Methodism suggests that Allen viewed his congregation and the connection that he founded as authentically Methodist as any American Methodist institution. Despite attempts by white Methodist elders to assert control over Bethel, Allen was respected as a Methodist and he in turn conducted himself as a direct heir to John Wesley.

In 1801, for example, the same year that his wife, Flora Allen, died, white Methodists tried to assert power within Bethel. Despite Allen's resistance, a retinue of Wesleyan preachers still came to Bethel to honor his wife. They included "the Reverend Messieurs McComb, Sneeth, Cavender, Green and several other Clergymen of the Methodist persuasion." This impressive aggregation of Philadelphia churchmen suggests the esteem in which the Allens were held and their peer position within the Methodist group. Moreover, *Poulson's American Advertiser* noted that these Wesleyan clergy acknowledged Flora Allen as a woman of "piety, charity, and other Christian virtues." Along with Allen's stature as a Methodist minister, his church was clearly described in this 1801 publication as the African Methodist Church, called Bethel. Hence, Allen's religious venture not only represented institutional independence in black religious life, but a serious move to revive the Wesleyanism that he thought American Methodism had abandoned.[13]

Whatever charges Allen leveled against American Methodists, he never wanted to be guilty of violating the general rules and regulations that governed the Wesleyan movement. This sentiment shaped the way in which he responded to Jarena Lee, a Bethel member who received a call to preach. Lee approached her pastor in around 1809 on this matter, and Allen responded in an oblique and uncertain manner. When he discovered that Lee wanted to pursue her call among the Methodists, Allen acknowledged "that a Mrs. Cook, a Methodist lady, had also some time before requested the same privilege; who, it was believed, had done much good in the way of exhortation, and holding prayer meetings; and who had been permitted to do so by the verbal license of the preacher in charge at the time." But, to Jarena Lee, Allen declared, "as to women preaching . . . our Discipline knew nothing at all about it . . . it did not call for women preachers."[14] Allen's seeming timidity on this momentous matter did not derive from any fear of criticism from white Methodists. That he already had engineered a legal separation from white Philadelphia Methodists showed his courage and independence. At the same time Allen was mindful of his reputation as a strict Methodist who adhered unwaveringly to Wesleyan doctrine and discipline. To license Jarena Lee to preach when no consensus existed about the wisdom of the practice seemed something that Allen chose to avoid. The legitimacy of African Methodism as a mainstream alternative to American Methodism was at stake.

In 1817, however, Jarena Lee, an exponent of sanctification, convinced Allen to authorize her to preach. During a service at Bethel, the Holy Spirit inspired her to stand at her pew and finish a sermon that a spiritually incapacitated preacher attempted to deliver. Allen, who was now the first elected and consecrated Bishop of the African Methodist Episcopal Church, "rose up in the assembly." Lee observed that Allen "related that I had called upon him eight years before, asking to be permitted to preach, and that he had put me off; but that he now as much believed that I was called to that work, as any of the preachers sent." Not only did Allen permit Lee to preach, but he also invited her to participate in the New York and Baltimore Annual Conferences. When Lee traveled as an evangelist, Allen and his second wife, Sarah Allen, took care of Lee's son.[15] Lee's resolve helped to change Allen's attitude, but the Bishop's growing confidence as a Methodist leader also accounted for his tardy support for a female preacher. Allen was the presiding prelate of a Wesleyan denomination that embraced four states during its first year of existence. How he defined Methodism mattered as much as the testimony of any peer within the family of Wesleyan churches.

Perhaps Richard Allen was too modest to assert explicitly that the Methodist movement he led had a better claim upon the Wesleyan tradition than mainstream American Methodism. The African Methodist Episcopal Church that Allen established sustained a dual egalitarian/evangelical thrust that John Wesley envisaged for the Methodist movement. Even Francis Asbury, the patriarch of American Methodism, lamented in 1796 "the superficial state of religion among the white people who are called Methodists."[16] Elsewhere, the author of this essay has written:

> How was African Methodism different from American Methodism? In the view of Richard Allen, white Wesleyans, as they gained status in American society, increasingly lost spiritual fervor. As a result their Christian witness diminished and their insurgency against slavery and other societal ills dissipated. Allen designed African Methodism to be different. He produced an A.M.E. Discipline in 1817, modeled it according to the Methodist Discipline, and zealously enforced it. His puritanical tendencies stemmed in part from an intense desire to convince followers to live soberly and uprightly. Although Allen devoted most of his time to church matters, he remained a vocal opponent against slavery and a conspicuous leader in a wide range of community and racial uplift activities. For Allen, a forthright social witness like that of John Wesley against bondage resulted from spiritual fervor. Also, for Allen, the Wesleyan witness pulled adherents beyond personal piety to public stands against individual and societal sins. This void which American Methodism left, African Methodism filled.[17]

Hence Richard Allen could justifiably view himself as John Wesley's truest American heir. In his devotion to spiritual fervor, social witness, and strict adherence to Methodist doctrine and discipline, Allen's claim as a quintessential Wesleyan is both compelling and credible.

Allen's efforts to reclaim the Wesleyan mission to the United States moved him formally to adopt the Methodist Discipline for the governance of his local congregation, Bethel African Methodist Episcopal Church, and to adapt it for the AME denomination after 1816. Similarly, he developed an AME hymnal in 1801 to affirm the evangelical character of his AME followers and to affirm their Wesleyan identity. Because the Methodists, around whom Allen was socialized, sang hymns and participated in the popular religious culture of evangelicalism, the manumitted minister heard the same stanzas that Asbury and others often recited. So familiar and commonplace were these hymns that Asbury, as he reflected in his journal on various religious experiences, inserted portions of hymns to illuminate his observations. In Allen's Delaware in 1773, Asbury traveled late into the night to reach a remote destination. "But, by the help of a good guide," he said, "I got there safe at last." Then, the itinerant preacher proclaimed: "In all my ways, Thy hand I own,— / Thy ruling providence I see: / Assist me still my course to run, / And still direct my paths to Thee."

Asbury, who was familiar with an impressive repertoire of hymns, in 1774 sojourned in Maryland and learned of the death of "a serious, faithful man," about whom he wrote: "Happy soul, who, free from harms, Rests within his Saviour's arms."

Asbury's hymnody was broad enough to speak to almost any occasion. His meditation on August 17, 1774, while in New York, moved poetically from free verse to the rhythmic rhyme of a hymn. He said, "my mind is free; and my soul delighteth in God. He taketh such possession of my heart, as to keep out all desire for created objects. In due time, I humbly hope, through Jesus Christ, to enter into the full fruition. O blessed day, when my soul shall be swallowed up in God!" Then, he repeated: "In hope of that immortal crown, / I now the cross sustain; / And gladly wander up and down, / And smile at toil and pain."

Still in New York, Asbury confessed to his diary that he was "grieved and ashamed that my soul is not more steadily and fervently devoted to God." Another hymn summed up his feelings, "And shall I ever live / At this poor, dying rate— / My love so faint, so cold to thee, / And thine to me so great?"[18]

Richard Allen's devotional life paralleled Asbury's blending of prayers, poetry, and hymns. His writings on Acts of Faith, Acts of Hope, and Acts of Love, like similar expressions of Asbury, showed Allen's Wesleyan attributes. "I believe, O God," Allen wrote in Acts of Faith, "that Thou art an eternal, incomprehensible spirit, infinite in all perfections; who didst make all things out of nothing, and dost govern them all by thy wise providence." He added: "let me always adore Thee with profound humility, as my Sovereign Lord; and help me to love and praise Thee with godlike affections and suitable devotion." As in a hymn in Acts of Hope Allen declared, "blessed hope! be thou my chief delight in life, and then I shall be steadfast and immovable, always abounding in the work of the Lord; be thou my comfort and support at the hour death, and then I shall contentedly leave this world, as a captive that is released from his imprisonment." And, in Acts of Love, Allen prayed, "O crucified Jesus! in whom I live, and without whom I die; mortify in me all sensual desires, inflame my heart with Thy holy love, that I may no longer esteem the vanities of this world, but place my affections entirely on Thee."[19]

Asbury surely supplied Allen with a devotional template the younger preacher could emulate. Moreover, Allen counted Asbury as a mentor, supporter, and occasional companion. Like Asbury, Allen traveled extensively in Pennsylvania, Delaware, New Jersey, and Maryland between 1783 and 1786. He was constantly in the company of fellow Methodists and other evangelicals where he surely heard and learned what hymns were often and familiarly sung. The several associations that Allen developed gave him a broad exposure to Methodist music and popular evangelical hymns that he later used in AME services. In 1783, Allen, newly freed from slavery, hauled salt from Sussex County, Delaware. In this area he "had regular stops and preaching places on the road . . . enjoyed many happy seasons in meditation and prayer while in this employment." After preaching widely, including in Wilmington, Delaware, Allen spent substantial time in New Jersey where "he strove to preach the Gospel until the spring of 1784." There he met "the good and great apostle," Benjamin Abbott, "who seldom preached but what there were souls added to his labor." In other parts of West Jersey and East Jersey, Allen worked cutting wood or laboring in some mill by day while he preached at night. In Pennsylvania, around Lancaster and York, Allen continued his preaching until he moved on to Maryland. He accompanied Methodist preachers on their circuits until he arrived in Baltimore to attend the Christmas Conference. He visited various services in the Baltimore area and returned to Pennsylvania. Later in Philadelphia at the invitation of the pastor at St. George Church, Allen preached "at different places in the city." Although he preached mainly to whites, he discovered that blacks had been neglected, and "he saw the necessity of erecting a place of worship for the colored people." When Allen reached this conclusion, his broad travels had exposed him to Wesleyan worship practices, orders of service, and the prominent place of hymns in Methodist gatherings.[20]

In Radnor, Pennsylvania, for example, Allen "stayed and labored" for several weeks. He recalled, "I was frequently called upon by many inquiring what they should do to be saved. I appointed them to prayer and supplication at the throne of grace, and to make use of all manner of prayer, and pointed them to the invitation of our Lord and Saviour, Jesus Christ, who has said: 'Come unto me, all ye that are weary and heavy laden, and I will give you rest.' Glory be to God! and now I know he was a God at hand and not afar off." Allen observed, "we spent a greater part of the night in singing and prayer with the mourners." He also noted that "there were but few colored people in the neighborhood—the most of my congregation was white."[21] What Allen learned and practiced as an itinerant Methodist preacher benefited this aggregation of Radnor whites. Later similar efforts would be applied to his nearly all-black following in Philadelphia.

Historian Dee Andrews, writing in *The Methodists and Revolutionary America, 1760–1800: The Shaping of an Evangelical Culture,* observed that John Wesley in his "invention of Wesleyan Methodism" published in 1737 *A Collection of Psalms and Hymns* by numerous authors. Andrews noted that in hymns "singers are beckoned to Christ, transformed into spiritual seekers in quest of the Divine, mourners longing for a return to the heights of sensate grace achieved at first awakening, triumphant victors over sin."[22] In his invention of African Methodism, Allen pursued the same process. Hence in 1801, Allen, the minister of the independent Bethel African Methodist Episcopal Church, published *A Collection of Hymns and Spiritual Songs from Various Authors.*[23]

Allen's volume contained fifty-four hymns in its first edition and another ten in a second edition. Although unknown authors wrote over half of the songs, he included others from such well-known English hymn writers as Isaac Watts, John Newton, and Charles Wesley. One scholar of Allen's hymnody noted that the *Collection* reprinted "popular evangelical hymns by English writers and a generous number of popular American hymns, many of which we might easily call 'folk hymns.'" Some of these hymns may have come from existing works, especially like Samson Occum's *A Choice Collection of Hymns and Spiritual Songs* (1774), Samuel Jones and Burgis Allison's *A Selection of Psalms and Hymns* (1790), and others. Music historian Eileen Southern, however, believed that "Allen had developed his own repertory of favorite hymns and turned to these when the occasion came to produce his own hymnal."[24]

Allen's travels within the Middle Atlantic states and his lengthy visits at several locations provided him with broad opportunities to hear numerous hymns and to sample a range of religious music. He knew many Methodist ministers and members including Benjamin Abbott and Joseph Budd in New Jersey; Caesar Water, Peter Morratte, and Irie Ellis in Pennsylvania; and Richard Whatcoat, Richard Mould, Richard Russell, Jonathan Forest, and Leari Coal in Maryland. Freeborn Garrettson and Francis Asbury, the nation's most noted Wesleyan leaders, were similarly familiar to Allen. In these extensive interactions with prominent preachers and parishioners Allen probably listened to their testimonies in sermon and in song and adapted many of their stanzas and sentences to articulate his own spirituality. They in turn learned from Allen who was in several instances their preacher of choice as he traveled their region. Allen's familiarity with William Colbert, a fellow Methodist clergyman, suggests another source for a hymn that appeared in Allen's *Collection*. Colbert often visited Allen and preached at Bethel Church. Since the hymnal included a song similar to one that Colbert composed, his influence seems plausible. Additionally, Allen drew hymns from the American camp meeting circuit. J. Roland Braithwaite, a scholar of Allen's hymnody, identified as camp meeting songs that the AME cleric included in his *Collection* such selections as "Saviour, I Do Feel Thy Merit," "Come All Ye Poor Sinners That from Adam Came," "The Great Tremendous Day's Approaching," "How Happy Every Child of Grace," "O God My Heart with Love Inflame," and "We've Found the Rock, the Trav'ler Cried." Braithwaite observed that these tunes were "often spontaneously created, passed on orally, (and) sometimes distributed in broadsides at meetings. Richard Allen was among those who pioneered the inclusion of such a repertory in published hymnals."[25]

Allen's search for consensus and common ground in hymnody is best illustrated in his insistence upon hymn singing as integral to Wesleyan worship. Allen would have agreed with Frederick Norwood, the noted historian of Methodism, who observed that Wesleyan services while they "consisted of preaching, aided by Bible, prayer, and hymn-singing" did not mean that they "were one gospel hymn-sing. The tunes were rather dignified, certainly not the popular ditties of the day, and the emphasis was on the theological content, not on emotional response."[26] Perhaps Allen's clearest sentiment about hymnody was expressed in the 1817 Discipline adopted for the newly established AME denomination. In sections on public worship and on the spirit and truth of singing were statements about black Wesleyan hymnody. The morning worship was to consist of "singing, prayer, the reading of a chapter out of the Old Testament, and another out of the New, and preaching." Afternoon and evening services followed a similar pattern. Although dignity in worship was important, formality was not. Hence, the AME Discipline asked, "how shall we guard against formality in singing?" The answer was, "by choosing such hymns as are proper for the congregation." Other rules included strictures against "singing too much at once; seldom more than five or six verses." The Discipline required that "the tune" should suit the words and that the minister should stop frequently to ask the people, "do you know what you said last? Did you speak no more than you felt?" Additionally, the minister should not "suffer the people to sing too slow. This naturally tends to formality."[27]

The importance of hymns in Allen's Bethel Church was demonstrated repeatedly. In 1822 the "male members" of the Bethel AME and Wesley AME

Zion congregations in Philadelphia gathered at Allen's church, "and after singing and praying, there was an exhortation given by Rev. Richard Allen of the utility of living (in) love and . . . union one with the other." On August 10, 1826, the monthly meeting of the Union Benevolent Sons of Bethel AME Church, a burial society, conducted its business only after "singing and praying."[28]

As he developed the African Methodist Episcopal Church, Richard Allen had to reconcile several religious realities. First, he was a committed Wesleyan. The Methodists had converted him to Christianity and had nurtured his evangelical ministry. Hence, he preached extensively and vigorously to rural and working-class whites and to slave and manumitted blacks throughout the Middle Atlantic States and believed that Methodism had special appeal to these groups. Moreover, Allen advocated the Methodist style of extemporaneous, evangelical preaching, spontaneous praying, and hymn singing. Allen strongly believed that "no religious sect or denomination would suit the capacity of colored people as well as the Methodist; for the plain and simple gospel suits best for any people; for the unlearned can understand, and the learned are sure to understand; and the reason that the Methodist is so successful in the awakening and conversion of the colored people, the plain doctrine and having a good discipline."[29] While he held tenaciously to these convictions, Allen also confronted several difficult challenges. American Methodists allowed racism to influence their newly established denomination in the 1780s and thereafter suffered a loss in religious zeal and spiritual fervor. Those Wesleyan attributes that attracted Allen to Methodism had to be rescued. Simultaneously, Allen, while he revived the Wesleyan mission to America through the development of African Methodism, had to fit it to the tastes and cultural characteristics of his largely black constituency. Hymn singing, an integral practice within Wesleyanism, needed to be maintained and adapted to the African Methodists Allen thought were John Wesley's true American heirs.

Although Allen believed that hymn singing was crucial to African Methodism, he creatively adjusted hymn style and structure to appeal to blacks. At the same time the theological content and the gospel message that were integral to Wesleyan hymnody remained the same. Hence, Allen included in the *Collection* such hymns as:

1. Saviour, I do feel thy merit,
   Sprinkled with redeeming blood;
   And now my troubled, weary spirit,
   Now finds rest in thee my God.

2. I am safe, and I am happy
   While in thy dear arms I lie:
   Sin nor Satan cannot harm me
   While my Saviour is so nigh.

3. Now I'll sing of Jesus' merit,
   Tell the world of his dear name,
   That if any wants his spirit,
   He is still the very same.[30]

Allen, whom Francis Asbury ordained as a deacon in 1800, perennially preached that the unsaved should accept Jesus Christ, acknowledge His sacrifice, and benefit from the salvation that He offered. Hymns communicated this fundamental Christian tenet, and never would Allen abandon such testimonies in song. The totality of the gospel seemed contained in another hymn that Allen included:

1. Come, Christian friends, and hear me tell
   The wonders of Immanuel
   He is the light of saints below,
   Their strength and comfort from him flow.

2. Tho' all the world should spread its wings,
   And tempt them with ten thousand things,
   They can't forget that heavn'ly love,
   Which brought a Saviour from above.

3. For us he bow'd his awful head,
   Down to the regions of the dead,
   To take away our weighty guilt,
   The Saviour's sacred blood was split.[31]

Allen's *Collection* could have been used by any American Methodist or African Methodist congregation. The lyrics proclaimed the same doctrinal position that evangelical Protestants anywhere within the United States would espouse. Yet Allen's *Collection* possessed peculiar characteristics that identified it as an AME hymnal. Notwithstanding Allen's fervent Methodism, he included few hymns from widely used Wesleyan hymnals. The *Collection* was Allen's own compilation of a "popular folk hymnal." The camp meeting songs that Allen included, for example, bore the influence of blacks who frequented these revival settings. J. Roland Braithwaite, an authority on Allen's hymnody, observed that "these camp meeting spiritual songs often reflect oral, responsorial practices, undoubtedly encouraged by circumstances in which a leader who would know the stanzas would sing them and all of the assembled participants in the meeting, who might know the chorus, would respond." Braithwaite identified four hymns in Allen's *Collection* that followed this pattern. These hymns used "wandering choruses." These were choruses "that could be attached to several different hymns and often might not seem to be particularly related textually to the hymns to which they are attached." Two hymns that Allen included in the *Collection* used the following "wandering chorus": "Hallelujah to the Lamb, / who has purchased our pardon, / We will praise him again / when we pass over Jordan." The other "wandering chorus" was: "Firm united let us be / In the bonds of charity; / As a band of brothers join'd / Loving God and all mankind."[32]

Perhaps the most important feature of Allen's *Collection* was the inclusion of a hymn that Allen most likely wrote. Even though the Discipline that he adopted for the denomination in 1817 advised that congregations should "sing no hymns of your own composing," clearly Allen had felt that way in 1801 when he published his hymnal.[33] Allen's hymn, "See! How the Nations Rage Together," struck an eschatological tone. Prophecies that foretold how national conflict presaged the second coming of Jesus shaped the thematic thrust of Allen's hymn. This prophetic context, however, allowed Allen to press a familiar message. Preaching was an urgent matter because sinners required immediate rescue lest the end would come before they were saved. The first of fourteen stanzas captures this urgency: 1. See! how the nations rage together, / Seeking of each others blood; / See how the scriptures are fulfilling! / Sinners awake and turn to God.[34]

As a Methodist and hymn writer, Allen structured services that accommodated demonstrative displays of religiosity within an order of service with scripturally substantive hymns. The cultural tastes of his black parishioners pursued the former as Allen instructed them to appreciate the latter. A Russian traveler, Paul Svin'in, reputedly visited a service at Allen's Bethel AME Church in Philadelphia in 1811. In his introduction to Allen's *Collection*, Braithwaite said that Svin'in observed the "singing of what was evidently some response to the reading of psalms as a 'loud, shrill monotone' which went on for extended periods of time and involved activities he thought curious such as falling on the knees, bowing to the ground, and engaging in 'an agonizing, heart-rending moaning.'"[35] Whatever the accuracy of Svin'in's description, it failed to capture the dialectic that Allen sought to establish in his services—the blending of black folk religion and ordered Methodist worship. Allen believed the African Methodist Episcopal Church could effect a marriage between the black religious experience and Wesleyan doctrine, discipline, and hymnody.

While wedded to an African Methodism that would become indigenously black, Allen maintained efforts to develop his congregation and then his denomination into thoroughly Wesleyan organizations. To all of his sermons and speeches, Allen appended poetry, some of which may have been stanzas borrowed from contemporary hymns. They allowed him to emphasize religious and public issues that clergymen like himself were compelled to address. In 1793, Richard Allen and Absalom Jones, a former black Methodist and later rector of St. Thomas Protestant Episcopal Church, offered their services to the City of Philadelphia during a devastating yellow fever epidemic. Because some disparaging comments had been made about the extent of participation by blacks in helping the sick and burying the dead, Allen and Jones wrote "A Narrative of the Proceedings of the Colored People during the Awful Calamity in Philadelphia, in the Year 1793; and a Refutation of Some Censures Thrown upon Them in Some Publications." The eloquent defense of the reputation of black Philadelphians and the chronicle of their extensive assistance to yellow fever victims ended with Allen and Jones pulling from their repertory of religious poetry and hymns what may have been familiar phraseology: "God and soldier all men do adore / In time of war and not before; / When the war is over, and all things righted, / God is forgotten, and the soldier slighted."[36]

Richard Allen, the former slave, remained an implacable foe of chattel bondage throughout his life. In his "Short Address to the Friend of Him Who Hath No Helper," Allen commended abolitionists who worked hard to end black slavery. "You feel our afflictions; you sympathize with us in the heartrending distress," he said. Additionally, Allen wrote: "may, He, who hath arisen to plead our cause and engaged you as volunteers in the service, add to your numbers, until princes shall come forth from Egypt, and Ethiopia stretch out her hands unto God." After these allusions to Afro-centric scriptures, Allen repeated a later version of a hymn that he probably wrote that closely resembled one in his 1801 Collection: 1. Ye ministers that are called to preaching, / Teachers and exhorters too, / Awake! behold your harvest wasting; / Arise! there is no rest for you. / 2. To think upon that strict commandment / That God has on his teachers laid / The sinners' blood, who die unwarned, / Shall fall upon their shepherd's head.[37]

In later years, Richard Allen, who died in 1831, wrote his autobiography, *The Life Experience and Gospel Labors of the Rt. Rev. Richard Allen*. Since 1816 he had served as the first consecrated and elected Bishop of the African Methodist Episcopal Church. In 1818 he and several associates published an expanded hymnal for denominational use. Now congregations that stretched northward to New England, westward into the Old Northwest Territory, southward to Charleston, South Carolina, and into the Caribbean benefited from Allen's hymnody. "I could not be anything else but a Methodist," he declared in his autobiography. So, not surprisingly, Bishop Francis Asbury, his mentor, dedicated in 1794 the edifice that his congregation erected at Sixth and Lombard Streets in Philadelphia. Asbury named it Bethel, and Allen accepted the appellation. Appropriately, Bishop Allen closed his autobiography with a hymn:

1. The God of Bethel heard her cries,
   He let his power be seen;
   He stopp'd the proud oppressor's frown,
   And proved himself a King.

2. Thou sav'd them in the trying hour,
   Ministers and councils joined,
   And all stood ready to retain
   That helpless church of Thine.

3. Bethel surrounded by her foes,
   But not yet in despair,
   Christ heard her supplicating cries;
   The God of Bethel heard.[38]

Notes

1. Elmer T. Clark, J. Manning Potts, and Jacob S. Payton, eds., *The Journal and Letters of Francis Asbury* (Nashville: Abington Press, 1958), 1: xiii, 6, 58–9, 156.

2. Gary B. Nash, "New Light on Richard Allen: The Early Years of Freedom," *William and Mary Quarterly* 46 (1989): 333.

3. Richard Allen, *The Life Experience and Gospel Labors of the Rt. Rev. Richard Allen* (Nashville: A.M.E. Sunday School Union/Legacy Publishing, 1990), 14, 16; Nash, "New Light on Richard Allen," 33.

4. Allen, *Life Experience and Gospel Labors*, 13–14.

5. D. Bruce Hindmarsh, "'My chains fell off, my heart was free': Early Methodist Conversion Narrative in England," *Church History* 68 (1999): 910.

6. Allen, *Life Experience and Gospel Labors,* 14–16, 20–21; Nash, "New Light on Richard Allen," 333, 336, 340.

7. Allen, *Life Experiences and Gospel Labors,* 16; Nash, "New Light on Richard Allen," 335.

8. Allen, *Life Experience and Gospel Labors,* 27–28.

9. Ibid., 20.

10. Ibid., 23.

11. Ibid., 28.

12. Ibid.

13. *Poulson's American Advertiser,* March 14, 1801.

14. Jarena Lee, *Religious Experiences and Journal of Mrs. Jarena Lee: "A Preach'in Woman"* (Nashville: A.M.E. Sunday School Union/Legacy Publishing, 1991), 13.

15. Lee, *Religious Experiences,* 22, 41, 48, 89–90.

16. *Journal of Rev. Francis Asbury,* (New York: Lane and Scott, 1852), 2: 291.

17. Dennis C. Dickerson, *Religion, Race, and Region: Research Notes on A.M.E. Church History* (Nashville: A.M.E. Sunday School Union/Legacy Publishing, 1995), 21.

18. Clark et al, *Journal and Letters of Francis Asbury,* 73, 108, 129–30.

19. Allen, *Life Experience and Gospel Labors,* 40, 43, 44.

20. Ibid., 17–22.

21. Ibid., 18–19.

22. Dee Andrews, *The Methodists and Revolutionary America, 1760–1800: The Shaping of an Evangelical Culture* (Princeton, NJ: Princeton University Press, 2000), 19, 78.

23. Richard Allen, *A Collection of Hymns and Spiritual Songs* (Philadelphia: T. L. Plowman, 1801).

24. J. Roland Braithwaite, ed., and Richard Allen, *A Collection of Hymns and Spiritual Songs* (Nashville: A.M.E. Sunday School Union, 1987), x–xii, 113–16.

25. Allen, *Life Experience and Gospel Labors,* 17–21; Braithwaite, ed., *Collection of Hymns and Spiritual Songs,* xii–xiii.

26. Frederick Norwood, *The Story of American Methodism: A History of the United Methodists and Their Relations* (Nashville: Abingdon Press, 1974), 34–35.

27. Richard Allen and Jacob Tapsico, *The Doctrine and Discipline of the African Methodist Episcopal Church* (Philadelphia: John H. Cunningham, 1817), 56–57.

28. Minutes, August 11, 1822, Minute and Trial Book, Bethel A.M.E. Church, 1822–1835, 1838–1851, copybook, n.p. written in MS; Minutes of the Union Benevolent Sons of Bethel A.M.E. Church, bound copybook, n.p. MS, c. 150 p.; Reel #5, microfilm, *Records of Mother Bethel African Methodist Episcopal Church.*

29. Allen, *Life Experience and Gospel Labors,* 27.

30. Braithwaite, ed., *Collection of Hymns and Spiritual Songs*, 29. There are three additional stanzas in this hymn. The author of this hymn is unknown.

31. Ibid., 41. There are two additional stanzas in this hymn. The author of this hymn is unknown.

32. Ibid., xi, xiii–xiv.

33. Allen and Tapsico, *Doctrine and Discipline*, 57.

34. Braithwaite, ed., *Collection of Hymns and Spiritual Songs*, 104.

35. Ibid., xlv.

36. Allen, *Life Experience and Gospel Labors*, 47–64.

37. Ibid., 75–6.

38. Ibid., 34; *A.M.E.C. Hymnal* (Nashville: A.M.E. Sunday School Union, 1954), 543.

9
Singing Pilgrims

Hymn Narratives of a Pilgrim Community's Progress from This World to That Which Is to Come, 1830–1890

Candy Gunther Brown

IN 1865, William Aitchison of the Presbyterian mission to China lay on his deathbed. When some of his "fellow-travelers" to "Zion," missionaries from several evangelical denominations, visited him for the last time, Aitchison used the opportunity for their mutual benefit in the way he best knew how: he exhorted his visitors to keep straining toward heaven, making their "calling and election sure." Aitchison requested that they sing together some of his favorite hymns: "All Hail the Power of Jesus' Name," "When I Can Read My Title Clear," and "There Is a Land of Pure Delight." As the group sang and read, Aitchison "attempted to join with his feeble faltering voice." The singers paused from time to time for Aitchison to repeat from memory "such passages as he was still able to recollect" in his weakened state. Aitchison's friends, fortified to persevere in their own pilgrimage by the corporate rehearsal of "exceeding great and precious promises," dismissed Aitchison to "rest from earth's toilsome strife, / till God shall wake me to endless life."[1]

In countless scenes such as this, mid-nineteenth-century evangelical Protestants used hymns to reiterate cohesive narratives of the Christian life: its beginnings, progress, and purpose. The hymns people sing reflect their culture's "narrative theology"—their story of how God orders the universe, the processes by which he leads people to fulfill his purposes, and the ends for which he does so; hymns thereby position individual and communal life stories within an overarching cosmic narrative. Aitchison's deathbed scene and the corpus of hymns popular among American evangelicals tell a common story, strikingly like that articulated in John Bunyan's *Pilgrim's Progress*.[2] This story metaphorically equates Christians with pilgrims, who encourage one another daily to pursue an arduous collective journey from sin to sanctification; the journey eventuates in perfect relationship with Jesus Christ in the land of pure delight.

American evangelical hymns offer a window onto evangelical culture(s). I use the term culture to suggest self-identified evangelicals' sense of membership in a Christian community that transcends time, space, and disputes over doctrine and practice.[3] The parenthetical "s" suggests the existence of overlapping, distinctive cultures and narratives within the rubric of evangelicalism, varying for instance by region, race, and denomination. Taking these differences into account, the evidence suggests that the narrative theology articulated by the most widely popular and enduring hymns is remarkably consistent, changing relatively little across space or time.[4]

In a way approached by no other cultural artifact, hymns reflect a universe of shared beliefs, values, and practices. Evangelicals understood hymns as the common property of the church universal and endowed them with a measure of cultural authority surpassed only by that afforded to the Bible.[5] Evangelicals sang and read hymns during worship services, prayer and praise meetings, family gatherings, and in private devotions; children memorized hymns before they could read, and the aged recited hymns on their deathbeds. Hymns that retained popularity across the boundaries of time, region, class, race, gender, and denomination expressed—and in turn shaped—the sentiments of all who sang its words as their own. Whereas periodical literature thrived on contention and novels voiced the preoccupations of individuals, hymns embodied the shared convictions and experiences that unified evangelical culture(s).

Evangelicalism was animated not only by concern for individual salvation and the moment of justification but also by interest in communal relationships and the life-long sanctification process. The hymn form is well suited to unfolding the contours of this process through storytelling. Hymn narratives, rather than replacing doctrine with emotional, subjective experience, embraced both within a collective story that details the process of traveling from sin to sanctification. After positioning itself in relation to other scholarship, this essay turns to the hymns themselves to retell the evangelical narrative.

Religious and cultural historians have too often treated theology and culture as distinct or antagonistic. Students of American religion interested in evangelical beliefs and practices have frequently used as their sources prescriptive texts such as ministers' sermons, treatises, or personal notes, coupled with an occasional lay conversion narrative. Based on this evidence, they have focused on the doctrine of justification, which describes the moment at which God absolves sinners of guilt from sin through the imputation of Christ's righteousness. Scholarship driven by this doctrine emphasizes the individual conversion experience—often in response to revival preaching—as the critical point when salvation occurs, and as the pivot around which evangelicalism revolves.[6] Cultural historians, for their part, have neglected the theological work done by evangelical narratives. Assuming an adversarial relationship between narrative and theology, these scholars argue that by the middle of the nineteenth century, narrative, emotion, and subjective experience had replaced doctrine as sources for cultural definition; these shifts in cultural authority produced and reflected the secularization, humanization, and feminization of religion.[7] Despite a wealth of hymn studies, many of them teasing out individual strands of theology, few scholars have examined the overarching narratives embodied in evangelical hymnody as a window onto the intersection between theology and culture-linking sermons preached on Sundays with weekday Christian living.[8]

Hymn narratives suggest that the doctrine of sanctification may be the core around which evangelical culture(s) have formed.[9] In sanctification, God sets apart individuals and the church as holy, free from the pollution and power of sin, restoring the now-severed relationship between creation and Creator. Whereas justification is completed in an instant, sanctification is progressive and involves continual growth in grace throughout the life cycle. Both justification and sanctification are necessary components of God's saving activity. While justification reflects a vertical relationship between God and the individual, sanctification also involves a horizontal relationship between members of the Christian community. Longing for sanctification permeates hymn texts; it is striking therefore how little scholars have to say about this critical doctrine in their expositions of evangelicalism. Hymn narratives begin with conversion and end with salvation, but the heart of the story depicts the life-long, communal process of growth in holiness. The salvation narrative is meaningful not only for its origins and outcome but also for the progression of the story itself.

Hymn narratives function culturally to integrate doctrine and experience. Narratives are not just stories, enjoyable in the telling and hearing, but means of communicating fundamental theological "truths" about life, God, and the universe. The narrative form, in contrast to more prescriptive forms of discourse, is particularly well attuned to express a community's collective growth process. The evangelical narrative extended sacred space and time beyond church ritual, lending universal and eternal, or what I term "cosmic," significance to daily experiences—any one of which God could use as a vehicle for growth in holiness. Repetition of the story by members of the community in one another's hearing reinforced its cultural power by redefining secular experiences in sacred terms. Every hymn singer was a theologian who used hymns to explain God, the world, and life experience. Through hymns repeatedly, evangelicals internalized the theological values embedded in the narratives and lived out the values they sang; hymns had a teaching function, even as they reflected shared values.

Individual hymn texts belong within the framework of a common narrative universe. I freely mix quotations from different hymns on the grounds that singers themselves made no sharp distinction between theology articulated by one hymn versus another. I adopt hymn diction to evoke the linguistic universe in which evangelicals viewed themselves as living. I now turn to the narrative theology embedded in hymn texts: beginning with conversion, as the start of the journey toward sanctification; progressing through the daily process of growth in holiness; and culminating with the fruit of sanctification in a pure relationship between Christ and the church in heaven.

Throughout evangelical hymnody, verbal metaphors define the Christian life as pursuing a journey, fighting a battle, and running a race. This constellation of action-oriented images reflects evangelicals' sense that sanctification is a lengthy, difficult process that commences with conversion and culminates with arrival in heaven. Prior to conversion, the "wanderer" cannot even find the "celestial road"—"the way I long have sought, and mourned because I found it not." But God provides a way for people, while still sinners, to find and enter the path to life: by coming to Jesus "just as I am and waiting not / to rid my soul of one dark blot." At the point of conversion, Jesus "led my roving feet / to tread the heav'nly road." But the story has just begun. Now, "introduced by thee, have I my race begun," and "in that light of life I'll walk, till all my journey's done."[10] Metaphors interpret the experience of living in this world within the framework of an overarching cosmic narrative, reminding converts that the Christian life is a process and exhorting the unconverted to cease wandering and begin traveling toward heaven.

Viewing their lives within this narrative framework, evangelicals envisioned themselves as "pilgrims" on an earthly mission, traveling through a foreign land toward their home in heaven. Pilgrims traverse a "barren wilderness" road, where fiery trials and dangers "stand thick." The rugged, devious, narrow path leads through darkness, scorching sand, a burning sky—at one moment climbing over a sharp crag, at the next, dipping deep into a "dark vale of tears." Travelers must cross a "troubled sea" during a dreadful tempest;

"storm after storm" of sorrow, sharp distress, toil, and pain repeatedly buffet weary pilgrims, threatening to swallow them beneath a "swelling tide of woes." Meanwhile, the lures of transitory things, the "world's bewitching snare," and even hopes threaten to deceive unwary travelers, causing them to lose their way. While traveling as pilgrims, Christians also fight as soldiers who must keep their "armor bright" and press onward, "marching as to war" to wrestle all their foes. Evangelicals similarly view themselves as long-distance runners who press with vigor and zeal in a "heavenly race." To win their prize and crown, they must never slacken in pace, but pursue their goal through every period of life—in "childhood, manhood, age, and death." All the while, time is of the essence, since none can know when the "short tale" of life will conclude.[11] All three metaphors of journeying, battling, and racing reflect evangelicals' understanding of the Christian life as a lengthy, difficult process. Completing this process successfully entails suffering and requires perseverance, watchfulness, and haste. While the beginning and anticipated end of the journey offer crucial points of reference and meaning, the tension-wrought drama of the journey itself constitutes the heart of the story.

Hymn theology pairs God's sovereignty with human responsibility in explaining how sanctification progresses. The cross represents God's role in the salvation drama. It is "in the cross of Christ I Glory," since "all the light of sacred story / gathers round its head sublime." At the center of the sacred story, the cross symbolically transforms suffering into the principal cure for sin. According to evangelical theology, Jesus Christ is God incarnate in human flesh. Jesus, the only sinless human ever to have lived, suffered and died on a wooden cross—symbolic of sin's shame—in order to make full atonement for human sin. On the cross, "Christ, the mighty Maker, died, / for man the creature's sin." Through Christ's suffering on the cross, God both justifies and sanctifies sinners: providing for "sin the double cure, / saving from wrath and making me pure." God completely justifies sinners at the time of conversion, clearing them from the guilt of sin that necessitates divine wrath. But God only gradually purifies converts from the pollution and power of sin inherent in human nature. Justified Christians continue to sing: "I am all unrighteousness; / vile and full of sin I am." Evangelicals who appropriate hymn texts as the language of their own prayers, ask Jesus for pardon from sins committed each day and for new supplies of grace to "make and keep me pure within." Hymns reveal the expectation that Christians will only cease to sin and be prepared for full relationship with God at the conclusion of life on earth: when "grace has purified my heart," "then, from sin and sorrow free, /

take us, Lord, to dwell with thee."[12] Until Christians arrive in heaven, the cross daily prepares them through the grace of growth in holiness.

Many hymns treat the process of purification from sin and growth in holiness. One of the best known, "Love Divine, All Loves Excelling," was written by Charles Wesley in the eighteenth century. The 1878 *Hymnal of the Methodist Episcopal Church with Tunes* indexes the hymn under the heading "The Christian—Sanctification and Growth." The hymnal also lists "Love Divine" under several subject entries: Christ—Author of Faith, Entire Sanctification and Christian Growth, Heaven Anticipated, Prayer for Entire Sanctification, and Social Worship—Consecration and Sanctification. *The Presbyterian Hymnal* of 1874 lists "Love Divine" under the heading "The Lord Jesus Christ —Affections and Duties," cross-referencing it under the subjects Sanctification, Holy Spirit, and Growth in Grace.[13] The hymn reads:

1. Love divine,
   all loves excelling,
   Joy of heaven, to earth come down;
   Fix in us thy humble dwelling,
   All thy faithful mercies crown:
   Jesus, thou art all compassion,
   Pure, unbounded love thou art;
   Visit us with thy salvation,
   Enter every trembling heart.

2. Breathe, O breathe thy loving Spirit
   Into every troubled breast!
   Let us all in thee inherit,
   Let us find that second rest:
   Take away our bent to sinning;
   Alpha and Omega be;
   End of faith, as its beginning,
   Set our hearts at liberty.

3. Come, almighty to deliver,
   Let us all thy life receive;
   Suddenly return, and never,
   Never more thy temples leave:
   Thee we would be always blessing,

Serve thee as thy hosts above,
Pray, and praise thee without ceasing,
Glory in thy perfect love.

4. Finish then thy new creation,
   Pure and spotless let us be;
   Let us see thy great salvation,
   Perfectly restored in thee:
   Changed from glory into glory,
   Till in heaven we take our place,
   Till we cast our crowns before thee,
   Lost in wonder, love, and praise.

The hymn pays specific attention to the work of each person of the Trinity: Jesus in bringing love to earth, the Holy Spirit in setting hearts free from the power of sin, and the Father in beginning and completing his creative work. "Love Divine," like most of its companion hymns, is full of Scriptural allusions. The Methodist hymnal for 1878 indexes the hymn's Scriptural references: Malachi 3:1 (prophecy of Jesus's arrival in his temple)—stanza one, line one and stanza three, line four; Matthew 14:4 (Jesus's compassion)—stanza one, line five; 2 Corinthians 3:18 (the Holy Spirit transforms Christians from one degree of glory to another)—stanza two, line one and stanza four, line five; Revelation 4:10 (crowns cast down in worship)—stanza four, line seven; Revelation 21:5 (God makes all things new)—stanza four, line one; and Revelation 21:6 (God is Alpha and Omega)—stanza two, line six. "Love Divine" weaves Scripture into a doctrinal and experiential testimony of the progress of the Christian life.

It is important to acknowledge nuances in sanctification narrative(s) from one hymn to the next. "Love Divine" can be contrasted doctrinally with other hymns appearing side-by-side in the same hymnals. Augustus Toplady's "Rock of Ages," for instance, suggests that Christians cannot in this life receive the purity implied by "Love Divine." Toplady, one of Wesley's contemporaries, agreed with Wesley about the importance of sanctification but disagreed about the timing. According to Toplady, the sinner-Christian must continually return to the cross for new grace, without ever receiving the perfect love anticipated by Wesley: "Thou must save, and thou alone! / Nothing in my hand I bring; / Simply to thy Cross I cling." In the nineteenth century, Methodist hymnals included a version of Toplady's hymn—heavily edited by Anglican Thomas Cotterill in 1815—alongside Wesley's. Cotterill elided entire lines that denied human ability to struggle against sin, cutting, for instance: "Not the labors of my hands / Can fulfill thy law's demands." Methodist hymnals indexed "Rock of Ages" under the heading "The Sinner—Repentance," rather than under the subject of sanctification. This example suggests the existence of doctrinal differences de-emphasized by the organizational strategies of hymnal editors who desired to promote evangelical unity through song. The example also hints at the important role played by editors, compilers, and translators in mediating hymn meaning.[14]

The symbol of the cross is a crucial point of contact between doctrine and emotional experience, or between theology and culture. The evangelical hope of salvation rests on Jesus's suffering as a human, and his sinlessness as God. Sings the congregation, "My hope is built on nothing less than Jesus' blood and righteousness; / I dare not trust the sweetest frame." Evangelicals grounded their sweetest emotional experiences in their theological convictions. Yet the cultural power of the cross stemmed not only from intellectual affirmation of doctrine but also from deeply personal and emotional appropriation of theology as a lens through which to interpret life. Christians reflected on their own moment of justification as a stimulus to greater present and future devotion. In one of the most popular justification hymns, "Alas! and Did My Saviour Bleed?" as the Christian remembers Christ's justifying activity, she responds: "Dissolve my heart in thankfulness, / And melt mine eyes to tears." Since there is no way to repay the "debt of love I owe: Here, Lord, I give myself away,—'Tis all that I can do."[15] Recalling the moment of justification encouraged Christians to pursue sanctification with renewed zeal.

Hymns employ the first person singular in speaking of the cross, exhorting each singer to reflect that Jesus's blood was "shed for me," and that "my sin . . . is nailed to His cross." Evangelicals claimed the "dear cross" as a sacred symbol suitable for personal meditation and devotion: "here it is I find my heaven / while upon the cross I gaze." The diction selected to focus meditation on the cross contemplates Jesus as an agonizing Savior and bleeding Lamb, and visualizes in turn the thorns on his brow, his precious bleeding side, and crucified feet. Hymns metaphorically transform the goriness of Jesus's blood into a purifying stream: "There is a fountain filled with blood," that "can make the foulest clean"; "plunge now into the crimson flood / that washes white as snow."[16] Through emotionally intense language, evangelicals personally appropriated Christ's sufferings as a curative for their sin. As scholars read the emotional tenor of devotion to the cross, it is essential to consider simultaneously hymns' constant theological allusions; the fervent emotion exhibited in crucifixion hymns may thereby be distinguished from mere sentimentalism or romanticism by the grounding of emotional experience in doctrine.

In symbolically transforming Christ's sufferings into a source of purity, the cross redefines all suffering as productive of holiness. All the "woes of life . . . by the cross are sanctified." Since Jesus endured the cross in order to reach heaven, his followers must also expect to suffer as they travel. Hymns ask rhetorically, "Must Jesus bear the cross alone? / No there's a cross . . . for me." Jesus not only brings good out of incidental suffering, but actually sends suffering in love and mercy to provide "steps unto heaven." Christians need not fear trials or distress, since "the flame shall not hurt thee,—I only design / thy dross to consume, and thy gold to refine." Hymns exhort Christians to trust God's purifying design even when this purpose is not apparent: "God moves in a mysterious way . . . the bud may have a bitter taste, but sweet will be the flower." Hymns envision Christians as gladly submitting to the trials God sends, and even praying for "disaster, scorn, and pain!" since "all must work for good to me" in making known God's full salvation.[17]

Without God's constant intervention, even suffering sent in mercy would quickly overwhelm the helpless pilgrim. As Jesus calls pilgrims to travel "through the deep waters," he promises that all along the way, "I will be with thee thy trials to bless, / and sanctify to thee thy deepest distress." In describing who Jesus is and how he involves himself in assisting Christian pilgrims, hymns draw on a wide range of metaphors, many of them apparently conflicting. The implication is that evangelicals sense the limitation of even figurative language fully to convey Jesus's identity and relationship to themselves. Jesus is Savior and Friend, King and Brother, Judge and Advocate, Almighty God and Man of Sorrows, Redeemer and Divine Instructor, Healer and Sacrifice, Father of Mercies and Son of God, Creator and Anointed, Messiah and Guide. These metaphors reflect the interfacing of doctrine and experience. Hymn imagery focuses on Jesus's role in Christian theology, in divinely saving, redeeming, and judging sinners; metaphors simultaneously emphasize a personal relationship between Christians and their friend, brother, and instructor. This juxtaposition of metaphors, rather than reflecting a humanized or secularized understanding of who Jesus is, correlates evangelicals' cosmic and personal narratives of Jesus's saving activity. The Holy Spirit was often invoked as the source of sanctifying grace. For instance, "Come Holy Spirit, Heavenly Dove," seeks "all thy quickening powers; / Kindle a flame of sacred love / In these cold hearts of ours."[18] Hymns addressed Jesus more frequently than either the Holy Spirit or God the Father, but evangelical narrative theology assumed that all three persons played critical roles in the salvation process.

The journey heavenward is too difficult for individual pilgrims; they must travel as a community. Hymn narratives reflect evangelicals' understanding of the Christian life as both individual and collective: "we share our mutual woes, / our mutual burdens bear."[19] Hymn language moves back and forth between first person singular and plural voices, intermixed with second person addresses to others in the singing community; individuals can personally own the words being sung, identify with the singing community, and participate in the mutual giving and receiving of encouragement.[20] Hymn narratives reinforce evangelicals' sense of cultural unity by affirming affection for the church through emotionally rich language: "I love Thy church, O God!" and "How sweet to the soul is communion with saints!" Hymns simultaneously deny the existence of divisions within the church: "we are not divided, / all one body we, / one in hope and doctrine, / one in charity." Even when sung or read by individuals in private, hymns evoke the community: "though sundered far, by faith they meet / around one common mercy-seat."[21] Hymns thus mirror evangelicals' longing to transcend theological and ecclesiological disputes, and function to cement singers' self-conception as members of a unified Christian community.

Hymns reflect evangelicals' sense that pilgrims in the Christian community must help one another progress toward sanctification. "Stand up stand up for Jesus / ye soldiers of the cross" and "Onward Christian soldiers" address other members in the congregation, urging them to keep moving toward holiness: "Like a mighty army / moves the Church of God, / brothers, we are treading / where the saints have trod." Hymns express a broadly inclusive definition of church as consisting of all who fight for Jesus—in contrast to a narrower, sacramental conception of church, defined by common participation in the Lord's Supper. Hymns offer a means by which soldiers of Christ admonish one another to maintain guard against sin, to ensure arrival at the goal of sanctification. "Leave no unguarded place, / no weakness of the soul," since "ten thousand foes arise; / and hosts of sins are pressing hard / to draw thee from the skies. / O watch, and fight, and pray; . . . Ne'er think the vict'ry won, / nor once at ease sit down; . . . till thou obtain the crown." The sufferings endured by past pilgrims prod current pilgrims to persevere for their prize in heaven. This "long cloud of witnesses / show the same path to heaven." The individual is encouraged by watching others and urged forward by the knowledge that others watch him: "A cloud of witnesses around / hold thee in full survey."[22] By recalling the timeless, collective narrative of which the Christian journey is a part, hymns point beyond the confines of the congregation—transcending geographic and temporal boundaries to foster perseverance in the journey through life.

The narrative quality of hymn texts interfaces evangelicals' collective sense of purpose with their past experiences and future expectations of participating in a cosmic drama. The collective repetition of hymns builds the faith of both singers and hearers in the doctrinal truth and experiential relevance of the cosmic story: "I love to tell the story / because I know 'tis true; it satisfies my longings, . . . what seems, each time I tell it, more wonderfully sweet . . . for those who know it best / seem hungering and thirsting / to hear it like the rest." Hymns, sweeter at each repetition, remind singers and hearers of the overarching narrative that frames their lives. At the same time, hymns recall past experiences of the story's relevance, thus reinforcing a future hope. In the very process of singing, congregations ritually performed a speech-act: "here I raise my Ebenezer," or symbolic marker, that "through many dangers, toils, and snares," "hither by Thy help I'm come; / and I hope, by Thy good pleasure, / safely to arrive at home." By recalling the past and anticipating the future, evangelicals built one another's faith that, through the cosmic story, their own life stories derived purpose and meaning.

Hymn narratives breathe with evangelicals' longing for sanctification as the means to experience a closer relationship with God. In emotionally rich language—reflective of the experiential appropriation of doctrine—hymns lament, "I sigh from this body of sin to be free, / which hinders my joy and communion with thee." Hymns offer impassioned prayers for purity from sin as productive of deeper relationship with Jesus: "Lord Jesus I long to be perfectly whole; / I want Thee forever, to live in my soul; / break down every idol, cast out every foe; / now wash me, and I shall be whiter than snow." The driving purpose of the Christian pilgrimage is "pressing on to God," for the "soul that's born of God, / pants to view his glorious face." Intimate relationship with God through Jesus can be experienced to some degree on earth, as well as in heaven: "Jesus the very thought of thee / with sweetness fills the breast; . . . Jesus be thou our glory now, / and through eternity."

Worship accompanies sanctification, as a response to work already accomplished by Jesus, and furthers growth in holiness, as preparation for the collective relationship between Christ and the church in heaven. Hymn texts call Christians to sing "thankful songs" with joy and cheer, in response to Jesus's justifying and sanctifying activity; since "the Son of God came down to die, / that we might be forgiven . . . join every tongue to praise the Lord." As God continually offers "perpetual blessings" and "streams of mercy never ceasing," these inevitably demand songs of "loudest praise." As Christians respond to God's blessings through worship, they take steps forward in the journey toward sanctification. "As we journey we will sing," and thus "begin the heavenly theme" that will grow "as to Canaan on ye move." The communal practice of congregational hymn singing, in particular, prepares Christians for heaven by foreshadowing the future relationship between Christ and the church. As Christians gather with the earthly church in "the dwellings of thy love . . . where God appoints to hear" prayer and praise, they find themselves "new graces ever gaining / from this our day of rest." The Sabbath, the day especially devoted to congregational worship, is an emblem and "dear pledge of glorious rest"—consisting not of inactivity but of the "holy duties" and "holy pleasures" of worship with the gathered church.[23] By repeatedly enacting the cycle of congregational, Sabbath worship, evangelicals gain a foretaste of heavenly relationship with Jesus; new graces received at each repetition assist individuals to lead a sanctified life throughout the week, especially when physically separated from the support of the pilgrim community.

Traveling the path to purity involves more than the performance of Sabbath rituals. Hymns reflect an understanding of Christian pilgrimage as holistic, transcending boundaries between sacred and profane times, spaces, or practices. As Christians take daily steps toward sanctification, they seek to consecrate their entire lives to God: "I am my Lord's, and He is mine." With this understanding of the Christian life, every ordinary, daily activity can be devoted to holy living: "Take my life and let it be / consecrated, Lord, to Thee; / take my hands and let them move / at the impulse of Thy love . . . take my lips and let them be / fill'd with messages from Thee; . . . take my moments and my days, / let them flow in ceaseless praise." At every moment and in every activity, Christians can live for Jesus. Holiness bears fruit not only in the individual's relationship with God but also in interpersonal relationships. The "fruits of thy salvation / in our hearts and lives abound" in kindly words and virtuous life, "some work of love begun, / some deed of kindness done, / some wand'rer sought and won."[24] In the context of daily human interactions, Christians can love God by demonstrating his love to others. Evangelicals' holistic understanding of pilgrimage infuses every activity and relationship with cosmic significance. It is inadequate, therefore, in studying evangelicalism, to focus solely on traditionally "religious" times, spaces, or activities, since the secular could be redefined as sacred.

The evangelical narrative reinterprets all of life—its Sabbaths, its weekdays, and even its conclusion—as pointing toward a sanctified relationship between Christ and his worshipping church. Death, the end point of pilgrims' earthly journey, is redefined by hymn theology as victory rather than tragedy. Pilgrims, paradoxically, "shall conquer, though they die." The story of Christ's crucifixion ends in the resurrection, which foreshadows the resurrection of all Christians: "See, the Saviour leaves the tomb . . . sin o'erthrown, and captive hell! Where, O death, is now thy sting?" Hymns metaphorically compare death to crossing the river Jordan, alluding to the Old Testament narrative of the Israelites' entrance to Canaan, the promised land. Death, like Jordan, is but a narrow sea, that "divides / this heavenly land from ours." Jesus, guiding the Christian across the sea, will "bid my anxious fears subside" and "make a dying bed / feel soft as downy pillows." Hymns remind both the dying and the living that the story of their lives continues after death. In fact, the story gets better: "There are depths of love that I cannot know / till I cross the narrow sea. / There are heights of joy that I may not reach / till I rest in peace with Thee."[25] Rather than remaining a thing to be dreaded, death—thus reenvisioned—becomes a passage to a better land.

The evangelical narrative culminates with arrival in heaven—which is not only an ending, but the beginning of a new story. Death demarcates the completion of the sanctification process, and the end of sin and suffering: "in heaven alone no sin is found," since saints will "never, never sin." Hymns picture heaven, like earth, metaphorically. In contrast to the verbal metaphors that describe the journey to heaven, nouns connoting the cessation of activity envision heaven itself: rest, home, and eternal day. Rather than indicating the domestication of religion, the feminization of God, or the humanization of divine hopes, pictures of heaven embedded in hymns suggest the power of narrative to use experience as a lens onto doctrinal meaning. At the end of their long journey from sin to sanctification, pilgrims hope for heaven as the place and time they will finally be able to rest from sin and suffering. Alluding to shared cultural experiences, hymns compare heaven to a Sabbath that "ne'er shall end," a dear land of rest, and "seas of heav'nly rest," free from all the toils and cares of life. Having lamented sin as a source of alienation between themselves and God, hymns envision heavenly rest as a close embrace with God: "how sweet to rest / forever on my Saviour's breast" and "in his bosom." Conceiving of life as a journey, hymns anticipate heaven as arrival at a happy home, the place of God's abode. Christians will dwell with him there in "mansions of glory and endless delight." Whereas the earthly journey leads through dark and dangerous pathways, God's presence in heaven "scatters night away," along with all its gloom. In heaven, there are rivers of life divine, trees of paradise, and an everlasting feast. Evangelicals borrow imagery from daily experience as successive linguistic approximations for their ultimately ineffable hopes. Metaphors describing heaven's pleasures are strikingly vague and sparse, compared with hymns' clear articulation of the hope for closer relationship with God himself: the source from whom "oceans of endless pleasure roll," and the only bliss for which the saint pants.[26] God is the center of the heavenly hope anticipated by hymn narratives.

The cosmic story reaches its climax when "God the Son forever reigns" in full glory. Jesus, once crucified, sits enthroned, surrounded by "glorified millions" in the Church above, who worship before the eternal throne with "united heart and voice." Hymns picture heaven as an everlasting worship service, "where congregations ne'er break up." Divisions between Christians are finally abolished; in "perfect love and friendship" the "saints of all ages in harmony meet." Having "conquered in the fight," sinners, transformed into purified saints, "reign with Christ in endless day" and sing a victor's song. The church, no longer alienated from God by sin, at last behold Christ on his throne and see the Father's face. Emotionally exuberant language describes heavenly worship, pointing to the core longing of evangelical culture for restored relationship with God. "Anthems of rapture" unceasingly roll in an everlasting song of saving grace. The "enraptured host" rejoice in "ecstasies unknown" and sing God's "loving-kindness in the skies!"[27] The pilgrim community's progress from sin to sanctification eventuates in perfect relationship between Jesus Christ and his worshipping church.

The narratives embedded in evangelical hymnody conflict with prevailing scholarly interpretations of evangelical theology and culture. Religious historians have emphasized the doctrine of justification, expressed in individual conversion experiences—often in the context of revivals. While these themes accurately reflect components of evangelical culture, the internal evidence of hymn texts suggests significantly stronger, more enduring concern for the doctrine of sanctification, its implications for daily living within Christian communities, and its culmination in restored relationship between Christ and the church. Justification marks the commencement rather than the consummation of the evangelical narrative. Sanctification offers a theological lens through which to view the daily, life-long process of growth in holiness, thus offering context for personal life stories within the broader framework of a cosmic narrative of origins, purpose, and destiny.

The texture of the Christian life, largely invisible in studies focused on the endpoints of conversion and salvation, materializes in the telling of the story. The evangelical narrative amplifies, in profoundly cosmic and deeply personal dimensions, Christians' step-by-step progression from sin to sanctification. The evidence of hymns' narrative theology suggests that a wider range of narrative texts do theological work. The theological positions articulated by ministers in their sermons and treatises reflect only certain aspects of evangelicalism; prescriptive texts must be read in conjunction with more popular texts, which are drenched in theology and narrative—including not only hymns, but poems, periodicals, memoirs, letters, and novels—that incarnate theology through the unfolding of the stories they tell. Verbal texts must also be read within the context of cultural uses: as embodied in music, books, commercial networks, and religious practices.

A corollary to the argument for expanding the range of "theological" texts is that a wider range of cultural practices than those often studied as religious do theological work. Scholars of evangelical culture, making sharp distinctions between sacred and secular practices, have posited a linear process of cultural declension, caused by and resulting in the domestication and secularization of religion. The narrative theology embodied in evangelical hymnody, rather than limiting itself to transactions conducted within the confines of sacred times, spaces, and practices, viewed the whole of life as directed toward heaven. For most evangelical Christians, revivals were never an everyday occurrence; specifically religious rituals of any sort occupied a relatively minor proportion of time each day and week. But gradual growth in holiness could occur constantly. By redefining secular experience in light of theology, hymn narratives served a sacralizing, rather than a secularizing function.[28] Completing the most mundane daily task or passively submitting to suffering could be as profoundly "religious" in this framework as clearly defined practices like evangelism or hymn singing. Hymn narratives—memorized in childhood and repeated by evangelicals innumerable times throughout their lives and even on their deathbeds—articulate a shared cultural longing for sanctification. Evangelical narrative theology offers meaning and purpose to past and present experiences, and anticipates its ultimate fulfillment in the future as the purified church unites in worship around the everlasting throne of Jesus Christ.

Notes

1. Rev. Charles P. Bush, AM, *Five Years in China; or, The Factory Boy Made a Missionary. The Life and Observations of Rev. William Aitchison, Late Missionary to China* (Philadelphia: Presbyterian Board of Publication, 1865), 147, 271, 274.

2. John Bunyan, *The Pilgrim's Progress from This World, to That Which Is to Come: Delivered under the Similitude of a Dream, Wherein Is Discovered the Manner of His Setting Out, His Dangerous Journey, and Safe Arrival at the Desired Country* (London:

Nathan Ponder, 1678). Bunyan's influence should be viewed alongside that exerted by Horace Bushnell's *Christian Nurture* (New York: C. Scribner, 1861; Hartford: Edwin Hunt, 1847), which presented an organic model of gradual, continuous growth, free from the crisis moments assumed by Bunyan.

3. For definitions of evangelical culture, see Joan Jacobs Brumberg, *Mission for Life: The Story of the Family of Adoniram Judson, the Dramatic Events of the First American Foreign Mission, and the Course of Evangelical Religion in the Nineteenth Century* (New York: Macmillan, 1980), xi, 11;, I use Brumberg's model in conjunction with theoretical work done by Clifford Geertz, *The Interpretation of Cultures: Selected Essays* (London: Fontana Press, 1994); Stanley Fish, "Interpreting the Variorum," *Critical Inquiry* 2 (1976): 465–85; Fish, *Is There a Text in This Class? The Authority of Interpretive Communities* (Cambridge, MA: Harvard University Press, 1980); Benedict Anderson, *Imagined Communities: Reflections on the Origin and Spread of Nationalism* (New York: Verso 1991 [1983]); James L. Machor, ed., *Readers in History: Nineteenth-Century American Literature and the Contexts of Response* (Baltimore: Johns Hopkins University Press, 1993); Brian Stock, *Listening for the Text: On the Uses of the Past* (Baltimore: Johns Hopkins University Press, 1990).

4. See my "Salt to the World: A Cultural History of Evangelical Reading, Writing, and Publishing Practices in Mid-Nineteenth-Century America" (PhD diss., Harvard University, 2000), 194–262.

5. Henry Ward Beecher, *Revival Hymns* (Boston: Phillips, Sampson and Company, 1858), iv; Rev. William H. Parker, *The Psalmody of the Church: Its Authors, Singers and Uses* (New York: Fleming H. Revell Company, 1889), v; James O. Murray, DD, *Christian Hymnology: A Sermon Preached in the Brick Church, New York, Dec. 12, 1869* (New York: Charles Scribner, 1870), 25.

6. William G. McLoughlin, *The American Evangelicals, 1800–1900: An Anthology* (New York: Harper and Row, 1968); Brumberg, *Mission for Life;* Virginia Lieson Brereton, *From Sin to Salvation: Stories of Women's Conversations, 1800 to the Present* (Bloomington: Indiana University Press, 1991); Mark A. Noll, et al., eds., *Evangelicalism: Comparative Studies of Popular Protestantism in North America, the British Isles, and Beyond, 1700–1990* (New York: Oxford University Press, 1994); Iain H. Murray, *Revival and Revivalism: The Making and Marriage of American Evangelicalism, 1750–1858* (Edinburgh: Banner of Truth Trust, 1994); Sang Hyun Lee and Allen Guelzo, eds., *Edwards in Our Time: Jonathan Edwards and Contemporary Theological Issues* (Grand Rapids, MI: Eerdmans, 1999); John Bealle, *Public Worship, Private Faith: Sacred Harp and American Folksong* (Athens: University of Georgia Press, 1997), 16; Ian Bradley, *Abide with Me: The World of Victorian Hymns* (London: SCM Press, 1997), 110.

7. Ann Douglas, *The Feminization of American Culture* (New York: Anchor Books, 1977), 5–10, 62, 68, 115, 347–49; David S. Reynolds, *Faith in Fiction: The Emer-*

gence of Religious Literature in America (Cambridge, MA: Harvard University Press, 1981); 2, 5, 71, 197; Karen Halttunen, *Confidence Men and Painted Women: A Study of Middle-Class Culture in America, 1830–1870* (New Haven: Yale University Press, 1982), 57; R. Laurence Moore, *Selling God: American Religion in the Marketplace of Culture* (New York: Oxford University Press, 1994), 5, 10; Amanda Porterfield, *Feminine Spirituality in America: From Sarah Edwards to Martha Graham* (Philadelphia: Temple University Press, 1980); June Hadden Hobbs, *"I Sing for I Cannot Be Silent": The Feminization of American Hymnody, 1870–1920* (Pittsburgh: University of Pittsburgh Press, 1997); Susan S. Tamke, *O For a Thousand Tongues, Make a Joyful Noise unto the Lord: Hymns as a Reflection of Victorian Social Attitudes* (Athens: Ohio University Press, 1978); Lionel Adey, *Class and Idol in the English Hymn* (Vancouver: University of British Columbia Press, 1988).

    8. Elizabeth Rundle Charles, *The Voice of Christian Life in Song; or, Hymns and Hymn-Writers of Many Lands and Ages* (New York: Robert Carter and Brothers, 1866); John Julian, *Dictionary of Hymnology* (London: J. Murray, 1892); Erik Routley, *Hymns and the Faith* (Greenwich, CT: Seabury Press, 1956); Sandra S. Sizer, *Gospel Hymns and Social Religion* (Philadelphia: Temple University Press, 1978); Ellen Jane Lorenz, *Glory Hallelujah: The Story of the Campmeeting Spiritual* (Nashville: Abingdon, 1978); Albert Christ-Janer, *American Hymns, Old and New* (New York: Columbia University Press, 1980); Frank Colquhoun, *Hymns That Live: Their Meaning and Message* (London: Hodder and Stoughton, 1980); Samuel J. Rogal, *Sisters of Sacred Song: A Select Listing of Women Hymnodists in Great Britain and America* (New York: Garland, 1981); S. Paul Schilling, *The Faith We Sing: How the Message of Hymns Can Enhance Christian Belief* (Philadelphia: Westminster Press, 1983); Jon Michael Spencer, *Black Hymnody: A Hymnological History of the African-American Church* (Knoxville: University of Tennessee Press, 1992).

    9. Melvin E. Dieter, et al., *Five Views on Sanctification* (Grand Rapids, MI: Zondervan, 1987), 51, 57, 72, 158.

    10. P. P. Bliss, "Almost Persuaded Now to Believe," 1880s: 126:3; Isaac Watts, "My Saviour My Almighty Friend," 129:25; John Cennick, "Jesus My All to Heaven Is Gone," 2:52; Charlotte Elliott, "Just as I Am without One Plea," 118:26; Philip Doddridge, "Grace 'Tis a Charming Sound," 26:39; Doddridge, "Awake and Stretch Every Nerve," 123:25; Horatius Bonar, "I Heard the Voice of Jesus Say," 333:15 and 1880s: 126:3.

    11. Henry Lyte, "Jesus I My Cross Have Taken," 45:35; Augustus Toplady, "Your Harps Ye Trembling Saints," 201:22; Joseph Addison, "The Lord My Pasture Will Supply," 152:24; George Keith, "How Firm a Foundation," 12:47; Watts, "Thee We Adore Eternal King," 202:21; Watts, "Broad Is the Road That Leads to Death," 58:34; Watts, "Early My God without Delay," 122:25; John Henry Newman, "Lead Kindly Light," 1880s: 48:4; Watts, "Lord of the Worlds Above," 168:22; J. H. Gilmore, "He Leadeth Me

O Blessed Thought," 1880s: 48:4; Addison, "How Are Thy Servants Blest O Lord," 202:21; William Muhlenberg, "I Would Not Live Alway," 37:37; Watts, "When I Can Read My Title Clear," 8:50; Watts, "God Is the Refuge of His People," 155:23; Helen Williams, "With Thee I Seek Protecting Power," 202:21; Hugh Stowell, "From Every Stormy Wind That Blows," 45:35; Robert Seagrave, "Rise My Soul and Stretch Thy Wings," 58:34; John Newton, "Savior Visit Thy Plantation," 168:22; Sir John Bowring, "In the Cross of Christ I Glory," 295:16; William Cowper, "What Various Hindrances We Meet," 155:23; Sabine Baring-Gould, "Onward Christian Soldiers," 1880s: 25:5; Samuel Medley, "Awake My Soul in Joyful Lays," 122:25; John Leland, "The Day Is Past and Gone," 78:31; Addison, "When All Thy Mercies O Lord," 45:35; Reginald Heber, "By Cool Siloams Shady Rill," 218:20; Newton, "While with Ceaseless Course," 92:29.

12. Charles Wesley, "Love Divine, All Loves Excelling," 16:42; Bowring, "In the Cross of Christ I Glory," 295:16; Newton, "Approach My Soul," 137:24; Charles Wesley, "Blow Ye the Trumpet," 13:45; Watts, "Alas and Did My Saviour Bleed," 13:45; Toplady, "Rock of Ages," 16:42; Charles Wesley, "Jesus, Lover of My Soul," 8:50; George Doane, "Softly Now the Light of Day," 253:18; Watts, "Plunged in a Gulf of Dark Despair," 81:30.

13. Levi Scott and Committee, *Hymnal of the Methodist Episcopal Church with Tunes* (New York: Nelson and Phillips, 1878); Rev. Joseph T. Duryea, *The Presbyterian Hymnal* (Philadelphia: Presbyterian Board of Publication, 1874).

14. Julian, *Dictionary of Hymnology,* 971.

15. Watts, "Alas and Did My Saviour Bleed," 13:45.

16. Edward Mote, "My Hope is Built on Nothing Less," 1880s: 126:3; Elliott, "Just as I Am without One Plea," 118:26; Watts, "Alas and Did My Saviour Bleed," 13:45; James Allen, "Sweet the Moments Rich with Blessing," 81:30; John Bakewell, "Hail Thou Once Despised Jesus," 155:23; Jonathan Evans, "Hark the Voice of Love," 115:26; William R. Featherstone, "My Jesus I Love Thee," 1750–1950: 108:56; Fanny Crosby, "I Am Thine O Lord," 1750–1950: 70:42; James Nicholson, "Lord Jesus I Long to Be Perfectly," 1880s: 126:3; Cowper, "There Is a Fountain," 37:37; Charles Wesley, "O for a Thousand Tongues to Sing," 21:41; Stockton, "Come Every Soul by Sin Oppressed," 1750–1950: 65:47.

17. Bowring, "In the Cross of Christ I Glory," 295:16; Thomas Shepherd, "Must Jesus Bear the Cross Alone," 253:18; Sarah Adams, "Nearer My God to Thee," 81:30; Watts, "Alas and Did My Saviour Bleed," 13:45; Cowper, "God Moves in a Mysterious Way," 31:38; Wesley, "And Let This Feeble Body Fail," 99:28; Lyte, "Jesus I My Cross Have Taken," 45:35.

18. Watts, "Come Holy Spirit, Heavenly Dove," 26:39.

19. John Fawcett, "Blest Be the Tie That Binds," 22:40.

20. Hymnal prefaces often claim to avoid including any sectarian hymns: "As the

object of the editor is, to aid the devotions of all true Christians, who may choose to avail themselves of his humble labours; he has not introduced into the work any hymns, which can properly be called sectarian; that is, such as can be sung only by one denomination of Christians. It is believed, that there is not a hymn in this whole collection, which may not be used by all persons of evangelical views and pious feelings," and every hymn "ought . . . to become the common property of Christendom"; Archibald Alexander, *A Selection of Hymns, Adapted to the Devotions of the Closet, the Family and the Social Circle; and Containing Subjects Appropriate to the Monthly Concerts of Prayer for the Success of Missions and Sunday Schools and Other Special Occasions,* 3rd ed. (New York: Jonathan Leavitt, 1832), iv; John Mason Neale, trans. and ed., *Hymns, Chiefly Mediaeval, on the Joys and Glories of Paradise* (London: J. T. Hayes, 1865), ix.

21. Timothy Dwight, "I Love Thy Kingdom Lord," 45:35; David Denham, " 'Mid Scenes of Confusion," 105:27; Baring-Gould, "Onward Christian Soldiers," 1880s: 25:5; Stowell, "From Every Stormy Wind That Blows," 45:35.

22. George Duffield Jr., "Stand Up Stand Up for Jesus," 333:15 and 1880s: 25:5; Baring-Gould, "Onward Christian Soldiers," 1880s: 25:5; Charles Wesley, "Soldiers of Christ Arise," 155:23; George Heath, "My Soul Be on Thy Guard," 99:28; Watts, "Am I a Soldier of the Cross," 7:52; Watts, "Give Me the Wings of Faith to Rise," 105:27; Doddridge, "Awake and Stretch Every Nerve," 122:25.

23. Watts, "Before Jehovah's Awful Throne," 42:36; John Cawood, "Hark What Mean Those Holy Voices," 273:17; Watts, "Come Let Us Join Our Cheerful Songs," 45:35; Joseph Hart, "Glory to God on High," 81:30; Watts, "My God How Endless Is Thy Love," 92:29; Robert Robinson, "Come Thou Fount of Ev'ry Blessing," 5:54; Cennick, "Children of the Heavenly King," 22:40; Martin Madan, "Now Begin the Heavenly Theme," 122:25; Watts, "Lord of the Worlds Above," 168:22; Christopher Wordsworth, "O Day of Rest," 1880s: 48:4; Newton, "Safely through Another Week," 99:28; Joseph Stennett, "Another Six Days Work Is Done," 137:24.

24. Doddridge, "O Happy Day That Fixed My Choice," 58:34; Frances Havergal, "Take My Life and Let It Be," 1880s: 126:3; Walter Shirley, "Lord Dismiss Us with Thy Blessing," 16:42; Frederick Faber, S. D. Phelps, "Savior Thy Dying Love," 1880s: 126:3.

25. Watts, "Am I a Soldier of the Cross," 7:52; Thomas Scott, "Angels Roll the Rock Away," 137:24; Watts, "There Is a Land of Pure Delight," 13:45; Watts, "Why Should We Start and Shrink," 65:33; Crosby, "I Am Thine O Lord," 1750–1950: 70:42.

26. Stennett, "Another Six Days Work Is Done," 137:24; Bernard of Cluny, "Jerusalem the Golden," 1880s: 48:4; Watts, "When I Can Read My Title Clear," 8:50; Dwight, "I Love Thy Kingdom Lord," 45:35; Seagraves, "Rise My Soul and Stretch Thy Wings," 58:34; John Keble, "Sun of My Soul Thou Savior," 333:15 and 1880s: 25:5; Stennett, "On Jordan's Stormy Banks I Stand," 6:53; Joseph Bromehead "Jerusalem My

Happy Home," 3:56; Stennett, "Majestic Sweetness Sits Enthroned," 115:26; Newton, "While with Ceaseless Course," 92:29; Featherstone, "My Jesus I Love Thee," 1750–1950: 108:56; Gilmore, "He Leadeth Me O Blessed Thought," 1880s: 48:4; Charles Wesley, "And Let This Feeble Body Fail," 99:28; Newton, "Safely through Another Week," 1880s: 25:5; Watts, "I Send the Joys of Earth Away," 168:22.

27. Stennett, "On Jordan's Stormy Banks I Stand," 6:53; Samuel Wesley, "Behold the Savior of Mankind," 105:27; Denham, "'Mid Scenes of Confusion," 105:27; Newton, "Safely through Another Week," 1880s: 25:5; Anne Steele, "Ye Wretched Hungry Starving Poor," 92:29; Bromehead, "Jerusalem My Happy Home," 3:56; Fawcett, "Blest Be the Tie That Binds," 22:40; Muhlenberg, "I Would Not Live Alway," 37:37; Bernard of Cluny, "Jerusalem the Golden," 1880s: 48:4; Perronet, "All Hail the Power of Jesus' Name," 4:55; Fawcett, "Lord Dismiss Us with Thy Blessing," 16:42; Duffield, "Stand Up Stand Up for Jesus," 333:15 and 1880s: 25:5; Toplady, "Rock of Ages," 16:42; Robert Lowry, "Shall We Gather at the River," 1880s: 48:4; Charles Wesley, "And Let This Feeble Body Fail," 92:28; Medley, "Awake My Soul in Joyful Lays," 122:25.

28. Leigh Schmidt, "Mixed Blessings: Christianization And Secularization," *Reviews in American History* 26, no. 4 (1998): 642. Secularization as the two alternatives for cultural progression. He observes admonition that it is dangerous to dichotomize Christianization and Secularization as the two alternatives for cultural progression.

10
Children of the Heavenly King

Hymns in the Religious and Social Experience of Children, 1780–1850

Heather D. Curtis

ON JULY 4, 1831, nearly 2,500 children, parents, and Sunday school teachers crowded into the sanctuary of Park Street Church in Boston, Massachusetts, to take part in an Independence Day celebration sponsored by the Boston Sabbath School Union. The ceremony opened with an original hymn sung by the juvenile choir, which was directed by the aspiring hymn writer Lowell Mason. Unlike the unruly hordes who gathered out on the adjacent Boston Common to witness the "infantry parade, ringing of the bells, and discharge of cannon," these children "all dressed so neat and gay" processed up the steps of the church in orderly fashion to celebrate the anniversary of American Independence by singing praises to God for the "sweet land of liberty" where "freedom's song" might ring out "from every mountain-side." "Our father's God!" they prayed, "to thee— / Author of Liberty! / To thee we sing; / Long may our land be bright / With freedom's holy light— / Protect us by thy might, / Great God, our King!"[1]

In future years, this hymn—Samuel Francis Smith's "America"—would be dubbed the "national hymn" of the United States. Generations of school children would come to know and celebrate their identity as Americans by singing the words "My country! 'tis of thee." For the young people assembled at Park Street Church in 1831, however, "America" was just one of several compositions sung during the ceremony. In the opening song, the juvenile choir proclaimed the blessings of both "peaceful home" and "Sabbath school."[2] Following the minister's "Address to the Children," which highlighted the way in which "the Bible so frequently speaks of children in language of parental kindness and affection," the entire congregation joined in singing a hymn that spoke of citizenship in a heavenly, rather than an earthly society; of the joys of salvation, rather than the duties of patriotism.[3] "Behold a youthful chorus sings / Hosanna to the King of kings," the congregation sang. "The Savior comes—and they proclaim / Salvation sent in Jesus' name." This hymn reminded the children present at Park Street Church that they were Christians called to profess the message of the gospel and to praise the Lord of heaven to whom they owed their ultimate allegiance.[4]

This brief recounting of the Boston Sabbath School Union's 1831 Fourth of July celebration suggests that hymnody played an important role in shaping the religious and social identities of children in the early republic. In repeating the words of particular hymns such as "America," children learned what it meant to be patriotic citizens. Through their participation in the rituals of Independence Day celebrations, children enacted the tenets expressed in the words of the songs they sang. The sweet, harmonious singing of Sunday school students in their neat, clean clothing set them apart from the disorderly crowds—including the unruly children—who used the Fourth of July as an occasion to engage in raucous behavior, and instead symbolized their status as respectable constituents of the democratic nation and their dedication to promoting an orderly society.[5] Hymns also encouraged children to be thankful for their families, obedient to their Sunday school teachers, and friendly with their classmates. Singing both with and about the important people in their lives reinforced the ties that bound children to parents, mentors, and friends. Finally, the practice of hymn singing was meant to draw young people into the community of saints. Hymns introduced children to the principles of Protestant theology, urged them to cultivate a relationship with God through the process of repentance and conversion, and trained them to set their hearts on heaven—the ultimate society to which they should desire to belong.

Drawing on Sunday school reports and tracts, broadsides, devotional books and hymnals written specifically for children, periodicals, and novels such as Susan Warner's enormously popular *The Wide, Wide Word* (1850), this chapter explores the various ways in which young people in the early American republic were encouraged to appropriate hymns as a means for translating Christian doctrine into religious and social experience.[6] By asking how the practice of hymn singing helped to incorporate children into the multiple communities—familial, political, and religious—in which adults wished them to be included, the study evaluates the ways in which hymns served as means of both cultural integration and spiritual transformation.

Many scholars have commented on the challenge of writing the history of "children's religion." Exploring children's inner spirituality is especially difficult since their experiences are most often related through "adult sources and adult eyes" or at best through reminiscences in which the adult subject's childhood appears through "the veil of memory and nostalgia."[7] Given these apparent obstacles, most historians have focused primarily upon adult ideas about children, rather than attempting to uncover the religious experience of children themselves.[8] Hymns offer a unique and rarely exploited opportunity to shed light upon the spiritual lives of Protestant young people. Although hymn texts themselves are "adult sources," examining the ways in which children were encouraged to use these texts can further our understanding of the texture of children's religious experience. Through careful attention to the actual practice of hymn singing in addition to the theological content of hymn lyrics, we can recover a fuller—albeit incomplete—picture of children's religion in the early nineteenth century.

This emphasis on the way hymns functioned in children's lived religious experience also serves to complicate scholarly narratives that chart a smooth transition in children's hymnody from an older, "Puritan" view that associated children with original sin and stressed the fearful consequences of an unrepentant state, to a newer, "romantic" or "sentimental" understanding of childhood that emphasized the child's purity, innocence, and special spiritual status. Although it is possible to discern a general liberalizing trend in attitudes toward childhood during the antebellum period through a focused study of hymn lyrics, attention to lived experience suggests that this theological progression was not as linear in practice as it may have been in theory. Hymns such as Isaac Watts's "Solemn Thoughts of God and Death"—a song that encouraged its young readers to "improve the hours" because death could come upon them unexpectedly, at any moment—were printed in the same hymnals and magazines that pictured children as innocent "lambs" specially loved by Jesus.[9] While most studies of early nineteenth-century children's hymnody highlight the shift from a rhetoric of terror (most often associated with Watts's *Divine Songs Attempted in Easy Language for the Use of Children*, 1715), to a rhetoric of guilt (embodied in the lyrics of Jane and Anne Taylor's *Hymns for Infant Minds*, 1809), to a rhetoric of love (manifest in Cecil Frances Alexander's *Hymns for Little Children*, 1848), I will emphasize the persistence of all these themes and explore the consequences of this ambiguity for the religious and social lives of children in the early Republic.[10]

That young people were the focus of intense concern—even anxiety—during the early national era has been cogently argued by historians of family ideology, education, political philosophy, and literature.[11] As the brief vignette of the Boston Sabbath School Union's Fourth of July celebration suggests, the belief that young people held the key to the success of the new nation stimulated adult worries about the rising generation. If the political experiment was to succeed, children needed to imbibe and embody the democratic ideals established in the Constitution. Hymns were seen as a primary means for accomplishing this goal of evoking patriotic sentiments among the young. Samuel Smith's "America" was only one of scores of original texts composed for annual Sunday school Independence Day ceremonies. The August 1839 edition of the *Sabbath School Treasury*, a Baptist children's magazine published in Boston, reprinted an "original hymn sung on the 4th of July at the Sunday school celebration, Charles St" that extolled the "blessed land" where Christians found freedom from tyranny, freedom to "breathe the spirit before it's Maker's throne" and to worship God as they saw fit.[12] The periodical also included a description of the ceremony that noted that "the exercises were interspersed by singing several hymns prepared for the occasion." The author praised the Sunday school teachers for organizing the event, and keeping the children from "yonder common" where they might have "engaged in hilarity and mirth, sipping the intoxicating bowl, or listening to the low and vulgar song." Instead, these children were gathered in the church, singing the nation's praises in "fine style" and evincing the "good order and decorum" that the occasion demanded. "Our pleasure was heightened," the author noted, "by the gratification [the singing] seemed to afford the children, and the animation with which they entered into it." Through their seemingly willing and active participation in this ritual event the young people gathered at Charles Street Meeting House manifested in their behavior the values they proclaimed in their song. The adult observers rejoiced that the rising generation was exhibiting the qualities necessary for the continued flourishing of the fledgling nation.[13]

If Independence Day hymns were meant to have a didactic purpose for the children who participated in the celebrations, they were also conceived as a means for influencing adults—particularly those who might be tempted to engage in "drunken revelries" and "vulgar song," or perhaps even to ignore the anniversary altogether. "Sing some hymns . . . call out the youth, and the fathers and mothers will follow," one author urged. "The effect is good upon the people." Through their orderly deportment, smiling faces, and spirited singing children demonstrated "proper observance" of the holiday to the adult spectators and to nonconforming children.[14] The content of the hymns was also designed to have an effect on both young people and their elders, reminding them of the link between freedom and faith: "For liberty, / Great God, to thee / Our grateful thanks we pay," the juvenile choir sang, "For thanks, we know, / To thee, we owe, / On Independent day."[15] Lyrics like these, when proclaimed by neatly clad, perfectly disciplined children, hymn writers believed, could not fail to touch the emotions of adult audiences and impress upon them the importance of cultivating virtue and propriety for the future of the republican experiment. "What is more calculated to inspire, and call forth the better feelings of parents," another Sunday school spokesperson asked, "than to see their children free and acknowledging the author of all their blessings?"[16]

While such sentiments admittedly reveal more about adult views of young people than they do about the inner spiritual lives of the children who were the objects of such intense scrutiny, the numerous descriptions of Independence Day celebrations do show that hymn singing was a central feature of children's participation in the religious and civic rituals of the early Republic. The reports also indicate that children's hymnody was considered an important means for the cultural integration of both children and adults. Although children's responses to the lyrics they sang and the practices in which they engaged most often remain obscured behind the veil of adult interpretation, some accounts of Fourth of July celebrations do offer a refracted glimpse of how children reacted. On one occasion, for example, a young girl watched her classmates entering the church "in orderly procession" and, looking up at her Sunday school teacher, exclaimed "O if these children should all meet in heaven, what a happy meeting that would be." Unlike the adult commentators, this little girl did not mention the orderly manner in which her fellow students conducted themselves. Nor did she discuss the political significance of the event. Instead, she construed the gathering of her schoolmates in primarily social and spiritual terms. While this response was certainly one that adults would have encouraged, it suggests that children were not only objects but also actors in these events, capable of interpreting them in different ways.[17]

In addition to impressing upon children the duties of patriotism, teaching them to model the values of the existing social order, and encouraging them to consider God's providential role in establishing and protecting their freedom, hymns composed for Independence Day often introduced young people to issues of social reform. Hymns promoting the virtue of temperance, for example, were a common feature of Sunday school celebrations. On July 4, 1840, Sabbath school children at "Cold Spring" joined in singing these words: "Our country's God! in thee we trust / The cause is holy, good and just / And in thy strength thy children must / Renew their pledge to thee. / Lead on, lead on, ye youthful band! / With joyful heart and willing hand, / Spread temperance banners through the land, / On this glad jubilee."[18] Through these temperance hymns, adults who participated in the movement endeavored to engage children as partners in this reform effort.

From the mid-1830s, the Cold Water Army—a children's temperance brigade that promoted the cause through parades and demonstrations—often marched out on the Fourth of July, singing songs to show their support for reform. Their presence quickly became an important symbol for the movement.[19]

Antislavery activists also wrote hymns for children to sing at Independence Day celebrations. A teacher at the Belknap Street Sabbath School in Boston composed a song for the school's 1834 Fourth of July ceremony that explicitly sought to promote antislavery sentiments among the students. "Dwells there a child upon *this* land, / Who joins not with the festive band? / Who strikes no note of jubilee, / On this the bright day of Liberty?" the singers rhetorically queried. "Yes," the chorus answered, "the poor SLAVE, in silence pines, / And weeps, and moans—for on him shines / From FREEDOM'S SUN, no Heaven-born ray, / No moral light, no mental day." Through these lines, the songwriter hoped to impress upon the young singers and their audience the fact that the blessings of liberty did not extend to everyone in the nation. The lyrics also insisted that slave children were the "brothers" and "sisters" of the Sunday school singers. They deserved to be free and to enjoy the privileges of knowing the Savior no less than did the children gathered to celebrate American Independence in Belknap Street.[20] In singing hymns like this one, children were introduced to the rhetoric of moral reform and political protest; a discourse that antislavery hymn writers hoped they would adopt for themselves.

In addition to attending meetings along with their parents and other adults, children were encouraged to form their own "juvenile" antislavery societies. The first of these organizations was chartered on August 14, 1836, at the Sabbath School of Chatham Street Chapel, New York City, under the leadership of the abolitionist Lewis Tappan, one of the founders of the American Anti-Slavery Society. At the charter ceremony for the children's association, Tappan argued that it was a "duty" for children to join reform societies promoting the causes of temperance, missions, peace, and abolition. The children present at the gathering then sang the hymn "Praise for Christian Birth," thanking God for their freedom and lamenting the plight of the slaves and others less fortunate than they.[21]

Through hymn-singing experiences such as these, young people learned to identify themselves as reformers. Rather than teaching children to uphold the values of the established order, abolitionist hymns attempted to enfold young people within an alternate community that was dedicated to challenging the institution of slavery, even if doing so meant violating socially accepted norms. "When our parents are called fanatics, incendiaries and enemies of their country, for being abolitionists," members of the juvenile antislavery societies pledged, "we will only love them the more, and try to imitate their example." Abolitionist hymn writers hoped that singing together in societies dedicated to the cause would help prepare these children to fulfill their vows and inspire them to continue fighting against injustice throughout their lives.[22] They were encouraged in this expectation by the story of slave-ship captain John Newton who reportedly attributed his decision to give up the slave trade and become a minister to his sudden recollection of "the hymns his mother had taught him when he was a little boy." Drawing on the maxim, "what is learned in childhood is seldom lost," abolitionist authors urged "every child in the land to read *The Slave's Friend,* learn the hymns, and fasten in the memory all that these little books contain."[23]

As the earlier analysis of hymnody's role in Independence Day celebrations suggests, reformers were not the only adults who put their confidence in the power of music and hymn singing to shape a child's character. In the early Republic, Protestants engaged in enterprises of all sorts advocated the practice of hymn singing as a crucial part of children's moral education. Music was believed to have an amiable effect on an individual's disposition and to provide a congenial mode of inculcating both practical and theological tenets. "Parents in cities are beginning to appreciate the salutary influence of the 'harmony of sounds' upon the minds of children," a Philadelphia newspaper reported in 1844. "It softens temper, sweetens the disposition, and tunes the heart in unison with all the better feelings of their nature. Its influence upon the rising generation would do more to elevate the standard of our national morality than all the pedagogical reproofs ever invented."[24] Sentiments like these led many common schools to incorporate music education within the larger curriculum. The school committee for the town of Chelmsford, Massachusetts, for example, argued that music not only improved students' minds and hearts but also increased attendance and reduced tardiness: "It has been found that the scholars, if possible, will be present at the time of singing; so that if the first lesson, morning and evening, be singing, it is believed none will play truant on the way, nor unnecessarily be absent."[25] Hymn singing, in this environment, was seen as an ideal pedagogical form.

This conviction helped fuel the composition and publication of literally hundreds of new hymns for children in the late-eighteenth and early-nineteenth centuries. While American authors lagged behind British composers such as Anne and Jane Taylor in producing original hymns for children until at least midcentury, the transatlantic nature of evangelical Protestant-ism in this period assured that young people in the United States had access to a wealth of material designed for their edification.[26] The Taylors' enor-mously popular *Hymns for Infant Minds*, first published in London in 1809, went through numerous reprintings in the United States. In 1817, the inter-denominational Sunday and Adult School Union (later the American Sunday School Union), produced the first version of *The Sunday School Hymn Book*, a collection of 187 hymns for children that went through nineteen editions in fewer than ten years. This volume contained many of Watts's Divine Songs alongside newer compositions.[27]

Undaunted by the popularity of the Union's hymnbook, regional and de-nominational Sunday school associations assembled their own hymnals for children.[28] Sometimes denominational considerations provided the central motivation for producing new children's hymnals, but often compilers argued that their collections were created out of a desire to provide better variety, suitability, or overall quality of hymns. In the preface to his *The Sabbath School Harp*, first published in 1837, Lowell Mason noted all these factors as "advantages which this work possesses over many other Sabbath school Hymn and Tune Books."[29]

Mason's comment suggests that children's hymnody was not only growing at a rapid pace in the early nineteenth century but was also becoming increas-ingly competitive, like the literary marketplace in general.[30] Publishers ac-cordingly marketed their products to parents, Sunday school teachers and ad-ministrators, and even directly to children, indicating that young people were viewed as consumers with the power to influence or even to make purchasing decisions. Advertisements for new hymnals were strategically placed on the inside back covers of Sunday school tracts, as well as in magazines aimed at young readers. "Children, have you seen the *Sabbath School Harp*?" one pro-motional notice inquired. "It is a neat little square book, with the picture of a golden harp on the cover . . . containing 144 Hymns, 78 of which are set to music. . . . What say you Sabbath school girls? What say you Sabbath school boys? Will you have the *Harp*?"[31] In addition to playing a role in their educa-tional and moral formation, hymnody also introduced children to the world of consumer goods. Hymns were pedagogical and devotional aids, but they were also commodities to be bought and sold. Hymnbooks for children came in many shapes and sizes, and young people were encouraged to consider these material qualities in making their selections. Illustrations also became increasingly important features. The American Sunday School Union's revised version of its *Hymns in Prose: For the Use of Children* (1829) embellished the earlier edition with "twenty or thirty excellent wood-cuts" in order to add to "its value as a child's book."[32]

While publishers produced increasingly elaborate hymnals designed to attract and capture the attention of young consumers, voluntary organizations like the American Tract Society and the American Sunday School Union also generated cheap, pamphlet editions that colporteurs and Sunday school teachers freely distributed.[33] On the occasions when students were asked to contribute to the cost of supplying hymnals for their classes, subsidies from the voluntary organizations ensured that the expense to them was usually quite minimal. A teacher who started a Sunday school in a rural area, for example, asked her students for 6 cents apiece so that she might procure them each a hymnbook from the American Sunday School Union. One little girl, who desperately wanted to participate, "brought a dozen of eggs to know if she could have a hymn book for them." Apparently, the offering was accepted.[34]

More often, these Union- or Tract Society–sponsored editions were given to Sunday school children as rewards for their academic achievements and good behavior, a practice that was especially common in the earlier decades of the century. One Sunday school tract tells of Susan Smith, a "country Sunday-school girl" who sang from her hymnal while walking through the fields on the way to her lessons. On the cover of her book, the narrator noted, her teacher had inscribed the following words: "This little book is given to Susan Smith, for regular attendance, constant good behavior, and great improvement in the Sunday School, by her affectionate Teacher, Martha Field."[35] That real children received these hymnbooks as rewards and gifts is evidenced by the extent of hymnals from the period that contain similar dedications inside their front covers.[36]

As the story of "Susan Smith" suggests, hymn singing was a central feature of the Sunday school experience. Teachers in the early Republic believed that hymns served an important ritual function in marking the beginning and end of the day, as well as transitions from one lesson to another. Many hymnals were divided into sections containing compositions appropriate to these different ritual moments in the Sabbath day, as well as hymns for a wide range of other events in which Sunday schools might participate. Thomas Whittemore's *The Sunday School Choir and Superintendent's Assistant* (1846), for example, consisted of "services . . . for the opening of Sunday Schools" and "for Christmas, Independence, for the death of teachers and pupils, and for Sunday School exhibitions, etc.," with a variety of hymns for each occasion.

The collection contains hymns for "rural celebrations" as well as for Sunday school anniversary outings.[37] If these hymnals accurately reflect experience, children learned and sang songs for nearly every circumstance and season. The Union's *Sunday School Hymn Book* (1824) even included a composition entitled "Dismission of an incorrigible scholar"![38]

Learning hymns "by heart" was presented as a means for cementing family bonds. One story, repeated in several different children's magazines, tells of a young girl named Regina who moved from Würtemburg to North America, only to be abducted by Indians in 1754, during the French-Indian war. Ten years later, Regina was rescued along with another group of children and taken to Pennsylvania to be united with her parents. Since so much time had passed, parents and children did not recognize one another. Only when her mother began to sing a favorite childhood hymn—"Alone, yet not alone am I, / Though in this solitude so drear; / I feel my Saviour always nigh, / He comes the weary hours to cheer. / I am with him, and he with me, / Even here alone I cannot be"—did Regina rush from the crowd, begin to sing it also, and throw herself "into her mother's arms."[39]

For Protestants in the early nineteenth century, this popular tale, which was supposedly translated from Danish and had an international circulation, illustrated the power of hymnody to create and sustain human relationships. Singing hymns together was therefore presumed to be an essential feature of family religion, and would have been part of many children's familial experience. Since the seventeenth century, devotional manuals recommended psalm singing as part of family devotion.[40] With the development of hymnody in the eighteenth century, the repertoire of hymns available for use in families broadened considerably. By the early nineteenth century, many children's hymnals such as Mason's *Sabbath School Harp* and the Baptist publication titled *New England Sabbath School Minstrel* were "adapted to the wants of . . . families."[41] Children's periodicals like *The Family Altar,* encouraged parents and children to "come to the place of prayer" in both the morning and evening hour to "raise with one consent the grateful song of praise."[42] Articles aimed at parents instructed them to assemble all members of the family at the close of the day, to have each read aloud, and to have the older family members "hear the younger lisp from memory its infant hymn of praise to God, while the parent closes the delightful scene by solemn prayer."[43] Lydia Sigourney maintained that, "young voices around the domestic altar, breathing sacred music at the hour of morning and evening devotion are a sweet and touching accompaniment."[44]

If hymn singing served to strengthen kinship ties, the practice also had other important implications for families. First, just as singing could promote good conduct in the classroom, it could also have a sanguine effect upon children's behavior in the home. One magazine recommended music education as a disciplinary strategy, recounting the tale of a clergyman who instructed his large family in the theory and practice of music, and encouraged his children to sing whenever they misbehaved. "When anything disturbs their temper," the minister reported, "I say to them, 'Sing'; and if I hear them speak against any person, I call them to sing to me; and so they have sung away all causes of discontent and every disposition to scandal."[45]

In addition to transforming children's demeanor, hymn singing could also have a profound influence upon the state of their souls. Although the Sunday school movement flourished partially in reaction to a perceived declension in the practice of family devotion, parents were still seen as primarily responsible for attending to their children's religious education. The rise of the domestic ideology, which insisted on the centrality of the home as the primary seat of religion, virtue, and morality heightened the emphasis on the importance of family worship for incorporating children within the community of Christian saints.[46] Horace Bushnell's influential work *Christian Nurture* (1847), reinforced this view, asserting that the "house, having a domestic Spirit of grace dwelling in it, should become the church of childhood." Bushnell suggested that hymn singing was one of the means by which the task of Christian nurture could be accomplished. In his chapter titled, "The Christian Teaching of Children," Bushnell argued that religious education should begin not with catechisms, which only served to worry small children, but instead with "the memorization of the ten commandments and the Lord's prayer, followed by the Apostle's creed and the simplest Christian hymns."[47]

Bushnell's views on Christian education were soon reflected in the works of hymn writers and promoters of children's hymnals, many of whom began to emphasize the advantages of hymnody as a more "tender" means for instilling piety and teaching doctrine. "It is due to those who we would train up for God, that their lips should be early taught to show forth his praise," the preface to one hymnal affirmed. "Being encouraged from childhood to join in public acts of devotion, their hearts will be sweetly and powerfully attracted to the cross, while their minds will be imbued with the saving principles of religious truth."[48]

While this gentler understanding of Christian nurture gained currency among evangelical Protestants in the middle decades of the nineteenth century, it never fully displaced more traditional understandings that stressed the pervasiveness of sin and the necessity of a "new birth." Hymns that warned of impending judgment for those who failed to devote their youth to God continued to appear in children's magazines and hymnals alongside newer compositions that smoothed over these starker teachings. One Baptist minister wrote a letter to the *Sabbath School Treasury* describing a revival among the children in his church, four of whom came forward for baptism upon profession of their faith. "The oldest of these children," the pastor explained, "was awakened by reading on the back of a printed Sabbath school ticket the lines of Dr. Watts: 'Broad is the road that leads to death, And thousands walk together there.' After reading, she began to reflect on her *own* course and was soon convinced that *she* was walking in the 'road to death.' She retired to pray, which she continued to do many times every day, till she obtained mercy, and felt assured."[49] For those who continued to advocate a model of spiritual life that emphasized a sharp transition from a state of sin to an experience of conversion that involved self-examination and repentance, hymns like Watts's were seen as effective means of grace that might awaken a child to her sinfulness and need for mercy, and enable her to take the next, necessary steps along the path of salvation.

Susan Warner's best-selling novel, *The Wide, Wide World,* published just three years after Bushnell's *Christian Nurture,* provides an excellent example of the persistence of more traditionally evangelical understandings of the spiritual life. The narrative details the spiritual pilgrimage of "little" Ellen Montgomery, a young girl who is forced to find her own way in the "wide, wide world" when her parents travel to Europe seeking a cure for Mrs. Montgomery's health. Left in the care of her appropriately named Aunt, "Miss Fortune," Ellen faces trials and tribulations of many sorts; all of which are necessary, Warner explains, to teach Ellen to trust and love God above all else, including her absent mother. Although Ellen's mother was extremely pious, and raised her in an atmosphere infused with a gentle form of Christian teaching, Ellen is still unable to feel that she is a child of God. Throughout the first half of the nearly six-hundred-page narrative, Ellen struggles to submit herself to God and to give Jesus the central place in her heart. Hymns play a crucial role in this battle. Beginning with her mother, nearly every adult figure who attempts to persuade Ellen to give herself to Christ employs hymns as a means of impressing the importance of this decision upon her. After Ellen tells Mr. George Marshman that she does not love the Savior best of all, for example, he gives her his hymnbook and asks her to look over one of the hymns. "Think carefully of what I have been saying, will you?—and resolve what you will do," he entreats. The hymn, which beseeches the singer to admit Jesus to her heart before the hour comes when she will be denied entry to "*his* door," ends with a stanza that enables her to take this action on the spot through the very act of singing: "Open my heart, Lord enter in; / Slay every foe, and conquer sin. / Here now to thee I all resign,— / My body, soul, and all are thine." Ellen's scrupulosity prevents her from singing this last line, but she *is* willing to pray that God would open her heart and enter in. Mr. Marshman, encouraged by this initial step, gives her the hymnbook as a gift, marking those selections that he believes will help lead her toward conversion. The hymnbook becomes a source of great comfort to Ellen in the challenging days to come, and she continually returns to the prayer of the last stanza, "open my heart, Lord, enter in," as she struggles to accept the promise of grace.[50] When she finally does resign her heart to God, Ellen herself becomes an evangelist, entreating others, like her Aunt's friend Mr. Van Brunt, to become "Christ's people." Again, hymns play a central role in this enterprise. When she is sick, Ellen asks Van Brunt to read her a hymn; a request he complies with hesitantly. "Don't *you* love hymns?" Ellen asks after he had finished, "Mr. Van Brunt are you one of the fold? . . . Because I wish you were, very much."[51]

Elsewhere in the story, Warner illustrates how the practice of hymn singing helped Ellen translate doctrinal principles into personal experience. At one point, Ellen asks another of her mentors, Alice Humphreys, to "talk over a hymn" with her, explaining its meaning. Alice and Ellen work through the hymn text line by line, discussing the proper interpretation of specific words and phrases, and then contemplating how they can apply these teachings to their daily lives. They begin with the first stanza: "A charge to keep I have— / A God to glorify; / A never-dying soul to save, / And fit it for the sky." Alice explains that this hymn calls the Christian to her responsibility (her charge) to glorify God through her "faithful, patient, self-denying performance of every duty as it comes to hand." Ellen's duty is both to prepare her own "never-dying soul" for heaven, and also, as the next stanza makes clear, to serve "the present age" by letting her "little rushlight" shine through her "sweetness of temper" and her efforts to do good. When Ellen asks for a specific example of how she might do good, Alice suggests that she find a way to amuse and cheer her elderly and neglected grandmother, a duty Ellen has often avoided. The final stanza of the hymn emphasizes the "strict account" that Ellen will give for her behavior. Alice explains that these lyrics refer to the final judgment described in Revelation 20, a passage that Ellen thinks is "dreadful" until Alice explains that she can avoid the horrible consequences of judgment through keeping Christ's commands and always "loving to please him." Ellen takes these words to heart, and seeks to implement their teaching in her everyday experience. When she next encounters her wearisome grand-parent, "the words came back upon her memory—'A charge to keep I have.'" Rather than going outside to play, as she had intended, Ellen decides to read to her grandmother from the Bible.[52]

Memoirs of pious children were a popular form of Protestant devotional literature for young people in the early American republic. James Janeway first introduced this genre in 1671, with the publication of his enormously successful collection *A Token for Children*.[53] By the early nineteenth century, accounts of godly children who died an early death were ubiquitous in children's magazines, Sunday school literature, and novels.[54] Many local Sunday schools produced short memoirs of their own pupils that were then reprinted in periodicals with a wider circulation. The particularity of many of these reports suggests that they are authentic, if idealized, accounts of real children whom some readers would have known personally. Refracted though they are through the "adult eyes" of the biographer, these accounts do offer at least a glimpse into the actual religious experiences of children in the late-eighteenth and early-nineteenth centuries.[55] More than any other source, these memoirs reveal the ways in which children themselves appropriated hymns as part of their devotional practice. Most children in these exemplary accounts made hymn singing a central feature of their daily experience. Martha Ann W., who died in Portland, Maine, on September 14, 1832, aged three years and nine months, for example, "was very fond of committing to memory little hymns" and "would never retire to rest, without first saying her prayers, and repeat-ing that beautiful little hymn of Watts, commencing—'And now another day is gone.'"[56] Just as they learned to mark the important moments in the Sab-bath day and Sunday school year with hymn singing, children like Martha also engaged in this practice at key points in their everyday lives. Hymns for "morning" and "evening," for "sun-set" and "sun-rise," for daily "self-examination" and for reflection at "the end of the year" or on a birthday were regularly featured in children's hymnals and periodicals.[57]

When they became ill, these model children found that familiar hymns like "O for a Thousand Tongues to Sing," "When I Can Read My Title Clear," and "Salvation! O the Joyful Sound" provided both comfort for the present ordeal and assurance about the eternal future.[58] Mary Ann Mitchell, who died on December 5, 1834, became anxious during her illness "to be fully prepared to meet her last enemy . . . and frequently her mind was much agitated by the fear of falling short at last." But then, her biographer reports, Mary Ann's "faith would rally" and she would sing with confidence, "How can I sink, with such a prop, / Which bears the world and all things up!"[59] Thomas Fletcher Sewell, from Charleston, South Carolina, died on June 25, 1836. While he was sick, he would sing his favorite hymn—"On Jordan's Stormy Banks I Stand"—so loudly, "that the sweet intonations of his voice could be heard in the next room."[60] On the last morning of her short life, thirteen-year-old "Miss S. H.," turned to her mother and sang this verse from "Come, Thou Fount of Every Blessing": "Jesus sought me when a stranger, / Wand'ring from the fold of God; / He, to save my soul from danger, / Interposed his precious blood." When her mother assured her that she need not fear death, the child replied, "Oh no," and sang "Safe folded in my Saviour's arms, / I'm safe from every fear." Just before she died, the little girl recited one last hymn—"I shall sing the song of grace, / And view my glorious hiding-place"—and said, "Yes, Mama . . . I know, I know his grace is sufficient for me."[61]

As these few examples suggest, children chose a wide variety of hymns as their personal "favorites." Although some texts, like "When I Can Read My Title Clear" and "On Jordan's Stormy Banks" were particularly popular and appeared in numerous deathbed narratives, the diversity of titles is more striking than the repetition of a few choice selections. Furthermore, few children—if any—sang the "starker" hymns like Watts's "Solemn Thoughts of God and Death," upon their sickbeds. Instead they chose songs that provided comfort in times of crisis, assuring them of Christ's love, God's grace, and the hope of heaven. Watts's "Why Should We Start and Shrink," reminded them that "Jesus can make a dying bed, / Feel soft as downy pillows."[62] When Abigail E. Dwight of Schenectady, New York, sang "When I can read my title clear, / To mansions in the skies," she was so focused on the vision of "heavenly rest" it offered that she "almost to forget she was a mortal inhabitant of earth."[63]

Through the practice of hymn singing, these children affirmed their membership in the community of saints, the most significant and enduring of the multiple societies—political, familial, and social—to which they belonged. From their youngest days, children learned that singing hymns reinforced the bonds that tied them to other people. As citizens of a young nation, children who participated in Independence Day celebrations sang and symbolized the virtues of the new republic. On some of these occasions, they were also introduced to issues such as temperance and antislavery through hymns that proclaimed the rhetoric of social reform. In their schools and families, hymn singing united children with loved ones, mentors, and classmates in an earthly fellowship that would someday be fulfilled in eternity. Upon their deathbeds, young people avowed their relationship to God through the songs they chose to sing. As "children of the heavenly king," they stood "on the borders of our land" ready to "gladly leave all below"—parents, teachers, friends, and fellow Americans—to "follow" Jesus.[64]

Notes

1. "Celebration of American Independence by the Boston Sabbath School Union at Park Street Church, July 4, 1831," broadside, American Antiquarian Society, Worcester, MA.

2. "Celebration of American Independence . . . at Park Street Church, July 4, 1831," broadside.

3. "Sabbath School Celebration the 4th of July," *Sabbath School Treasury* 4 (August 1831): 168.

4. "Celebration of American Independence . . . at Park Street Church, July 4, 1831," broadside.

5. The lyrics in the first song in particular stressed this distinction between those outside the church and those within: "This is the youthful choir that sings, / When all the town is gay; / That praises God with gratitude / On Independent day." See "Celebration of American Independence . . . at Park Street Church, July 4, 1831," broadside.

6. This study included a survey of ten children's and Sunday school periodicals from the years 1789 to 1850. The denominations represented by these publications include Congregationalists (*Sabbath School Treasury*, 1st ser., and *Sabbath School Visitor*); Baptists (*The Sabbath School Treasury*, 1st–3rd ser.); Methodists (*The Sunday School Magazine*); Episcopalians (*The Children's Magazine*, New York); and Unitarians (*The Juvenile Miscellany*, edited by Lydia Maria Child from 1826 to 1834, later by Sarah Josepha Buell Hale). Presbyterians are also represented by virtue of their participation in the American Sunday School Union, which published the *American Sunday School Magazine* and the *Infant's Magazine*. Nondenominational periodicals examined include the *Children's Magazine* (the "first American magazine for children" published in Hartford, CT, in 1789); *The Slave's Friend*, published by the American Anti-Slavery Society; and *Parley's Magazine*, published by Samuel Goodrich. While all of these periodicals were published in the Northeast (Philadelphia, New York, Hartford, and Boston), they included letters, Sunday school annual reports, and excerpts from newspapers and other magazines that gave them a much wider geographical range. The

incorporation of materials from British sources testifies to the transatlantic nature of Protestantism in this period.

7. Anne M. Boylan, review of *From Virtue to Character: American Childhood, 1775–1850,* by Jacqueline S. Reinier, *American Historical Review* 103 (1998): 580.

8. Historical studies that address aspects of children's religion in the early nineteenth century include Anne M. Boylan, *Sunday School: The Formation of an American Institution, 1790–1850* (New Haven: Yale University Press, 1988); Philip Greven, *Patterns of Child-Rearing, Religious Experience, and the Self in Early America* (Chicago: University of Chicago Press, 1977); Thomas W. Laqueur, *Religion and Respectability: Sunday Schools and Working Class Culture* (New Haven: Yale University Press, 1976); and Gerald F. Moran and Maris A. Vinovskis, *Religion, Family, and the Life Course* (Ann Arbor: University of Michigan Press, 1992). Literary historians have explored this topic from a slightly different perspective. Helpful works include Penny Brown, *The Captured World: The Child and Childhood in Nineteenth-Century Women's Writing in England* (New York: Harvester Wheatsheaf, 1993); Ruth Bottigheimer, *The Bible for Children: From the Age of Gutenberg to the Present* (New Haven: Yale University Press, 1996); Patricia Demers, *Heaven upon Earth: The Form of Moral and Religious Children's Literature, to 1850* (Knoxville: University of Tennessee Press, 1993); David Gryllis, *Guardians and Angels: Parents and Children in Nineteenth-Century Literature* (Boston: Faber and Faber, 1978); Anne Scott Macleod, *A Moral Tale: Children's Fiction and American Culture, 1820–1860* (Hamden, CT: Archon, 1975); and Samuel F. Pickering, *Moral Instruction and Fiction for Children, 1749–1820* (Athens: University of Georgia Press, 1993).

9. Song 10 in Isaac Watts, *Divine Songs Attempted in Easy Language for the Use of Children* (London, 1715). For an example of the juxtaposition of Watts's hymns alongside newer compositions, see *The New Sunday School Hymn Book* (Philadelphia: American Sunday School Union, 1832).

10. Susan S. Tamke, *Make a Joyful Noise unto the Lord: Hymns as a Reflection of Victorian Social Attitudes* (Athens: University of Ohio Press, 1978), 75–90; Mary Louise VanDyke, "Children's Hymnody in America: Furniture for the Mind," *The Hymn* 50 (July 1999): 26–31. Samuel J. Rogal challenges this interpretation of Watts in the introduction to *The Children's Jubilee: A Bibliographical Survey of Hymnals for Infants, Youth and Sunday Schools Published in Britain and America, 1655–1900* (Westport, CT: Greenwood Press, 1983), ix–xliv. For another more balanced reading of Watts's hymns for children, see Laqueur, *Religion and Respectability,* 11–14.

11. Paul Boyer, *Urban Masses and Moral Order in America, 1820–1920* (Cambridge, MA: Harvard University Press, 1978); Boylan, *Sunday School;* Jay Fliegelman, *Prodigals and Pilgrims: The American Revolution against Patriarchal Authority, 1750–1800* (New York: Cambridge University Press, 1982); Carl F. Kaestle, *Pillars of the Republic:*

Common Schools and American Society, 1780–1860 (New York: Hill and Wang, 1983); Jacqueline S. Reinier, *From Virtue to Character: American Childhood, 1775–1850* (New York: Twayne Publishers, 1996); and Melvin Yazawa, *From Colonies to Commonwealth: Familial Ideology and the Beginnings of the American Republic* (Baltimore: Johns Hopkins University Press, 1985).

12. "Original Hymn," *Sabbath School Treasury,* 2nd ser., 3 (August 1939): 177.

13. "Sabbath School Celebrations: Boston," *Sabbath School Treasury,* 2nd ser., 3 (August 1939): 172–73.

14. "Fourth of July," *Sabbath School Treasury* 7 (June 1834): 144; and "The Fourth of July," *Sabbath School Treasury,* 3rd ser., 4 (June 1840): 125.

15. "Celebration of American Independence . . . at Park Street Church, July 4, 1831," broadside.

16. "The Fourth of July," *Sabbath School Treasury,* 3rd ser., 4 (June 1840): 125.

17. "Celebration of Independence," *Sabbath School Treasury,* 3 (August 1830): 160.

18. "The Temperance Jubilee," *Sabbath School Visitor* 9 (September 1841).

19. Robert L. Hampel, *Temperance and Prohibition in Massachusetts, 1813–1852* (Ann Arbor, MI: UMI Research Press, 1982), 92; and Joseph R. Gusfield, *Symbolic Crusade: Status Politics and the American Temperance Movement* (Urbana: University of Illinois Press, 1963), 49.

20. "Celebration of American Independence by the Belknap Street Sabbath School, Boston, July 4, 1834," broadside, American Antiquarian Society, Worcester, MA.

21. "Juvenile Anti-Slavery Society," *The Slave's Friend* 2 (May 1837).

22. Ibid.

23. "Remarkable Fact," *The Slave's Friend* 2 (August 1837).

24. *Philadelphia Saturday Courier,* quoted in "Music in Children," *Sabbath School Treasury,* 3rd ser., 8 (June 1844): 129.

25. *Report of the School Committee of the Town of Chelmsford,* quoted in "Music in Common Schools," *Sabbath School Treasury,* 3rd ser., 7 (May 1843): 101.

26. Rogal, *Children's Jubilee,* ix–xxxviii.

27. Ibid., xx and 23.

28. *The Sabbath School Lyre: A Collection of Hymns and Music, Original and Selected, for General Use in Sabbath Schools* (Boston: New England Sabbath School Union, 1849); John Albro, *The Massachusetts Sabbath School Hymn Book* (Boston: Massachusetts Sabbath School Society, 1843); and *Hymns for Sunday-Schools, Youth, and Children* (Cincinnati, OH: Sunday School Union of the Methodist Episcopal Church, 1851).

29. Lowell Mason, preface to *The Sabbath School Harp: Being a Selection of Tunes and Hymns, Adapted to the Wants of Sabbath Schools, Families and Social Meetings,* 3rd ed. (Boston: Massachusetts Sabbath School Society, 1841).

30. David Paul Nord, *The Evangelical Origins of Mass Media in America, 1815–1835*

(Columbia, SC: Association for Education in Journalism and Mass Communication, c.1984); and David Paul Nord, "Religious Reading and Readers in Antebellum America," *Journal of the Early Republic* 15 (1995): 241–272.

31. "Sabbath School Harp," *Sabbath School Visitor* 5 (April 1837).

32. Review of *Hymns in Prose: for the Use of Children, American Sunday School Magazine* 6 (December 1829).

33. See Nord, "Religious Reading and Readers," 241–72.

34. "The Sunday-School in a Barn," *American Sunday School Magazine* 6 (August 1829): 244–46.

35. "Susan Smith; Or, The Country Sunday School Girl," in *The Child's Library; Embracing the Smaller Publications of the American Sunday School Union,* 7 (Philadelphia: American Sunday School Union, 1828).

36. Mary E. Tucker's copy of *Hymns for Sunday-Schools, Youth and Children* (Cincinnati: Sunday School Union of the Methodist Episcopal Church, 1851), American Antiquarian Society, Worcester, Massachusetts, that contains this inscription: "These are pretty hymns to learn, if you learn them now you are young you will remember them when you are old. Sarah can learn them too."

37. Thomas Whittemore, *The Sunday School Choir and Superintendent's Assistant* (Boston, 1846). In addition to designating hymns for specific occasions and ritual moments, hymnals often categorized their contents according to age appropriateness such as "hymns for children not over six years," and/or theological topic, such as "God's Omnipotence." *Hymns for Sunday Schools* (Boston: Boston Sunday School Society, 1828); *The Sunday School Hymn Book* (Philadelphia: American Sunday School Union, 1828).

38. "Dismission of an incorrigible scholar," in *The Sunday School Hymn Book* (Philadelphia: Sunday and Adult School Union, 1824).

39. "Account of Regina. A little girl of Würtemburg, who was carried away from her mother by the savages in North America, and after nine years' absence restored to her. Taken from a narrative, written in Danish, by Pastor Ronne, of Elsinore," *The Children's Magazine* 6 (July 1834): 147. See also, "Remarkable Fact," *The Slave's Friend* 20 (August 1837): 4.

40. Charles Hambrick-Stowe, *The Practice of Piety: Puritan Devotional Disciplines in Seventeenth-Century New England* (Chapel Hill: University of North Carolina Press, 1982), 143–50.

41. Mason, *Sabbath School Harp,* title page; *New England Sabbath School Minstrel: A Collection of Music and Hymns adapted to Sabbath Schools, Families and Social Meetings* (Boston: New England Sabbath School Union, 1846).

42. "The Family Altar," *Sabbath School Treasury,* 3d ser., 2 (February 1838).

43. *Sabbath School Treasury,* 3rd ser., 4 (June 1840): 124.

44. Lydia Huntley Sigourney, "Music," *The Sunday School Magazine* 3 (1836): 178.

45. Ibid.

46. Linda Kerber, "Separate Spheres, Female Worlds, Woman's Place: The Rhetoric of Women's History," *Journal of American History* 75 (January 1988): 9–39; Kathryn Kish Sklar, *Catharine Beecher: A Study in American Domesticity* (New Haven: Yale University Press, 1973); Nancy F. Cott, *The Bonds of Womanhood: 'Woman's Sphere' in New England, 1780–1835* (New Haven: Yale University Press, 1977).

47. Horace Bushnell, *Christian Nurture* (1847; reprint, with a foreword by Robert L. Edwards, Cleveland, OH: Pilgrim Press, 1994), 19–20, 30–32, 90–122, 387, 360, 369.

48. Preface to *Hymns for Sunday-Schools, Youth and Children* (Cincinnati: Sunday School Union of the Methodist Episcopal Church, 1851). The preface is dated 1849.

49. "Revival in Willington, Conn.," *Sabbath School Treasury* 3 (October 1830).

50. Susan Warner, *The Wide, Wide World* (New York: The Feminist Press, 1997 [1850]), 70–78, 88.

51. Ibid., 207, 214–16.

52. Ibid., 238–45.

53. James Janeway's *A Token for Children* (London, 1671), was extraordinarily and enduringly popular among Protestant readers for at least 150 years. Cotton Mather and John Wesley both produced their own versions of this text, as did numerous other ministers who added "new" accounts in order to update Janeway's work.

54. The most famous of these narratives is the deathbed scene of Little Eva in Harriet Beecher Stowe's *Uncle Tom's Cabin; or, Life among the Lowly* (New York: Penguin Books, 1986 [1852]), 412–28.

55. E. P. Thompson, *The Making of the English Working Class* (New York: Pantheon, 1964), 378.

56. "Martha Ann W.," *Sabbath School Visitor* 5 (October 1837).

57. *The New Sunday School Hymn Book* (Philadelphia: American Sunday School Union, 1832); "The Child's Morning Hymn," *Infant's Magazine* 3 (May 1831); "Little Willie's Hymn," *The Children's Magazine* 10 (September 1838); "Hymn for the New Year," *The Juvenile Miscellany*, 2nd ser., 2 (January 1829); and "A Child's Hymn on Its Birth-Day," *The Children's Magazine* 2 (November 1830).

58. George Hendley, "Joseph Stones," in *A Memorial for Children* (New Haven, 1806), 40; "Franklin Byrant Howard," *Sabbath School Treasury*, 3rd ser., 4 (May 1840); and Mathews, "Triumph Amidst Sorrow," 221.

59. "Mary Ann Mitchell," *The Sunday School Magazine* 1 (1835): 60–63.

60. James Sewell, "An Interesting Biography," *The Sunday School Magazine* 2 (1836): 55–62.

61. "Happy Death of Miss S. H., Aged Thirteen Years and Ten Months," *The Sunday School Magazine* 3 (1837): 151–57.

62. *Sabbath School Treasury,* 3rd ser., 3 (December 1839).

63. "Abigail E. Dwight," *Sabbath School Visitor* 5 (June 1837).

64. "Children of the Heavenly King," in James Janeway, *A Token for Children; Extracted from a Late Author,* by John Wesley, 2nd American ed. (Philadelphia: J. Pounder, 1814) 80.

11
Domesticity in American Hymns, 1820–1870

Susan VanZanten Gallagher

SOCIAL HISTORIANS HAVE identified a common nineteenth-century structure of norms called the "cult of domesticity," which emerged during an economic period when middle-class women were losing their status as independent managers of home industries and becoming instead the social repository of moral virtue. Excluded from the newly emerging business world, women were relegated to the sphere of the home. While men were active in political and economic life, women were to maintain religious and ethical ideals within the home, training children in the proper religious path and exercising a beneficent influence on men. The cult of domesticity relies on the notion of gender-defined "separate spheres," a phrase that originated, as Linda Kerber has demonstrated, in Alexis de Tocqueville's analysis of American society in *Democracy in America* (1838).[1] Subsequent twentieth-century cultural historians have used the concept of separate spheres to explain such phenomena as the rise of the nineteenth-century woman writer and the creation of a middle-class American culture. Separate spheres theory also has influenced the claim that America became increasingly secularized during the nineteenth century as religion was privatized and politics and business took over the public arena. Consequently, several studies of nineteenth-century hymns draw on the separate spheres model as a useful paradigm for discussing hymnody, focusing on the differences between hymns written by women and those written by men.[2]

However, more recently separate spheres theory as well as the secularization thesis have come under attack. Social scientists such as Christian Smith and José Casanova have challenged the Weberian model of secularization in new studies of contemporary society that should cause us to reexamine some common assumptions about the nineteenth century.[3] The "separate spheres" paradigm has been identified as a misleading binary structure that is too simplistic to explain adequately more complex facets of American society or literary production. Labels such as "the domestic" and "separate spheres" reflect nineteenth-century ideology but not necessarily nineteenth-century reality. Amy Kaplan comments, "Most studies of this paradigm have revealed the permeability of the border that separates the spheres, demonstrating that the private feminized space of the home both infused and bolstered the public male arena of the market, and that the sentimental values attached to maternal influence were used to sanction women's entry into the wider civic realm from which those same values theoretically excluded them."[4] Other categories of analysis, such as race, class, nationality, or theological tradition, further complicate the separate spheres paradigm. Both men and women drew on the ideology of domesticity, which was employed in complex and contradictory ways, depending on the context. As Laura Romero asserts, "No one group owns domesticity."[5]

Some studies of American culture have relied upon the cult of domesticity to argue for the increasing marginalization of American Protestantism in the mid-nineteenth century. Ann Douglas's monumental *The Feminization of American Culture* traces the similar economic disestablishment of ministers and women, and claims that both were confined to the private sphere from which they were to exercise "influence" rather than power.[6] However, religious disestablishment did not necessarily lead to a loss of public visibility or social power. During his 1833 tour of the United States, Tocqueville noted that religion was "the foremost of the political institutions of the country."[7] While the New England Congregationalists and Unitarians were dwindling in numbers and influence, Baptists, Methodists, and Presbyterians were experiencing massive growth in church membership as a result of the Second Great Awakening.[8] New interest in denominational unity and the Wesleyan holiness movement further strengthened clergy and women as arbiters of public morals and agitators for social change. Timothy Smith insists, "the churches were making a far greater impact upon American society than their numbers or separation from the state would imply."[9] Antebellum churches' refusal to be marginalized in a sacralized sphere suggests one way in which Christianity sometimes challenged and undermined the separate sphere paradigm. Hymn writing and singing demonstrates a further challenge to separate spheres ideology, particularly in the way the hymns from this period take up the domestic trope of home. Historical accounts and literary analysis reveal that the public nature of hymns and the complexity of their domestic references thwart the separate spheres paradigm. In both the hymns that were published and the hymns that were written during this period, we find frequent domestic references. Yet the ways in which this imagery is employed are varied, and specific examples reveal some striking tensions that suggest that gender is not always the best or only way to map nineteenth-century thought.

The Cult of Domesticity

Many nineteenth-century Americans endorsed the cult of domesticity, which was articulated and promoted in the rapidly expanding American publishing industry. Between 1790 and 1820 the number of newspapers in the United States grew from ninety to 370, and their character became increasingly democratic and less elitist.[10] American book sales quintupled between 1820 and 1850, while magazines increased their circulation sixfold between 1825 and 1860.[11] This burgeoning democratic market was dominated by women's magazines dispensing domestic counsel. *Godey's Lady's Book, Graham's Magazine,* and *Peterson's*—predecessors of such publications as *Lady's Home Journal, Redbook,* and *Good Housekeeping*—were some of the most widely circulated magazines of this period, easily outselling literary periodicals such as *North American Review* or *Harper's.*[12] Two of the most articulate spokeswomen for domestic ideology were Sarah Josepha Hale, the influential editor for half a century of *Godey's Lady's Book,* and Catherine Beecher—writer, educator, and author of *A Treatise on Domestic Economy* (1841). Both advocated the rule of wives and mothers over "the empire of the home," from which they were to effect social change by means of moral and psychological influence. An advice manual called *The Lady at Home* (1847), counseled, "even if we cannot reform the world in a moment, we can begin the work by reforming ourselves and our households—It is woman's mission. Let her not look away from her own little family circle for the means of producing moral and social reforms, but begin at home."[13] Gregg Camfield explains, "This sphere [the domestic] was defined as one of influence rather than power, of kindness and love rather than work, of educating children, of developing spiritual values in the face of the declining power and importance of the church, of maintaining cultural continuity in the home in the face of change in the market—in general, of providing 'haven in a heartless world.'"[14] Such a haven was created via domestic skills such as cooking, sewing, nursing, and gardening, all of which functioned to make home a cheerful and welcoming place in which men might be brought back to God. The women's magazines, cookbooks, and domestic how-to manuals—such as Lydia Maria Child's *The Frugal Housewife* (1830)—exemplified the domestic obsession with detail by providing meticulous instructions concerning the most basic household tasks.

Domestic ideology also appeared in the nineteenth-century American novel. Nina Baym's analysis of popular fiction written by women between 1820 and 1870 identifies a specific genre of the domestic novel, which emerged in the 1820s, dominated American literature by midcentury, and had run its course by the late 1860s and 1870s. Nineteenth-century reviewers recognized the domestic novel as a distinct genre, distinguished by means of its subject matter, setting, and "low-key, quiet style."[15] The domestic novel "is mostly about social relations, generally set in homes and other social spaces that are fully described."[16] The interiors and exteriors of the physical structure are extensively illustrated in these stories, with detailed accounts of "cool parlors, clean dairies, cozy kitchens, graceful well-sweeps, sunny meadows, [and] pleasant meadows."[17] Domestic geography emphasizes a pleasing physical and natural environment that provides a retreat from the urbanization and industrialization of America. The primary theme of the domestic novel is "the whole network of human attachments based on love, support, and mutual responsibility."[18] What Sandra Sizer terms "evangelical domesticity" characterized "home and woman as primary vehicles of redemptive power, as embodiments of a pure community of feeling."[19] In these novels, the home was the most significant center of spiritual development.

Baym says that men did not write in this genre, but other studies have demonstrated the ways in which male authors, as well as female, employed domestic ideology and rhetoric. For example, Nathaniel Hawthorne notoriously complained in a letter written in 1855 to his publisher about the "d——d mob of scribbling women" dominating public taste and diverting readers from his own work, but he had written in the domestic genre himself in *The House of Seven Gables* (1851) after the more gloomy romance of *The Scarlet Letter* (1850).[20] The cult of domesticity, then, assigned to the separate sphere of the home and presided over by women, played an important role in nineteenth-century thought. With the trope of the home at its center, the domestic rhetoric of novels includes detailed descriptions of homes and their natural surroundings, affirmations of networks of human relationships, and the parental succor of a loving God. In this way the novels reinforced and reflected the ideology created by the etiquette books and the advice dispensed in women's magazines.

The ideal qualities of the home are further sustained by the frequently employed metaphor of heaven as home. In the popular advice manual called *The Mother's Book* (1831), Lydia Maria Child recommends that children be taught to view death as "like going to a happy *home*."[21] The attractive display of a corpse at a funeral, as well as the parklike settings of the public cemeteries replacing churchyard plots at this time, were also intended to invoke such pleasing associations. George Cheever, a respected New York Congregationalist minister, in *The Powers of the World to Come* (1853) claimed that heaven "is not the dim incomprehensible universality of omnipresence merely, but a place for our abode, as determinate as place is for us now, and with as intimate a home circle, as the dearest fireside on this earth can have, nay incomparably more intimate and personal and definitely local in our Father's House in Heaven." [22] The domestic vision of heaven reached its apex in Elizabeth Stuart Phelps's celebrated account of the afterlife in her best-selling novel, *The Gates Ajar* (1868), in which heaven looks like Kansas, is stocked with Aunt Winifred's favorite cookies, and resembles, in Douglas's apt phrase, "a celestial retirement village." [23] For these nineteenth-century writers, heaven is a peaceful domestic realm in which physical homes and their possessions are restored, families and friends are reunited, and the private triumphs over the public.

Nineteenth-Century Hymnody: Public or Private?

Domesticity and hymnody are linked in such best-selling novels as Susan Warner's *The Wide, Wide World* (1850), Harriet Beecher Stowe's *Uncle Tom's Cabin* (1852), and Louisa May Alcott's *Little Women* (1868), which include hymns sung and discussed by female characters in domestic settings. June Hobbs argues such novels "established the idea that hymns themselves are the cultural property of women to be used in the home." She claims that in the first half of the nineteenth century, "Hymns were published as devotional material to be used privately, in the sacralized female sphere of the home and the emotions." [24] It was not until 1870, she concludes, that hymns were commonly sung corporately, prompting the development of simple, narrative-driven gospel hymns written by women such as Fanny Crosby. [25] However, although some novels depicted hymn singing as a feminine, domestic affair, the actual social practice of hymn singing was both public and inclusive, transcending alleged separate spheres. Customary congregational hymn singing in the United States occurred well before 1870. In *Three Centuries of American Hymnody*, Henry Wilder Foote identifies the major shift from psalmody to hymnody in American churches as taking place during the first half of the nineteenth century, with the "flood-tide" occurring between 1831 and 1865. Most American denominations began publishing their own hymnals, often incorporating British hymns, in the early nineteenth century. The first Presbyterian denominational hymnal appeared in 1830, while the Methodist Episcopal Church published hymnals based primarily on John Wesley's collections, in 1820 and 1832. In 1843, the Baptists published a huge volume with 1,180 hymns, and between 1830 and 1865, Congregationalists of the liberal persuasion published fifteen different hymnbooks. Foote recounts, "by 1820, a desire for a wider range of hymnody for evangelistic services began to make itself manifest among the Congregational and Presbyterian churches of Connecticut and New York," which was met in 1824 with the advent of *Village Hymns for Social Worship*, edited by the Reverend Asahel Nettleton. Although neither the Congregationalist nor the Presbyterian denominations formally adopted *Village Hymns*, this collection became exceptionally popular, going through seven editions in three years.[26]

At the same time, religious folk music associated with revival movements and the growing influence of African American churches was flourishing. Antebellum gospel music was first an oral phenomenon and was only later compiled and printed.[27] But both folk music and hymn singing flourished at urban revivals, rural camp meetings, and the emergent Sunday school movement, as well in the more established churches. The fashionable minister Henry Ward Beecher advocated congregational singing and sponsored the publication of a congregational hymn and tune book in 1851 (*Temple Melodies*) and again in 1855 (*The Plymouth Collection*). Louis Benson reports, "The hearty singing of the vast congregation [of Beecher's Plymouth Church] became almost as much of an attraction as his preaching."[28] The first treatise on American hymnology, *Hymns and Choirs*, published by two Andover professors in 1860, outlined the way in which hymns were to supplement the intellectual presentation of the sermon by giving voice to "the *heart* of the church."[29] *The Hymn Text Database*, drawn from 175 historic American hymnals published between 1731 and 1950, reveals that between 1820 and 1850, forty-six hymnals were published, containing 16,691 hymns; while between 1850 and 1870, twenty-nine hymnals with 12,684 hymns appeared. Although a few collections, such as Anna Warner's *Wayfaring Hymns* (1869), were intended primarily for private devotional use, public hymn singing was a prevalent practice in the first half of the nineteenth century.

Heaven: Home or Fortress?

The hymnals published in antebellum America relied heavily on British hymns written in the previous century; as one might expect, hymns by Isaac Watts and Charles Wesley were especially popular. From the hundreds of hymns written by Watts and Wesley, nineteenth-century compilers chose those that spoke best to their generation's concerns and ways of thinking. In the twenty most frequently appearing hymns published between 1820 and 1850 according to *The Hymn Text Database*, the predominant themes are (1) an intimate relationship between God and humanity, (2) God's strength and power, (3) the passion narrative, and (4) the joys of heaven. Austin Phelps, writing in *Hymns and Choirs* (1860), advises that "sacred song instinctively looks heavenward" and comments that "hymns on heaven are innumerable."[30] In these hymns, the domestic trope of home appears repeatedly, but heaven also is often depicted in nationalistic and militaristic terms, in what we might call "public sphere" rhetoric. Routinely, one hymn will evoke both vocabularies. Watts's "Come Ye That Love the Lord," for instance, the most frequently published hymn during this period, celebrates the joyful love of those in heaven surrounding the throne with "a song with sweet accord." Heaven consists of an intimate relationship between God and humanity characterized in geographic, economic, and aesthetic terms drawn from scripture: "The hill of Zion yields / A thousand sacred sweets / Before we reach the heavenly fields, / Or walk the golden streets." Yet God is also titled "the heavenly King," and "we're marching through Immanuel's ground,"—rhetoric that echoes some of the militaristic, triumphal imagery more typical of the hymns focusing on God's power.[31]

The second most popular hymn, Wesley's "Blow Ye the Trumpet," announces God's reign to "all the nations," celebrating the year of jubilee and pleading, "Return, ye ransomed sinners, home." Heaven as home in this hymn is the ultimate nation in which all debts are forgiven; yet it also provides rest, joy, and the sight of the Savior's face.[32] We find here a curious blend of domestic and nationalistic rhetoric. A more typical domestic plot evoking the story of the Prodigal Son is found in "Come, Thou Fount," in which the sinner is depicted as a wandering stranger, tenderly pursued by Jesus and hoping "safely to arrive at home." Yet the final three words of this hymn once again evoke the royal image of heaven by describing "thy courts above" (*Hymns and Hymn Writers of the Church* [HHW] #19). "He dies! The Friend of sinners dies!" relates the passion story with reference to home. When Christ rises from the dead, "Cherubic legions guard him home, / And shout him welcome to the skies." The "great Deliverer" now reigns on high, a "wondrous King!" (HHW #165). Guarded by legions of angel-soldiers, heaven as home is the ultimate military outpost. Nonetheless, hymns that focus on heaven as their primary topic typically employ imagery more characteristic of domestic ideology. "Jerusalem, My Happy Home" celebrates the urban beauty, the welcome rest from labor, and the warm human relationships found in heaven:

Jerusalem, my happy home!
Name ever dear to me!
When shall my labors have an end,
In joy and peace, and thee?

When shall these eyes thy heaven-built walls
And pearly gates behold?
Thy bulwarks with salvation strong,
And streets of shining gold?

Apostles, martyrs, prophets, there
Around my Savior stand;
And soon my friends in Christ below
Will join the glorious band.

The fellowship, lack of labor (mentioned twice), happiness, joy, and peace of heaven provide the key domestic ingredients. But this heaven is less a quiet domestic space than a busy thriving city, while the "bulwarks with salvation strong" introduce a subtle militaristic note (HHW #608).

Similarly, in "When I Can Read My Title Clear," by Watts, the poet anticipates receiving the legal deed to "mansions in the skies." Then even if "cares like a wild deluge come, / And storms of sorrow fall," he will "safely reach my home, / My God, my heaven, my all" (HHW #440). Heaven, as described by Methodist Samuel Stennett in "On Jordan's Stormy Banks," is once again limned in geographical and domestic terms: "On Jordan's stormy banks I stand, / And cast a wishful eye / To Canaan's fair and happy land, / Where my possessions lie." The third and fourth stanzas highlight the physical health, joyous celebration, and spiritual fellowship one will find in heaven: "No chilling winds, or poisonous breath, / Can reach that healthful shore; / Sickness and sorrow, pain and death, / Are felt and feared no more. / Filled with delight, my raptured soul / Would here no longer stay: / Though Jordan's waves around me roll, / Fearless I'd launch away." Charles Nutter and Wilbur Tillett comment that "this favorite hymn [in the Methodist tradition] was evidently modeled upon Dr. Watts's 'There is a land of pure delight.' The fathers used to sing this hymn to 'Exhortation,' an old-fashioned 'fugue tune'; and to hear them go through the six stanzas, at some of the Conferences, *like a whirlwind* was an experience never to be forgotten."[33] Even stronger domestic imagery occurs in "Children of the Heavenly King," which, despite its reference to royalty, depicts heaven as a family reunion: "We are traveling home to God, / In the way our fathers trod; / They are happy now, and we / Soon their happiness shall see" (HHW #547).

In these popular nineteenth-century hymns, heaven is both a home and a garrison, a place of divine love and holy rule, a pastoral countryside and a triumphal capital. Christ is Friend and King, Lamb and Lord. This combination of domestic and political rhetoric demonstrates the permeability of separate spheres. For if heaven is home as well as kingdom, earthly homes might be kingdoms with public roles. We thus find in the hymns about heaven a relationship between domesticity and imperialism similar to that identified by Kaplan in other discourses of this period as "manifest domesticity." Noting "the development of domestic discourse in American is contemporaneous with the discourse of Manifest Destiny," Kaplan suggests that "the ideology of separate spheres in antebellum America contributed to creating an American empire by imagining the nation as a home." She continues, "When we contrast the domestic sphere with the market or political realm, men and women inhabit a divided social terrain, but when we oppose the domestic to the foreign, men and women become national allies against the alien, and the determining division is not gender but racial demarcations of otherness."[34] Kaplan would probably equate the Christian rhetoric of kingdom-rule with American racism and imperialism, and it is true that postmillennial Protestantism supported Jacksonian expansionism as well as the international missionary movement. Yet the activities of denominations and voluntary societies were directed toward reforming domestic and foreign practices, with numerous efforts aimed at abolishing or alleviating urban poverty, alcoholism, homelessness, child labor, slavery, and women's disenfranchisement. For most nineteenth-century Protestants, postmillennial kingdom language was more a stimulus for social reform than a sedative for social complacency. The dual imagery of home and kingdom in hymns about heaven implies that the domestic and the political, women and men, Americans and foreigners, whites and blacks, will all be united in human fellowship and eternal worship in the celestial sphere. The private and the public are thus deconstructed in the depiction of heaven as home.

Home: Heaven or Hovel?

The need for internal reform or "home missions," as such activities are often termed, is strongly reflected in the hymns written during this period. The increasing political divisions climaxing in the Civil War, along with the increased complexity of urban and industrial life, prompted many Christians to long for the peace and order of heaven, even as they labored to bring in the millennium. Hymns written during this period do not always idealize earthly homes; at times they manifest an unflinching realism that cuts through romantic idealizations and challenges separate spheres ideology. Although the listings in *The Hymn Text Database* consist only of those hymns that repeatedly were printed over many years and so cannot be seen necessarily as representative, the forty-four hymns found in the database that were written between 1820 and 1870 reveal a number of different uses of the imagery of home. Heaven, as depicted in these hymns, is seldom described as a kingdom, and the domestic trope of home is not always associated with heaven. Domestic and nationalistic (or military) rhetoric rarely occur in the same hymn, although both remain prominent. Rather, some hymns clearly are anticipatory celebrations of the home provided by heaven, and others marshal military terminology to promote missionary activity (such as "From Greenland's Icy Mountains," "Stand Up, Stand Up, for Jesus," and "Onward Christian Soldiers"). Women wrote eleven of the forty-four hymns, but domestic imagery is used by men as well as women. The heaven celebrated in these hymns is seldom described in either the simply homely detail that we find in the fiction and sermons of the time or the lavish gem-and-mineral imagery of Revelations that was more popular in earlier hymns. Rather than physical or aesthetic comforts, these heavens hold emotional and spiritual comforts: joy, peace, rest, healing, and fellowship. Heaven does provide a haven in a heartless world, but that heartless world often includes the home.

Some of the hidden tensions of domestic ideology emerge vividly in the first enduring hymn written by an American woman: "I Love to Steal Awhile Away," by Phoebe Hinsdale Brown, a woman who had grown up in poverty and with little formal education. In 1818, Brown was living with her housepainter husband, an invalid sister, and four young children in a small, unfinished frame house on the edge of Ellington, Connecticut. In her autobiography, she describes the lack of what Virginia Woolf called "a room of one's own": "there was not a place, above or below, where I could retire for devotion without a liability to be interrupted. There was no retired room, rock, or grove where I could go."[35] Frazzled by her trying domestic circumstances, Brown would retreat each evening to the aromatic garden of a large residence down the road from her. She describes how she "used to steal away from all within doors, and, going out of our gate, stroll along under the elms that were planted for shade on each side of the road. And, as there was seldom anyone passing that way after dark, I felt quite retired and alone with God. I often walked quite up that beautiful garden, and snuffed the fragrance of the peach, the grape, and the ripening apple, if not the flowers. I never saw any one in the garden and felt that I could have the privilege of those few moments of uninterrupted communion with God without encroaching upon any one."[36] The luxurious garden and the time with God provided an escape from a crowded home, needy children, and demanding domestic duties.

One August evening when Brown was visiting a friend, she met the wealthy woman living in the neighboring house, who asked Brown why she walked so often in a garden that did not belong to her. "There was something in her manner more than in her words, that grieved me," Brown wrote. "I went home, and that evening was left alone. After my children were all in bed, except my baby, I sat down in the kitchen, with my child in my arms, when the grief of my heart burst forth in a flood of tears. I took pen and paper, and gave vent to my oppressed heart in what I called 'My Apology for My Twilight Rambles, Addressed to a Lady.'"[37] Written with one arm while she was holding a child in the other, this poem was later published in *Village Hymns* in 1824 under the title, "Twilight Hymn," with some significant changes. It originally began: "Yes, when the toilsome day is gone, / And night with banners gray, / Steals silently the glade along / In twilight's soft array, / I love to steal awhile away / From little ones and care, / And spend the hours of setting day / In gratitude and prayer" (HHW #498). As the verse subsequently appears in many hymnals, four stanzas, including the first with its reference to "the toilsome day," are eliminated. The editorial changes functioned to mute the implied domestic criticism and make the retreat more gender inclusive; "from little ones and care" was changed to "From every cumbering care." Another omitted stanza proposes an alternative home: "I love to meditate on death! / When shall his message come / With friendly smiles to steal my breath / And take an exile home?" The following stanza was preserved: "I love by faith to take a view / Of blissful scenes in heaven; / The sight doth all my strength renew, / While here by storms I'm driven." Heaven as home, in this hymn, provides a haven from the daily domestic demands of "little ones and care"; the silence and solitude of the garden "where none can see or hear" allows a communion with God not possible in the small cramped house, a space for penitence, prayer, meditation, and hope. Rather than idealizing the earthly domestic space, "I Love to Steal Awhile Away" posits an alternative domestic space in heaven that will release the homebound woman from "life's toilsome day." The domestic setting for a poverty-ridden, working-class woman such as Phoebe Brown is not a spiritually refreshing location. Rather, the home, for Brown and many others, was a crowded, noisy, demanding arena of hard labor.

A similar challenge to women's domestic bliss from a different social location occurs in the still-popular "Just as I Am," written in 1834 by Charlotte Elliott, and published in 1836 with the title, "Him That Cometh to Me I Will in No Wise Cast Out." Elliott was British, but this hymn soon appeared in many American hymnals, and ranks in *The Hymn Text Database* as the most frequently reprinted hymn written by a woman. A long-time invalid, Elliott one day felt particularly depressed because she was unable to perform one of the customary devotional duties of a nineteenth-century middle-class woman: charity work. Her mother and sisters were busily engaged in organizing a benefit bazaar for St. Mary's Hall, a school for the education of clergymen's daughters, founded and administered by her brother, but Elliott was too ill to assist. Bishop Moule tells the story of the hymn's composition:

> The night before the bazaar she was kept wakeful by distressing thoughts of her apparent uselessness; and these thoughts passed into a spiritual conflict till she questioned the reality of her whole spiritual life and wondered whether it were anything better, after all, than an illusion of the emotions. . . . The next day, the busy day of the bazaar, the troubles of the night came back upon her with such force that she felt they must be met and conquered in the grace of God. She gathered up in her soul the grand certainties, not of her emotions, but of her salvation: her Lord, his power, his promise. And taking pen and paper from the table, she deliberately set down in writing for her own comfort the formulae of her faith.[38]

When Elliott writes that she is "tossed about / With many a conflict, many a doubt, / Fightings within, and fears without," she is referring to her inability to perform the works of charity that were expected of a middle-class Christian woman. She is "poor, wretched, blind" as an invalid, unable to contribute to the domestic economy of bazaars and good-doing. This causes an emotional turmoil that can only be resolved with an intellectual assertion. "Just as I Am" affirms the fact that Elliott's salvation rests not on her ability to do good works but on the shed blood of Jesus Christ, the Lamb "whose blood can cleanse each spot" (HHW #272). This hymn is not a simple sentimental effusion but rather a sound theological declaration about the inability of domestic good works to provide salvation.

Often in mid-nineteenth-century hymns by women, the characterization of heaven as home functions not to idealize family life and the domestic realm but rather to criticize it. Such imagery establishes heaven as a place of ultimate fulfillment and reconciliation, a place in which work, pain, suffering, and the storms of life will be eliminated. What Watson terms a "hymnody of affliction" often operates to undermine the domestic ideal.[39] "Nearer My God to Thee," written in England in 1841 by Sarah Adams and published in the United States in 1844, casts the Christian in the role of the outcast Jacob, wandering without a shelter or a home, "my rest a stone" (HHW #315). Like Elliott, Adams also suffered from poor health. She depicts life as a *via dolorosa*, with one brought closer to God through bearing a cross, dreaming—like Jacob—of a stairway to heaven, enduring woes, and, eventually, dying. Heaven is not depicted in any concrete detail other than the fact that it will provide an ultimate proximity to God. Similarly, in Cecil Francis Alexander's "Jesus Calls Us O'er the Tumult" (1852), life is a "wild, restless sea" in which we too often "worship . . . the vain world's golden store." The call the Christian receives is compared to that of the disciple Andrew in a verse that is often omitted in modern hymnals: "As of old St. Andrew heard it / By the Galilean lake, / Turned from home, and toil, and kindred, / Leaving all for His dear sake" (HHW #545). Once again home is connected with toil, and the Christian is asked to give up family for the sake of Jesus, rather than finding Jesus within the family. Given the fact that Alexander was best known for the many hymns for children that she wrote, such as "All Things Bright and Beautiful" and "Once in Royal David's City," I imagine that the "tumult" she invokes in this hymn may include the often loud and demanding voices of children.

Nineteenth-century male hymnists also frequently used the domestic trope to represent heaven. In "Sweet Hour of Prayer" (1842), the Reverend William W. Walford, like Phoebe Brown, delights in a quiet time of prayer "that calls me from a world of care" and provides relief "in seasons of distress and grief." As in "I Like to Steal Awhile Away," this meditative time on earth is depicted as a foretaste of the heavenly life. "Sweet hour of prayer, sweet hour of prayer, / May I thy consolation share, / Till, from Mount Pisgah's lofty height, / I view my home, and take my flight: / This robe of flesh I'll drop, and rise, / To seize the everlasting prize; / And shout, while passing through the air. / Farewell, farewell, sweet hour of prayer!" (HHW #516). Once again the Christian is a wanderer in the wilderness, like Moses on Mt. Pisgah, waiting to enter his true home, which contains a "prize" and a "throne." The spatial distance that separates "home" from "Mount Pisgah," heaven from earth, is indicated in the actions of "flight," "rising," and "passing through the air." Walford was working class, like Brown, and was blind and so was disabled, like Elliott and Adams. From these social locations, a heavenly home often looked more appealing than the earthly one.

One of the most intense invocations of heaven as home appears in "Holy Spirit, Faithful Guide" (1858), by the American Marcus M. Wells, in which the third member of the Trinity is depicted as a kindly friend who leads the Christian by the hand through "a desert land" and "darkness drear." The weary pilgrim souls are heartened by the sound of "that sweetest voice," at the conclusion of each stanza, "whispering softly, 'Wanderer, come! / Follow me, I'll guide thee home'" (HHW #193). Once again the safety and security of heaven is contrasted with the difficulties of the earthly journey. Heaven is a home not because of its physical comforts or lavish beauty but because it provides a place where one is welcomed and comforted. A similar picture appears in the more famous "Lead, Kindly Light," written by John Henry Newman in 1833: "The night is dark, and I am far from home." Divine guidance leads to heaven, again characterized by human fellowship and reunion: "The night is gone, / And with the morn those angel faces smile, / Which I have loved long since, and lost awhile" (HHW #460). Repeatedly in these hymns, heaven as home is envisioned as a place of rest, fellowship, and harmony—both social and musical. William A. Muhlenberg's "I Would Not Live Alway" written in 1825 for a lady's album and then published in the American Episcopal *Hymnal* of 1826, is typical: "Who, who would live alway, away from his God? / Away from yon heaven, that blissful abode, / Where the rivers of pleasure flow o'er the bright plains, / And the noontide of glory eternally reigns; / Where the saints of all ages in harmony meet, / Their Saviour and brethren transported to greet; / While the anthems of rapture unceasingly roll, / And the smile of the Lord is the feast of the soul" (HHW #584). Muhlenberg's picture is strangely devoid of concrete physical details, with its abstract "rivers of pleasure," "noontide of glory," and "feast of the soul," rather than refreshing cool water, piercingly blue skies, or delectable meals of milk and honey.

The hymns from *The Hymn Text Database* are typical of their period in their use of the domestic trope and characterizations of heaven, but the sheer number of nineteenth-century hymns about heaven means that many did not last into the twentieth century. The American poet Phoebe Cary, for example, who incredibly succeeded in supporting herself as a professional writer during the mid-nineteenth century, but fell into later disregard, wrote a poem called "Nearer Home" in 1852 that subsequently became a popular hymn: "One sweetly solemn thought / Comes to me o'er and oe'er— / I am nearer home to-day / Than I ever have been before, / Nearer my Father's house, / Where the many mansions be; / Nearer the great white throne; / Nearer the crystal sea" (HHW #620).

When her sister Alice died in 1871 after a long illness, Cary wrote a companion piece called "Nearing Home": "I thought to find some healing clime / For her I loved; she found that shore, / That city, whose inhabitants / Are sick and sorrowful no more."[40] The contrast between the earthly and the heavenly are similarly outlined in the first hymn Fanny Crosby wrote in 1858: "We are going, we are going / To a home beyond the skies, / Where the fields are robed in beauty / And the sunlight never dies."[41] The American Methodist pastor William Hunter also employed the domestic trope of the Father's house, but he gives greater detail in his contrast of the celestial home with the earthly one:

> My heavenly home is bright and fair:
> Nor pain nor death can enter there;
> Its glittering towers the sun outshine;
> That heavenly mansion shall be mine.
>
> My Father's house is built on high,
> Far, far above the starry sky.
> When from this earthly prison free,
> That heavenly mansion mine shall be.
>
> Let others seek a home below,
> Which flames devour, or waves o'erflow,
> Be mine the happier lot to own
> A heavenly mansion near the throne. (HHW #628)

The simple imagery and diction in these hymns explain their ephemeral fame, yet these accounts of heaven as home maintain a kind of realism that recognizes that earthly homes are not always the romantic ideal. The heavenly mansion will endure even when illness, fire, and flood overwhelm the temporal home.

Conclusion

American hymnody of 1820 to 1870, both those hymns frequently published and those written during the period, reveals that Christianity at times defied the separate spheres mentality. Both men and women wrote hymns, for private consumption but also for public use. Poems first intended for the eyes of only one reader soon became more widely distributed and used in congregational singing, camp meetings, Methodist conferences, or urban revivals. Private and public, the sacred and the secular, came together in these hymns. The most popular hymns of this period, primarily written in the eighteenth century, drew upon the domestic trope to characterize heaven, but they also often included regal, military, or urban imagery in their account of the heavenly realm, thus suggesting the amalgamation of the domestic and the social, breaking down the barriers between private and public.

Hymns composed during this period employ the trope of home differently from that found in prescriptive domestic literature and novels. Heaven is not described in physical terms of consumption; rather, the focus is on the positive restructuring of social relationships; heaven is a place where human beings are reunited with loved ones, where laborers will find rest, and where natural and urban beauty peacefully coexist. While Douglas argues that the conflation of heaven and home serves to reinforce the domestic ideology of the earthly home as spiritual center and haven, we more commonly find the heavenly home of hymns contrasted with an earthly home of trouble, toil, and tears. The pilgrim imagery made prominent by John Bunyan in the eighteenth century persists in the hymns of the nineteenth century, casting the earthly home in a less idealized light. The democratization of American religion that accompanied the substantial antebellum growth in Baptist, Methodist, and Holiness associations and denominations contributed to this increased realism, as women from all classes and lower-class men began writing hymns. While the domestic description of heaven in nineteenth-century hymns might at times reinforce the idealized possibilities of the earthly home, it more often envisions a better home in the world to come.

Notes

1. Linda K. Kerber, "Separate Spheres, Female Worlds, Woman's Place: The Rhetoric of Women's History," *Journal of American History* 75 (1988): 9–39.

2. For example, see June Hadden Hobbs, *"I Sing for I Cannot Be Silent": The Feminization of American Hymnody, 1870–1920* (Pittsburgh: University of Pittsburgh Press, 1997). A similar approach to British hymnody is found in Susan S. Tamke, *Make a Joyful Noise unto the Lord: Hymns as a Reflection of Victorian Social Attitudes* (Athens: Ohio University Press, 1978).

3. Christian Smith, et al., *American Evangelicalism: Embattled and Thriving* (Chicago: University of Chicago Press, 1998); José Casanova, *Public Religions in the Modern World* (Chicago: University of Chicago Press, 1994).

4. Amy Kaplan, "Manifest Domesticity," *American Literature* 70 (1998): 581. Vol-

ume 70, number 3 is a special topics issue of *American Literature* with the theme "No More Separate Spheres."

5. Laura Romero, *Homefronts: Domesticity and Its Critics in the Antebellum United States* (Durham, NC: Duke University Press, 1997), 112.

6. Ann Douglas, *The Feminization of American Culture* (New York: Avon, 1977); Amanda Porterfield, *Feminine Spirituality in America: From Sarah Edwards to Martha Graham* (Philadelphia: Temple University Press, 1980), 78.

7. Alexis de Tocqueville, *Democracy in America,* trans. Henry Reeve (New York: G. and H. G. Langley, 1900), 1: 310.

8. Douglas bases her study on this particular subgroup, New England Congregationalists and Unitarians, which she admits is not representative.

9. Timothy L. Smith, *Revivalism and Social Reform: American Protestantism on the Eve of the Civil War* (Gloucester, MA: Peter Smith, 1976), 44.

10. Nathan O. Hatch, *The Democratization of American Christianity* (New Haven: Yale University Press, 1989), 25.

11. Porterfield, *Feminine Spirituality in America,* 70.

12. Douglas, *Feminization of American Culture,* 275.

13. Quoted in Barbara Welter, *Dimity Convictions: The American Woman in the Nineteenth Century* (Athens: Ohio University Press, 1976), 31.

14. Gregg Camfield, *Necessary Madness: The Humor of Domesticity in Nineteenth-Century American Literature* (New York: Oxford, 1997), 15.

15. Nina Baym, *Novels, Readers, and Reviewers: Responses to Fiction in Antebellum America* (Ithaca, NY: Cornell University Press, 1984), 201. Baym analyzes the domestic novel, which she prefers to call "woman's fiction," in *Woman's Fiction: A Guide to Novels by and about Women in America, 1820–1870* (Ithaca, NY: Cornell University Press, 1978).

16. Baym, *Woman's Fiction,* 26.

17. Herbert Ross Brown, *The Sentimental Novel in America, 1789–1860* (Durham, NC: Duke University Press, 1940), 383–34.

18. Baym, *Woman's Fiction,* 27.

19. Sandra S. Sizer, *Gospel Hymns and Social Religion: The Rhetoric of Nineteenth-Century Revivalism* (Philadelphia: Temple University Press, 1978), 87.

20. Letter to William Davis Ticknor, quoted in Caroline Ticknor, *Hawthorne and His Publisher* (Boston: Houghton Mifflin, 1913), 141. David Reynolds, *Beneath the American Renaissance: The Subversive Imagination in the Age of Emerson and Melville* (New York: Alfred A. Knopf, 1988), 338; Susan Gallagher, "A Domestic Reading of *The House of Seven Gables,*" *Studies in the Novel* 21 (1989): 1–13.

21. Lydia Maria Child, *The Mother's Book* (Cambridge, MA: Applewood, 1989 [1831]), 81, her emphasis.

22. Quoted in Douglas, *Feminization of American Culture*, 267–68.

23. Ibid., 272.

24. Hobbs, "I Sing for I Cannot Be Silent," 77, 35.

25. Douglas, *Feminization of American Culture*, 261–62.

26. Henry Wilder Foote, *Three Centuries of American Hymnody* (New York: Archon, 1968), 189.

27. See Hatch, *Democratization of American Christianity*, 146–47.

28. Louis F. Benson, *The English Hymn: Its Development and Use in Worship* (Richmond, VA: John Knox Press, 1962 [1915]), 474.

29. Austin Phelps, Edwards A. Park, and Daniel L. Furber, *Hymns and Choirs* (Andover, MA, 1860), 52, their emphasis.

30. Ibid., 82.

31. *Hymns of Faith and Life* (Winona Lake, IN: Light and Life Press and The Wesley Press, 1976), #50.

32. Charles S. Nutter and Wilbur F. Tillett, eds., *The Hymns and Hymn Writers of the Church: An Annotated Edition of The Methodist Hymnal* (New York: Methodist Book Concern, 1911), #294.

33. Nutter and Tillett, eds., *Hymns and Hymn Writers*, 323, their emphasis. Later versions have an additional gospel-like refrain: "We will rest in the fair and happy land, by and by, / Just across on the evergreen shore; / Sing the song of Moses and the Lamb by and by, / And dwell with Jesus evermore." *Hymns of the Living Faith* (Winona Lake, IN: Light and Life Press, 1951), #532.

34. Kaplan, "Manifest Domesticity," 582–83.

35. Quoted in Nutter and Tillett, eds., *Hymns and Hymn Writers*, 264.

36. Ibid.

37. Quoted in Edward S. Ninde, *The Story of the American Hymn* (New York: Abingdon Press, 1921), 179.

38. Nutter and Tillett, eds., *Hymns and Hymn Writers*, 146.

39. J. R. Watson, *The English Hymn: A Critical and Historical Study* (Oxford: Clarendon Press, 1997), 428. Tamke, *Make a Joyful Noise*, 142–45, argues that family life is idealized in British Victorian hymns at the same time that family life is becoming less cohesive.

40. Nutter and Tillett, eds., *Hymns and Hymn Writers*, 325.

41. Ninde, *Story of the American Hymn*, 347.

Contributors

Edith L. Blumhofer is professor of history and director of the Institute for the Study of American Evangelicals at Wheaton College. She is the author of *"Her Heart Can See": The Life and Hymns of Fanny J. Crosby.*

Candy Gunther Brown is assistant professor of American Studies at St. Louis University. She is the author of *Word in the World: Evangelical Writing, Publishing, and Reading in America, 1789–1880.*

Heather D. Curtis is a doctoral candidate in the History of Christianity at Harvard University. Her dissertation is entitled "'Acting Faith': The Devotional Ethics of Religious Healing in Late Nineteenth-Century Protestantism."

Mary De Jong is associate professor of English and Women's Studies at Penn State University, Altoona College. She has published several articles on the composition and performance of hymns.

Dennis C. Dickerson is professor of history at Vanderbilt University. He is the author of *Religion, Race, and Region: Research notes on A.M.E. Church History* and *Militant Mediator: Whitney M. Young, Jr.*

Susan VanZanten Gallagher is professor of English at Seattle Pacific University. She is the author of *A Story of South Africa: J. M. Coetzee's Fiction in Context* and *Truth and Reconciliation: The Confessional Mode in South African Literature.*

D. Bruce Hindmarsh is James Houston Associate Professor of Spiritual Theology at Regent College in Vancouver, Canada. He is the author of *John Newton and the English Evangelical Tradition: Between the Conversions of Wesley and Wilberforce.*

Mark A. Noll is McManis Professor of Christian Thought at Wheaton College. Among his many books is *America's God.*

Samuel J. Rogal is Chair Emeritus of the Division of Humanities and Fine Arts at Illinois Valley Community College. He is the compiler of the ten-volume *Biographical Dictionary of 18th-Century Methodism and the Sourcebook of Popular American Hymns, Sing Glory and Hallelujah!: Historical and Biographical Guide to Gospel Hymns Nos. 1 to 6 Complete.*

John R. Tyson is professor of theology at Houghton College. A founding member of the Charles Wesley Society, he is the editor of *Charles Wesley: A Reader* and the author of *Charles Wesley on Sanctification.*

Mary Louise VanDyke is coordinator of the Dictionary of American Hymnology Project at Oberlin College. She is an editor of the CD-ROM *Dictionary of North American Hymnology: A Comprehensive Bibliography and Master Index of Hymns and Hymnals Published in the United States and Canada, 1640–1978.*

Index

vance in church, 154; publishing of, 163–164; and evangelical culture, 195–196; as evangelical narratives, 196–208; and conversion, 197; and justification, 198, 201, 207; and sanctification, 198, 200, 203–208; and salvation, 201–202; and imagery of Jesus, 202–203; as collective narratives, 203–204; as individual narrative, 203; and death, 205–206; and heaven, 206–207; and children, 214–229; and Independence Day, 217–218; and family relationships, 223–224

Hymns Ancient and Modern, 99, 101, 103, 112

Hymns and Spiritual Songs for the Use of Real Christians of All Denominations, 22

Hymns for Infant Minds, 221

Hymns for Social Worship, 124–125

Hymns for Today's Church, 63

Hymns of Faith, 63

Hymns of Truth and Praise, 63

"I am Thine, O Lord," 159
"I Would Not Live Alway," 248

Jackson, Mahalia, 13
"Jesus, Keep Me Near the Cross," 159–160
"Jesus, Lover of My Soul," 87, 89
Jones, Absalom, 179, 190
Jones, Sam P., 12
Judson, Ann Hasseltine, 77
Julian, John, 8
"Just as I Am," 246
justification, 196

Kremser, Edward, 117

"Lead, Kindly Light," 248
Leavitt, Joshua, 86
Lee, Jesse, 25
Lesser Hymnal, The, 33
Lorenz, Jane Ellen, 27
"Love Divine, All Loves Excelling," 82, 199–200

Lowry, Robert, 163
Lutheran Book of Worship, The, 63

Make His Praise Glorious, 13
Manhattan, New York, 156
Manley, Kenneth, 48
Marty, Martin, 62
Mason, Lowell, 59, 79, 86–87, 214; and children's hymnody, 221
McClellan, General George Brinton, 107
MEC. *See* Methodist Episcopal Church
Methodist Church School Hymnal, The, 30
Methodist Episcopal Church (MEC), 23, 25; and Christmas Conference of 1784, 24; and first standard hymnbook, 29; and second hymnbook, 30; and Social hymnbooks, 30; schisms and new Methodist denominations, 32–33; post-Civil War and consolidation of, 33–34
Methodist Episcopal Hymnal, 123–125
Methodist Hymnal, The, 34–35, 124–125
Methodist Quarterly Review, 29, 80
Methodists, 10; and American Hymnody, 24; and expression in camp meetings, 24–28; general conference of May 1876, 135; committee formed for hymns, 135–136; changes in Wesleyan movement, 178; founding of African, 178–179; African vs. American, 182
Metrical psalmody, 132–133
Milton, John, 102
M'Kown, C. F., 35
Montgomery, James, 78–79
Moody, Dwight L., 12, 60, 103, 137, 140, 153–154; use of evangelical hymnody, 140–141; hymnbook topics, 148–150; use of Crosby-Doane hymns, 160–161
"More Like Jesus Would I Be," 152–153
Moyers, Bill, 11
Muhlenberg, William A., 248
Music, David, 23
Myers, Peter D., 10

Nash, Gary, 177
"Nearer My God to Thee," 81, 247
Nettleton, Asahel, 137, 141–142, 239